Restoring
My
Soul

Joyce

Restoring
My
Soul

A Workbook for
Finding and Living the
Authentic Self

Andrea Mathews, LPC, NCC

Enjoy You !
Andrea Mathews

iUniverse, Inc.
New York Lincoln Shanghai

Restoring My Soul
A Workbook for Finding and Living the Authentic Self

iUniverse books may be ordered through booksellers or by contacting:

iUniverse
2021 Pine Lake Road, Suite 100
Lincoln, NE 68512
www.iuniverse.com
1-800-Authors (1-800-288-4677)

The views expressed in this work are solely those of the author
and do not necessarily reflect the views of the publisher,
and the publisher hereby disclaims any responsibility for them.

ISBN-13: 978-0-595-42671-3 (pbk)
ISBN-13: 978-0-595-87001-1 (ebk)
ISBN-10: 0-595-42671-9 (pbk)
ISBN-10: 0-595-87001-5 (ebk)

Printed in the United States of America

Man's main task in life is
to give birth to himself.

—Erich Fromm

Dedicated to my children
to whom I gave birth, in hopes
that one day they might give birth to themselves,
and through whom
I gave birth to myself.

Contents

Contents ix

Introduction xi

An Image Of The Authentic Self 1

Defining The Role 15

Distinctions: The Role, The Authentic Self 59

Breaking Down The Barriers To Living Authentically 81

Diagnosis And The Authentic Self 143

Relying On The Authentic Self 182

Authenticity & Spirituality 280

Celebrating Authenticity 300

References 311

Introduction

Terrible or not, difficult or not, the only thing that is beautiful, noble, religious, and mystical is to be happy.—Arnaud Desjardins

Does it seem inconceivable that you could live the rest of your life in relative peace and happiness? Does anyone really ever live in peace? What is peace? Is it just not having any wars to fight? Or, is it something deeper, something one can feel, something that is primary to the perception of the world? This workbook will become, as you work it, a new paradigm for living a life of peace and, yes, even joy.

Are we talking about some kind of religious experience here? No, religion has nothing to do with this peace, though it may be experienced on all levels, including the spiritual level of awareness. But this peace is more than just an experience; it is a place. It is a place to stand, to breathe, to live. It is a peaceful and joyful place that is already inside each of us, but one which we do not even know how to access, much less live out. It is the *Authentic Self*.

What is it like to live life authentically? We've heard, since childhood, the adage, "be yourself." But no one ever told us who that self is, or how to know when we are being ourselves as opposed to being safe, or pleasing, etc. Even if we came from the most functional homes, which we all know are very rare, no one taught us how to find and live out of the authentic self. "Be yourself" has come to mean something like, "be natural, don't fake it." And so, if we practice this adage, we may find that we have to work with the tension between behaving like what others would have us behave and something that is more like our current mood or agenda. Therefore, if Mom, the wife, or everyone else wants us to wear a suit and tie to an event and we feel like wearing blue jeans and sneakers, then we should wear blue jeans and sneakers.

The problem then is: How do I mesh my seemingly natural inclinations with a society that does not approve of my inclinations? A bigger question is:

Do my inclinations come from an identity, or from my Authentic Self? Before we go fighting any battles with society, it might be best to understand this thing of inclination, this thing of identity and this thing of authenticity. In the next few paragraphs we will define these terms as they are used in this workbook.

Inclination is just what it sounds like, an incline, an uphill slope towards something. Often we get inclination and authentic desire mixed up, mostly because we rarely-to-never tap into authentic desire. Inclination is not authentic desire. Instead, it just seems like the next best thing to do. In other words, if I am on a path toward a goal, I am inclined in that direction. If the path is alcoholism and I have an inclination to go get a drink then that is precisely what I will do. Have I put any thought into this seeming decision? Have I considered it at all? Usually not. And this inclination is conducted without regard to the consequences. But up the slop I go. Or suppose that I am angry and someone says something irritating to me, well, I'm already on the path, so I'll say or do whatever comes next. I'm not really consciously choosing, I am just doing what seems to come next, often to my own demise.

Or, let's consider it from the angle of "goodness." Suppose we are talking about a person who sees himself as good, always there for others, always trying to do the "right thing." He is, thereby, inclined in his behavior to what he perceives as goodness. He is headed up the slop to the mountain top of goodness and someone offers him a choice, what will he do? He will look up to his goal of goodness, consider this choice from the perspective of goal attainment, and just do what he's always done. Is it real? Well, at least, we say, it isn't "bad." In my practice as a therapist, I find many people who have this goal, which has become an identity. They do all manner of "bad" things to themselves in order to stay on the path up the mountain to goodness.

Often these inclinations come from our identity. An identity is something with which we identify. This word gets thrown around quite a bit, so let's clarify. We hear people say, "I identified with that," when someone says something they understand on an emotional level. What they really mean is that they could easily empathize with some part of someone else's life usually because they have literally been in their shoes. Identity is something different. Suppose, as a child, I am playing near my mother one day, as she is discussing with the neighbor, the latest drug bust in town. I watch her, from my fairly preverbal perspective on life, more than I really listen to her, and as I watch I notice that she has a look of disgust on her face as she is declaring her opinions on "these teenagers today." I am reading that look as one of utter distaste, utter revulsion. Though I may have no words for this, I got the meaning.

Then a few hours later, she tells me to go change clothes because we are going out. I go put on some clothes that I really like, but when I walk out ready to go, she looks at me with that same look of disgust on her face that I saw earlier. She tells me that I'm not going to wear *that* and hurries me back into my room to change into something of her choice. As I note that look of revulsion on her face, I suddenly feel as if I am disgusting, I am revolting to my mother. Now, what has happened is that I have identified with her facial expression, *as if it is who I am.* Now, it is true that I am not that disgust, but I sure do feel as if I am. I have put my "I AM" in front of that feeling, and for all practical purposes at this moment, *I AM disgusting and revolting.* If I *continue* (key word)to identify with that feeling over and over again, then it will eventually harden into an identity. In other words it becomes who I think I am. And if I ever end up in therapy, I will eventually tell the therapist that this is who I am. Prior to therapy, however, I will have spent many years acting out disgust and revulsion, so that I lose friends and relationships either because I am acting disgusting and revolting, or because deep down I feel that if they don't already know that I am disgusting, they will eventually find out and then it will all be over. Or, I may act out my disgusting identity privately so no one will ever find out how truly bad I am. Or, I may find people to relate to who will keep me "cleaned up" so that I don't feel so disgusting.

If, once I am in therapy, my therapist asks me to tell her about myself, I will tell her that I do this and that for a job, I have this and that relationship and I am disgusting. But, have I told my therapist who I really am, or have I just told her what I have identified with? Now, let us clarify here, that one incident, such as the one sited above, does not make a child pick up an identity. Please note that we said, If I *continue* to identify with that feeling over and over again, *then* it will eventually harden into an identity.

Let's do another example. I've treated many adolescents who tell me, "*They don't understand; this is me!*" A great example is the adolescent boy, who doesn't want to cut his hair. We will call him Joey. Now let me hasten to say, that I have no aversion to long hair on males. I often find it quite attractive. However, that is not the point. The point for Joey is, "this is me!" In truth the Joeys of the world quite often haven't a clue what or who "me" is, but this thing of the hair has become a symbol of independence. They have identified with the concept of independence, often misguiding that concept all the way down to outright rebellion. The fact is, that as long as Joey is living in rebellion, he is not living in independence. Rebellion implies an "other" against whom he *must* rebel. He is thereby bound to his rebellion. Where is the independence in that? Independence needs no "other" to define itself against or with. It simply is. But

Joey doesn't know this. He just knows he must not lose the hair to that "other" or he will feel as if he has been robbed of an identity. So, you see, what he thinks is "me," isn't "me" at all. It's just a concept with which he has identified.

I've treated adults in couple's therapy, when one party takes the stand, "this is just me, s/he is just going to have to deal with it." Is this "me," or is it an identity? This is the question of course, but often when someone takes this stance, what s/he is really saying is, "I'm not willing to change." Change is scary, so it helps to know *what* one is changing. Therefore, at this point it helps to have the person resisting change to define what it is that s/he thinks will change. But eventually, if the relationship is to heal, we are going to have to come to terms with two identities and two authentic selves. Knowing the difference could save the relationship.

So, that's a bit about identity now, and we will discuss it in much greater depth within the chapters of this book. Now, how do we define the Authentic Self? Well, let's start with an image. Let's consider the tree. The tree we see everyday on the way to work or play is a living entity. It is living life. It is not made up of mask or costume, it is not trying to do anything; it simply is. This is "being." That beingness comes from itself before it is even visible to the world. Without revealing the workbook material, let me say that we all have a place of beingness inside of us. It is a place that is wise, knows the best direction for our lives and, most importantly, this is the place inside of us that has never been wounded. It is the vital source of our life energy. It is the raw essence of the real "me." In the first several pages of the book you will do exercises which will help you to get a very clear working image of your own personal Authentic Self.

Now that we've got at least a very basic overview of the terms used in this book, let us consider why it is that this Authentic Self seems so illusive. Most, if not all of us have been taught that it is our job, nay, our mission to ignore the impulses of the Authentic Self, thinking that they are at worst something dark and evil, and at best something with which our world does not need to be bothered. In various overt and covert patterns of behavior our primary caretakers provided us with the mirrors into which we were to look. In the invisible worlds beyond the rational, conscious mind, in the nonverbal messages that pass between people constantly, we picked up the messages that told us who to be. Very rarely did our worlds *really* want us to be ourselves. Mostly we heard this message: *Don't be who you are, be who I need you to be!* And we complied. We did this to survive, sometimes horrendous environments. So now we wear the masks and the costumes provided for us, without even knowing we are wearing them, until one day we hit the proverbial wall, and we find out that what was once a survival technique is now killing us.

All the while we were wearing these masks and costumes that others needed for us to wear, we were always secretly wondering what would happen if they ever really knew who we are. Would they run screaming out of the room, tearing their hair? Would they just take advantage of us, one more time? Would they even recognize us if we, suddenly, without warning tore off the masks and costumes? We have held the hands and wiped the brows of many other masks and costumes, never really being sure that we were with someone we could trust. We have jumped higher, longer, faster than anyone else in the department, the building, the house, for so long, that we have no clue what it's like to stand still and breathe. We have carried massive amounts of guilt, chagrin and shame for years, so that by now our backs are slumped with the enormity of pain, both ours and others, and we cannot see anything but the ground before us. We have faded into so many walls and halls that we have become them, so that people walk around us or through us, until we find that we are longing for fame, just to be visible again. We have run so long, so far away from family that they have no clue that we are even still on planet earth, and we hate them so hard that they chase us in our dreams at night. We have injured others in the name of self-preservation, or just plain rage. We have not known where to put our feelings because we are absolutely certain that if we ever once really experience them we will burn to dust in a nanosecond of actuality. We may know every nasal hair on our partner's face, but we have no clue what we like to eat, or how we like to spend our time. We are lost. Lost to any recognition of ourselves, and feel no hope that there is any way of finding our way back home to our own souls.

What we seem to know best is this deep distance from all that is of experiencing life, especially when it comes to joy. Do people ever really have joy? No, people can't know joy. If we could we'd feel guilty for having what so many others were so desperately missing. There is simply too much suffering in the world for any one of us to ever feel joy. But what if it were possible? What if it were possible to experience life beyond chaos and pathos? What if finding joy meant we found clarity of intention, compassionate reason, and meaning behind our labor? And what if the path to finding such a life were already inside us? Well, it's a different path for sure. It looks very different from circling the wagons, stopping our sojourn and leaping backwards in time to those awful moments we have wanted to avoid forever. And it is far more than just learning to be assertive, or changing habitual behavior. This path looks inward, not backward and not outward. You do not have to find that one last memory which, if found, promises release and healing. There is no such memory. There is, in fact, nothing in our past that offers healing, and just so, there is nothing external to us, not even our own behavior that is, in and of itself, healing. It is, instead, in our present. And inside of us. As a matter of fact, we carry our potential healing around with us all of the time, often never knowing it is there.

This workbook offers an opportunity to go there, to find the Authentic Self and peace. It is a life-changing book, if you do the work. So it is ill-advised reading for anyone who does not want life change. Once we have faced and welcomed the challenge of life change, it offers the potential of peace, and joy, to those who do the work of finding, identifying with and beginning to live out of the Authentic Self. Together we will seek and if you are willing you may find your Authentic Self, individualized but able to relate, strong but vulnerable, strange but somehow familiar. If you are willing, take the risk to challenge your own thinking.

We will use art, poetry, story, metaphor, role-play and image work to find, define and identify with the Authentic Self. You may find that the journey* is far more pleasant than you would imagine a healing experience to be. It is strange, but true, that we have come to believe that we cannot find healing unless we first put ourselves through excruciating pain. We are a little like the physicians of old who thought that we had to leech the disease out of the patient. Well, we can give ourselves a break. We are as new to therapy, as once physicians were to medicine. This book, therefore, will not ask you to go back and relive painful memories or events in your life, nor will it ask you to change behavior without a strong, willing internal component of Self-investment. It will, instead, ask that you look inside yourself, to find your own personal Authentic Self, to identify with it and to begin to trust and live out of it. All you need is some magic markers, a pen and willingness to consider new paradigms. And so, we begin.

*On your journey through this book, take your time, relax into your work and use as many colors, backgrounds, nuances of meaning as you would like. You may look back on this work after it is done, to find new meanings, even years after you have done the work. This is your book. For you and by you. Enjoy.

An
Image
Of
The
Authentic
Self

Begin with some art work.

On this page, draw a picture of your favorite animal. After you have finished the picture, write in at least 3 words describing what it is about this animal that you like. (This picture can be a pet, animal in the zoo, or an animal you've only seen on TV or in a book, but admire.)

On this page, draw a picture of your favorite place. After you have completed the picture, write in beside it at least 3 words which describe how you feel when you go to this place.

On this page, draw a picture of your favorite, or most admired person. (This can be a historical, fictional, or real person you know, or someone you've never met but have seen on TV or read about. Search yourself for a person who you would like to imitate, or who you first think of when the word favorite comes to mind.) After you have finished the picture, write in beside it, at least 3 words describing what it is that you like or admire about this person.

On this page, draw a picture of your favorite color, in a shape. (For example, if your favorite color is purple, you might draw a purple circle, triangle, square, or rectangle.) After you have finished the picture, write in beside it at least 3 descriptors of how you feel when you look at this color.

On this page, draw a picture of yourself. After you have completed the picture, write in beside it at least 3 words that describe you or how you feel about yourself both inside and out.

NOW, Read aloud to yourself, the descriptive words you used on each of the preceding exercises.

Ponderings: Do you hear a difference between the words you used to describe yourself and the words you used to describe the favorites in your life? Is it a big difference or a small one? What are your thoughts about that? <u>Do not write</u> down those thoughts just yet, just consider. Do you think that this means that you really are different by degree or all together different, or less than, equal to, better than those favorites that you thought of? Would that not mean that you have identified with the descriptors you place on the page beside your picture of yourself?

To a greater or lesser degree, we all identify with certain characteristics or self-images; and we call those traits "me." We hang our nametags on those traits and we say that this is who we are. Some of you have jobs in which you must wear a nametag, which displays your name and your job title and attaches you to your particular company, agency or institution. It is like that. We attach our names and our identity to certain characteristics, whether likable or unlikable and we say this is who we are. But are we? It's almost as if we assume that once we have decided on an identity, it becomes a box around us that cannot contain anything else beyond that which we have already decided.

Before we go any further, let us first ask, why is identity important? Well, it is important mostly because it is through the eyes of this identity that we view every other concern, commitment and effort in our lives. It is as if we are looking through a kaleidoscope of a certain pattern of color and design. We know that pattern well, since we have looked at it for years. Both of our eyes have become transfixed on that one picture and if someone were to ask us to turn the kaleidoscope to another pattern, we would be totally disoriented. Our pattern is the one we know. And while we are looking at that pattern, we have formulated relationships with our world that look just like that pattern. In other words, we have designed our entire lives around that one pattern—our identity.

Why would this be important? Well, we think, rather, we have been taught that the primary issue of healing is looking at the trauma(s) or bad experiences of our lives and the feelings around these experiences. And so, some of us have spent years trying to get to the bottom of our pasts, or change that one behavior that seems to be the big problem. And sometimes we find that even if we remember every last memory, we still are feeling out of touch with life and paralyzed in despair. Even when we finally manage to change that one behavior that's been sticking us to the wall, we now feel lost and absent from a keen living experience. What if the past or the behavior just isn't the problem? What if, instead, the problem is that because we have spent our lives trying so hard to do the right thing, work harder, run faster, be better, be worse, we have lost touch with any identification with the Authentic Self?

Let us take the example of traumatic experience. It works here simply because it is so outstanding to us. Many of us know already that quite often persons experiencing a trauma report having what has come to be known as an "out of body experience." We leave our bodies as a defense mechanism to avoid experiencing the trauma. We may elect after that, to go to a therapist who will allow us to go back into the past and experience the trauma, thinking that this will make us better. Yet, though we may have been very brave in our valiant efforts to salvage for ourselves those moments, hours, days of terror we lost in the trauma, it doesn't get us back our whole selves. For we know, that we don't typically just lose the memory of those moments, we lose touch with whole childhoods, in which, surely there was some laughter, some fun stuff.

The fact is that we didn't just lose touch with those moments, we lost touch with the Authentic Self. During the trauma we externalized. We went outside of us. How, then do we survive after that? We stay outside of us. We ask the world, without knowing we are asking, who it would like for us to be. And then we become that. Why would we do this? Because our survival is at stake. For some it is a literal survival. For others it is a sense of impending abandonment that feels like it could become an emotional death. We put on a costume and a mask and we wear it all day every day. It smiles for us when the world seems to need it to smile, it appears brave and strong, even super-strong, or weak and incapable or whatever else it appears that the world needs for it to be. The only time it comes off is in our dreams at night, when we experience and re-experience the trauma.

Now, that is the outstanding example of trauma, but the fact is we all do it. As infants and little children, we all inherently understand that abandonment by our primary caretakers means death. It is animal instinct for us to understand this. So, what will we do to stay alive? What compromises will we make to fit into a dysfunctional family system, simply because to not fit in is either an emotional or a physical death to us? The better question is: Where in the world do we gain the strength to simply stay alive? If the Authentic Self is told either overtly or covertly to get lost, go to its room, stay away, hide, duck, placate, manipulate, what will it do? Does it die? In some kind of metaphorical way, does it hear the message to go away and obey?

Well, maybe. But maybe that is the smartest thing to do. Maybe if the Authentic Self goes underground for several years, puts on a mask and costume for those who tell it to go away, maybe it will get to be here long enough to get to adulthood, where it will then come out and flourish. Maybe, the Authentic Self, in its wisdom says, "Okay, I know what to do. I'll stay invisible like the roots of the tree I am." So maybe it says to us, "Now, you must live. You must! So, here's what we're going to do. You go down on that stage, and you put on this costume and mask and you play out that role. And I will tell you when it is safe to come down off the stage and be me." The Authentic Self, sort of becomes the Director for the play, but no one knows, everyone just sees the actor.

Fig. 1:

Permission by membership to graphicsfactory.com

There's only one problem with this. When is the time to take off the mask and costume? How do we know? How will we hear the voice of the Authentic Self through the cacophony and drama? How will the mask suddenly grow ears that hear beyond the stage? The truth for most of us is that we can't. By the time we are safe enough to take off the mask and costume, we can no longer hear the voice of the Authentic Self. We have become so attached to the role that we think that this is who we are.

Thus, for many of us, it takes a crisis to get us to start questioning. Now I truly hope that one day we will reach a time in our evolutionary process in which having a crisis will no longer be necessary to get us to stop and listen a little to the voice of the Authentic Self. But for now, pain is often the ONLY thing we will listen to. Sometimes it takes more than one crisis. Why? Because in the first two or three crises we are just trying to do the same old thing harder. We are not asking those questions that take us to the Authentic Self. We have adapted so well to lives of chaos and disruption that we know what to do: We just do the same old thing we've always done, but just do it harder.

Something has to hit a nerve. Sad but true. Something has to say to us, "This isn't working anymore." Then we start listening.

Now, what has this got to do with the exercises we did above in which we drew pictures of our favorites? Once upon a time a psychiatrist, named Sigmund Freud, came up with a term: Projection. We don't have to like anything else about Mr. Freud to appreciate the term. Let's use the example of the TV tower and the TV. (See Fig. 2, below).

Fig. 2:

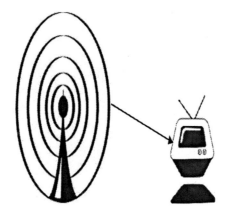

Permission by membership to graphicsfactory.com

The picture on our TV is really coming to us from the TV tower, (to which the picture is often really coming from a satellite, and which has been sent to the satellite from a studio somewhere). But when something goes wrong with our picture on the TV at home, we kick the TV. If it's the cable, we call the cable company, though the picture is really not coming from either of these two sources. Projection is like that. Another analogy that fits is the movie projector in a theatre. The film passes over the light and is reflected onto a mirror, which reflects it back onto a screen. We project onto others, the way the film is projected onto the screen. We have the ability to say that other people, places and things have certain traits, carry certain emotions, or give off certain attitudes. The question is, how do we know where that is coming from? Is it from them, or do we see it in them because it is in us?

Above, we looked at favorite animals, places, colors and most admired people. Because they are *our* favorites, they are some of our projections. The question to be asked is, is it possible for me to even recognize the traits I projected onto my favorites, if I don't also have those same traits somewhere in me? How could we recognize something we are not even familiar with? How would we know how to name it, or even qualify its goodness or badness for us? The truth is, we wouldn't. We can't recognize a trait with which we do not even resonate. How would we resonate with something that has no point of recognition within us?

So, let's say, you projected "peace" onto a beach scene, which you picked to be your favorite place. Now, you and I both know that the beach doesn't have peace. The truth is that you allow yourself to feel peace when you go to the beach. You, sort of, *let the peace out of its cage* at the beach. It has really been in you all along, but you open yourself to the possibility of peace when you go to the beach. If peace were not already in you, you would not even recognize it when it hit you. So, the real story is that you carry your peace around with you all of the time, and you allow yourself to experience it only sometimes. All of our projections are just like that. Pause and consider this for a moment.

Now, let's try something else. Imagine for a minute, that you have all of the traits inside of you that you projected onto your favorite animal, place, color and most admired person, along with the traits you described as yourself. Hold that thought and turn the page.

Draw below a picture or a symbol, which encapsulates all of the traits you just imagined or that you wrote beside all of your favorites. (This does not have to be a picture of a person, it can be a symbol that carries the traits you imagined. It might help to draw the first image that comes to mind. Thinking too hard often means you are editing your own soul.)

You have just created your first working image of the Authentic Self. You may alter this image as we progress through the exercises. But for now, this is a real image of the real you.

Ponderings: Now, we know that if we have created an image such as an angel, a mountain range, an ocean, or something equally expansive, that it is going to be hard to believe that this symbol really does represent your Authentic Self. But try this on. We are defining the Authentic Self as that part of each of us which has never been wounded, is wise, and knows the direction for our lives. Say it again. The Authentic Self has *never been wounded.* How can this be? Try this: What is missing from our view of this tree?

Fig. 3:

Permission by membership to graphicsfactory.com

Did you think of Roots? Many times we don't. So, if you didn't, that's okay. But just for clarity's sake, add the roots to the picture now, writing in over these words.

Now, let's just think about this tree. Can you see it clearly, in your mind's eye? If you can, then you know that the tree, as it exists above ground, may experience all manner of problems and blessings. The wind blows, sometimes gracefully, sometimes violently. Storms come, sometimes violently. Sun shines, rain falls. Snow falls, ice captures the branches. Sometimes lightning strikes the tree. Sometimes people put nails in the bark, creating a cancer where the nail is. Sometimes, branches break off and fall. Leaves come and go. All of this and more happens to the tree.

Now, we might look at this tree and say that the tree is the sum total of all of its experiences. We may say that it grew the way it did because it had some very bad experiences. We may even forecast the future of this tree, saying that it will never make a very big or beautiful tree, because it has had such a hard life. But what about the roots?

See, everyday of that tree's life, regardless of what was happening above ground, the tree's roots are doing just fine, thank you very much. And they are doing the same thing, all day, every day. All day, everyday they just send life energy to the tree. Though the tree is experiencing a branch falling, the roots are experiencing life energy. (Now, hang with me here. Maybe you don't believe a tree experiences at all. But this is just an analogy.) Whatever is going on above ground, the roots are still doing the same thing every day, every night, all the time. And the strength of the roots is amazing. Even if the tree is chopped down, the roots may create new growth, may even grow new branches. The tree may even begin to look like a whole new tree. In fact, it is very hard to kill a tree. In order to kill a tree, one has to dig deeply all around the roots, and then dig out the roots even as far down as the tap root goes. And even when the tree is dead, it can become mulch for the next generations of trees. For us, the truth is that we have most probably already been through the worst that we can go through. And we survived it. How? We had the strength of the Authentic Self (the roots) working for us.

The Authentic Self is like the roots of the tree. Though the tree may have been wounded above ground, the roots have never been wounded. Though the tree may grow in an odd shaped way, the roots carry in them the pathway to the sun. And so the Authentic Self is wise and knows the direction for our lives, because it has no wounds to misguide it.

Your roots are your authenticity.

Now, you have a workable image of your own Authentic Self. Let's go find out what role you've been playing.

Defining

The

Role

Now, what about the Role we've played. Let's try a few out. As you are looking through the next several pages, see if any of the characteristics of the roles fit you. Don't try too quickly to pick one. Wait until you get to the end. Then go back and survey them and see which one or two fit the _best_ of all of them:

Fig. 4:

Party Dude(tte)
is Mercury personified.
Tricking the world by tricking the
self, Party Dude(ttes) survive by
masking the sad, lost face
with the makeup and
mirrors of a clown.

Permission by membership to graphicsfactory.com

The class clown, the drunk wearing a lamp-shade (instead of crying in his/her beer), the first to crack a joke at the wake, the Party Dude is always on the look out for a party. But there is no music for this dance. The Party Dude knows how to run on empty with electric wit and contagious humor. His/her motto, like Peter Pan's is: I won't grow up! And while the world is laughing, the person behind the mask is hiding between the dry, empty cracks in the floor.

Fig. 5:

The Runaway Child

may have successfully run from family or past shame through geographic therapy. They move to Australia when they grow up. Or, they just distance themselves emotionally from family and/or problems. Sometimes this role takes on the form of "invisible woman/man," as the ultimate distancer.

Permission by membership to graphicsfactory.com

Again, the archetype is Mercury, the trickster, for, in effect, this person has chosen to separate from the family, perpetrator, past history and/or emotions, assuming that this is, in and of itself, the cure. Mentally the Runaway is an expert at compartmentalization. They fear that to feel, to know, to be associated with, to remember *is* the identity; so they choose another identity, which is completely separate from their own repressed emotional world.

Fig. 6:

The Scapegoat

is a complex identification, which combines Superhero
with super-sinner. The archetype is the devil himself. It is based on
the old Hebrew myth, in which a goat is sacrificed for the sins of a
community.

Permission by membership to graphicsfactory.com

Scapegoats may take one of two possible routes: that of righteous sacrifice
(Priest) or that of evil personified (Black Sheep). In the first, they try very hard
to be very good, because inside they feel guilty for everything. We call these the
Priest roles, because they are always sacrificing the self for the sins of others.
They actually empathically absorb the guilt for which others are responsible.
They then carry it around in their psyche and body as if it is theirs. In so doing,
they rescue others from having to take responsibility for their own guilt. In the
second, those with the Black Sheep role identify with "badness," getting themselves in trouble with the law, or other authorities, or just doing things that
embarrass the family. Like the Priest, they have absorbed guilt from others, but
unlike the Priest, instead of trying to compensate for it, they act it out. The
reality is that whether the Black Sheep or the Priest, these persons carry an
internal sense of shame for simply being alive.

Fig. 7:

The Superhero

"Bring me your poor, your tired,
your hungry ..."

Permission by membership to graphicsfactory.com

Superheroes have projected their entire ego-state onto their social world. While they feel authentic compassion, it is displaced. The archetype is Dionysus who rescued his mother from Hades and also rescued many other women. As children, Superheroes developed the ability to keep themselves alive by saving their world in some kind of psychological or real way. Superheroes can be very nurturing (somehow salvaging the feminine archetype within), but the archetype is the still masculine. Superheroes, whether male or female, live out a very tough masculine role that expends an exorbitant amount of time and energy in the external world, in order to avoid having to save the Self. Superheroes cannot be nurtured because the rest of the world needs it more. Often they do not make it into therapy until they are in very poor health or in immense pain, having carried the world around in their very bodies for so many years. It is the ultimate trickery to seduce ourselves into the belief that saving others is the same as rescuing the Self. This role is difficult to let go of, for who doesn't want to be seen by others as heroic?

Fig. 8:

Superwoman:

Like the Superhero, this role is based on a male
archetype. This one is Hercules, for indeed, the profound efforts
and feats that this woman performs are Herculean.

Permission by membership to graphicsfactory.com

The role has very few truly compassionate responses, for these come from the
Authentic Self. Rather it is based on fear, fear of loss, which feels so enormous
that it controls all behavior by impulse and compulsion. Often it covers up and
is compensation for it's opposite, the helpless child. "I must show you I can do
this, and maybe then I'll believe that I can do it." This woman can jump higher,
faster, longer than her peers, with both hands and feet tied behind her back.
She is not surprised that others expect this of her. She expects it of herself. She
is not the Martyr, who resents all that she does, for she may actually be enjoying it on some level. The problem is that her mental and physical health are
declining, often unknown to her, so that one day all of the pain she has
repressed may erupt in a deep feeling of helplessness and hopelessness. Notice
that this image lacks a head. That is because the Superwoman demonstrates a
large chasm between the head and the heart. She simply does not allow herself
to recognize her own sensations, feelings, emotions. They are a waste of time.
This person may also be a man (Superman). More often then not men choose
the Superhero, rather than superman, but it's possible. But regardless of gender, this role always lives out the masculine archetype.

Fig. 9:

For the *Victim,* everything always spells Victim.
The Archetype is Prometheus who saved the world
by giving it fire, only to experience the agony of death over
and over again as his punishment.

Permission by membership in graphicsfactory.com

Victims protect the world from being victimized (thus keeping it neatly constructed along the lines of their own understanding) by becoming the ultimate Victim. While they may know that they feel imprisoned, or boxed in, they are certain that someone else holds the key to their release. Even their very bodies betray and victimize them through illness. Yet, they dare not let go of the role, for to stop being victimized means that someone else will be. And that someone may be the Victim's victim as s/he turns Bully/Perpetrator. Often the chief feeling is that life is very hard, it's always an uphill battle, and I'm always battling with someone or something that is bigger and stronger than I. I cannot do what I want or fulfill my dreams because "he," "she," or "it" will stop me. Feeling overwhelmed is much easier than taking responsibility for one's life. "Yes, but ..." and "I had no choice" are favorite phrases.

Fig. 10:

The Bully/Perpetrator:
The archetype is that of the night monster,
the big, the bad and the ugly. Leviathan.
But the truth is that the Bully identifies
him or herself as such because s/he
inherently understands that to take such as
role means s/he cannot be victimized.

Permission by membership to graphicsfactory.com

Identity is the primary issue for the Bully or Perpetrator though this is not often
how it is viewed by society. They identify with the "evil" side of the good/evil
polarity, which has become a psychic complex of monumental proportions. In
actuality, what has happened is that all of the "evil" they see in their world has
been absorbed into their own identity. This has two purposes: It protects both
the Bully/Perpetrator's bully or perpetrator, and it protects the
Bully/Perpetrator. In the first, if I absorb your identity and act like you act, then
I really can't say much to you about what you did wrong, thereby protecting you
from my rage. Often, Bullies or Perpetrators were bullied or perpetrated by a
person or persons whom they loved or admired deeply. They need to continue
to love and admire this person, so they take on the person's "sins." In the second,
if I hurt you, then you can't hurt me, because I've made myself invulnerable, or
so I think, by hurting you first. In fact, Bully/Perpetrators are not "evil" at all,
though they certainly act the part. Instead they are very frightened, and carry
immense portions of shame though these have been repressed deeply.
Bully/Perpetrators often become addicted to the abuse cycle, as they depend
more and more on the role to help them find their way out of desperation.

These are just a few of the possibilities, but many find themselves in one or two of these roles. Which role(s) fit you best? Describe and/or draw that role here as you experience it.

On this page, write down all of the behaviors, feelings or thoughts that you have that match the role you chose. (For example: If you chose Scapegoat, one example might be, "I feel guilty all of the time." "I say 'I'm sorry'" when I bump into inanimate objects. "I feel as if everything is always my fault." If the Victim: "I feel that life is always too hard for me," "Others always have it better," "People are mean and unhelpful," or, "I keep finding myself being taken advantage of, or Victimized again by others," etc.)

_____

_____

_____

_____

_____

_____

_____

_____

_____

_____

_____

_____

_____

_____

_____

_____

_____

_____

_____

_____

_____

_____

_____

_____

_____

_____

_____

_____

Now, you have a picture of the Authentic Self and a picture of the role that you have played. We will continue to get clearer on these as we go.

Ponderings: The truth is that as we have said, we all develop roles to some degree. We do this because we all come from family systems in which we develop a role in order to stay attached to our primary caretakers. It would be a very different world if children received appropriate mirroring for their Authentic Selves instead of being subtly and overtly expected to play a certain role in the family. For example, if a child were to come to mother or father during play and express anger over being hit on the head with a truck, they might be told, "Oh, that really hurt, didn't it. Sometimes when we hurt we get really mad." Instead, they are often told, "Oh, you don't really hate Johnny, he didn't mean to hurt you." Or, "Don't cry."

In fact, our families subtly assign us roles, because they can. As we have said, we all fear the abandonment of our primary caretakers instinctively knowing that without them we will die. This fear is tremendous. Thus, we adapt to the roles assigned to us, in order to maintain that safe feeling of belonging that we think we need so badly. As we grow, we measure ourselves by how well we are playing the role assigned to us. And, in fact, we think that we are good or bad in exact correlation to how well or badly we are playing the assigned role. For example, if, as Superwoman (or in this instance, superchild) we take care of younger siblings, cook supper for Dad when he gets home from work, and can always manage to keep a smile on our faces, we believe that we have done well. If, on the other hand, we burn Dad's super one night, we think that we are truly bad people for having done this. We feel guilty in exact proportion to our fear because we know that our families are measuring us by how well we provide the role we are assigned. If as I grow older, I try to relinquish this role, there will be many ways in which my family, particularly Dad, may try to get me to take it back on.

Imagine, in the picture below, (Fig. 11) that one of the roles hanging on the end decides to jump off.

Fig. 11:

We measure ourselves by how well we play the roles, how true we are to our assigned and agreed upon identity. Not by the authenticity of our identities, but by how well we are pleasing those around us. We are like puppets on strings, all attached to the same measuring stick. Those on the ends of the measuring stick are those who can see the outside world and make comparisons between it and the family system. Those in the middle have a harder time seeing the outside world. (This does *not* imply that Party Dude(tte)s and Bully Perpetrators—as the image depicts—are more likely to do this, only that *whoever* is able to see beyond the family drama is closer to jumping off the stick.) Once one of those two on the end decide to live authentically, jumping off the stick, the stick tilts, leaving the rest in the family to swing and bang into each other for a while until they establish a new homeostasis. While this may be uncomfortable for everyone, it also provides an opportunity for everyone left hanging on the stick to jump off too. Their discomfort gives them options that they never had before. Now, they may choose to become authentic also. Or they may not. In fact, they may never change, but rather go seek out another person to fill the role you used to play. But at least now they have a choice. Therefore, though there may be considerable gnashing of teeth when one member changes, the person who changes is actually doing each other member a favor: giving them the opportunity to choose.

However, before anyone else does any changing, the person who jumped off the stick may experience both internal and external resistance to the change. Family members, out of their discomfort, may try to coerce those who jumped off to get back up into their positions, and/or those who jumped off may feel guilty for doing so. More on this later. For now, suffice it to say that one of the chief payoffs we get from staying in the role is avoiding this terrible gnashing of teeth that we suspect will come if we ever stop doing the expected. But we lose the Authentic Self, when we choose to stay stuck and the price we pay is something akin to an inner death, or a dead-like existence in which we stay dissociated from every part of us that says, **"Live, be alive, be fully alive! Where's your passion? What do you love? What do you hate? Is anyone home???"**

Ponderings: REMEMBER THIS: You are not being asked to take off the role, but to invite into your awareness the Authentic Self. *It is not what we say "no" to in life that makes us different, it is what we say "yes" to that makes for permanent change.* It is very frightening to most of us to think of changing our roles, taking off the old costume and mask and…. And, then what? Therefore, you will not be asked, through the working of this book, to take off the role. You will simply be asked to recognize it. You will come to know it, and its messages to you, intimately. At the same time, you will be becoming aware of another, yet unrecognized, part of yourself, the Authentic Self. And you will learn how to say, "yes" to it. As you do that, the old role will just naturally have less and less room in your life. Why? Because your authenticity gives you peace and joy.

Yes, we said the J-word. JOY. Joy is not that small satisfaction that comes from living the role well. Joy is not small at all. And joy is not that Bible School phrase we heard: J-esus first, O-thers second and Y-ou last. First, it is very important to understand that it is utterly impossible to put anything or anyone before yourself. Why? Because you are always there, experiencing whatever it is that you are doing. You may put yourself in a dissociative state so that you do not thoroughly experience it, but even the choice to put yourself in a dissociative state is *you* choosing an experience. You cannot put someone else in that space or in your own experience. It is impossible. You may choose to negate your own needs, yet *you* are still there in the experience of negation. You cannot go away to a second or third place. It is impossible.

Second, you are always getting something out of every action and reaction you have. It may be "Primary Gain" which is a direct gain, such as a paycheck for work done; or it may be "Secondary Gain," which is a more unconscious gain. An unconscious gain might look like this: I scratch your back and ignore my own needs because to do so means that you will keep me around. Secondary gain is what living the role is all about. Still, though you may have decided to negate your Self, behind the mask and costume of your choice, you did not go away. Therefore, you cannot put anyone else ahead of yourself, not your partner, not your children, not Jesus, not anyone. You are always first in the experience of your life, regardless of what other things, people or places you may also choose to experience.

One of the primary problems we have, and will discuss in more detail in the latter part of this book, is that when others try to manipulate us into coming back into the role, or into anything, they often use the phrase, "You are being so selfish!" Guilt trip coming, duck!! We then feel guilty and do whatever it is that the family member, friend, relative or spouse wishes for us to do. Then we have not been selfish. Whatever else has happened, at least we have not had to say to ourselves that we were selfish. So, who was selfish, now?

However, as we've said, it is important to recognize that family members may choose to become more conscious and authentic in response to your choice to become authentic as well. Authenticity is never selfish, for it always has the potential for positive impact on others. In my practice, I quite often see a client who is having trouble with his/her primary relationship. The partner refuses to come to therapy, but the client comes and proceeds to become more authentic. At first the more authentic client reports that the spouse is uncomfortable with the changes that the client is making. But sometimes the client comes in later with stories that the spouse sat down with them one day and said something like: You know, I've noticed all the changes you've been making and I'm really very impressed. I'd like to talk with you about our relationship and begin to work on it with you." It won't sound just like that, but it's the same message. Of course, it doesn't always happen just like that. Sometimes, in fact, the spouse decides to leave. The fact is that whichever way it goes, authenticity does create changes in the external world, which match by degree and intensity the changes in our internal world. Though others may not change as a result of our becoming more authentic, at least they are offered the opportunity to do so. And the clarity we gain from their choice NOT to change, is very empowering. We will discuss this more later.

Let's talk about Dual Roles for a while. If you chose two roles, both of which seem to fit almost equally, then you have played dual roles. Or, you may have played one role for a while, and then played another. For example, you may have played the Superwoman, or Superhero role throughout your childhood, and into your adulthood. Then a crisis comes along, a taller building than you can leap this time, and you fall flat on your face into a Victim identity. Where before, you could accomplish almost anything, now it is almost impossible to get up in the morning. You feel that everything is an uphill journey, with City Hall sitting at the top of the hill, and you still have to fight City Hall to go any further. And everyone knows that "you can't fight City Hall." You feel defeated before you start.

Linda Leonard, wrote a book called, *The Wounded Woman*, in which she talks about this very thing. She says that "The Amazon Woman," (her name for what I call the Superwoman), has a "Puella" (her word that closest fits our definition of the Victim, though the word means "little girl") living underneath it. In fact, the Amazon Woman is trying to "fix" or rescue the little girl, or the Victim, by being so big, brave and capable. But something will eventually happen which sends the Amazon Woman reeling backwards in time and space to the little girl or the Victim she's been desperately trying to rescue all along. Now instead of acting like Superwoman, she is cowering in the corners of her life, unable to move. At this point, she may even become suicidal. (Leonard, 1983). Now, we know that she is talking about women here, but the same exact phenomena happen to men, with different labels. The Superhero, (often a male role) can become a Victim, for the same exact reason.

Of course, what such a crisis ultimately does is give us the opportunity to move beyond the role and into the Authentic Self. Essentially the crisis informs us that the role won't work anymore. The intent of our emotional response to this crisis is to give us information about what is and is not working in our lives. If people wish to have happy lives, they must do something other than overcompensate for woundedness, or become woundedness. We will see, through the working of this book, that if we are going to live authentically we can not live our whole lives responding only to a few moments, hours, days, years of our history. In fact, in order to really grow up, we must outgrow our upbringing. As we do this our lives will become fresh and new each day.

So this is how the dual role transitions through time. It changes to its opposite. The Superwoman, Superhero changes to Victim. The Perpetrator changes to Victim, or the Victim changes to Perpetrator. The Runaway (trying to escape shame, blame, guilt, responsibility) changes to the Scapegoat (acceptor of all guilt and responsibility). The Party Dude changes to the Runaway, usually about the time s/he gets caught crying somewhere. And on and on, over time, and through crises, the roles may change accordingly.

It is also possible to have two roles at the same time. This may happen through piecing together parts of two roles. For example, you may be a Runaway, because you have, in some way, dissociated yourself from family, but you may also try hard, as the Superhero, to rescue others, who remind you of the family from which you dissociated. Or you may feel guilty and responsible for everything as the Scapegoat, and put on the Superwoman, or Superhero identity in order to compensate for the guilt. You may feel victimized constantly, yet also, on occasion act out the Perpetrator role. You may act out the Party Dude(tte) role, but do so because you feel you need a break from playing the Superhero role. Or, you may play the Party Dude(tte) and the Runaway roles simultaneously, running away to the party. Dual roles are not terribly uncommon, but your job is to figure out the role(s) and the messages you get from them.

In the assignment below, you will be asked to become a bit clearer about your role. While you are doing this assignment, please remember that this is a role. It is not who you really are. You are the Authentic Self. You put on the role in order to survive your circumstances. This role truly did fit your own unique circumstances in a way that no other role could have. You intuitively knew what would work the best in your life and family and you chose and were simultaneously assigned your role accordingly. Also, after a few attempts at trying it, you found that it worked to accomplish whatever you needed for it to accomplish. So, you kept it. Now, however, your role is more in the way than anything. It keeps you from the very thing you are seeking: happiness. So, congratulate yourself on being smart enough to pick out a role which would keep you alive long enough to get you to the point where you don't need the role anymore. And then move into the assignment.

You should also know before you start, how we are defining behaviors, thoughts and messages. *Behaviors* are simply the things that you do and the things that you say. They are often things that we can account for consciously, but sometimes we are not aware of our own behaviors. In this case, you may need to ask others for input about your behaviors. *Thoughts* are the opinions we have of ourselves, others and life. We may be conscious or unconscious of these. However, as you are doing this exercise, you may just have a feeling that one particular thought resonates with something inside. If that is so, then it is probably an unconscious thought. Thoughts are also sometimes associated with our behaviors in that we may be thinking about what we do. These will generally be more accessible. *Messages* are extremely important. Ultimately, they become our *mantra*. A mantra is a statement (perhaps not in words, but in thoughts) that you make over and over again to yourself day in and day out. A mantra may be conscious or unconscious, but either way it is extremely powerful. These mantras translate into attitudes, emotions, moods and behaviors. They can create depression, defeat and hopelessness, or they can create happiness and self-confidence. Very often they are created as a part of the development of the identity itself. The messages that we picked up from our environment when we were very young, along with the unresolved issues we absorbed became part of the psychological makeup of the mask and costume.

For example, if Mom used to say "I don't give a damn" every time I asked her for something or needed her, then later when I am an adult playing out the Scapegoat/Priest role, I may hear that message every time I feel need come up inside me. Then I may repeat the mantra, "I don't give a damn what you need." As I do this I feel more and more powerless over my life. No one gives a damn about me, not even God. I am then trapped behind a wall of people who don't care about me at all. How will I ever get what I need without some help from these people who don't care? That is the power of the message that becomes a mantra. Sometimes we don't notice that we are giving ourselves these mantras until we stop and think about it, which is precisely why we are stopping to think about it. So, stop and consider. If this message resonates inside of you with a feeling of "oh yes, that's how I feel," then it's probably a message you give to yourself or a mantra you repeat to yourself, of which you are not conscious. Circle or highlight it.

If you end up circling/highlighting almost everything under all of the roles, you are doing something that we clinicians have come to know as, Bibliohypochondriasis. It is an over-identification with just about every diagnostic thing that you read. It is based on fear that you are ultimately the sickest of the sick and the most villainous of the villains. You are not. You are your Authentic Self. You have simply been playing a role to keep yourself alive. More often then not, the idea of being the sickest of the sick is a Scapegoat theme, so you may want to go back and look harder at that one. If you need to, sit with the picture you drew of the Authentic Self in front of you, while you do this assignment. Circle then, everything that *truly* fits your behavior and thoughts and messages. If you cannot get clear on the mantras, just use the behaviors and thoughts here. You can come back to the mantras later. If you still cannot get clear, take the book to your Therapist and ask for assistance in completing this assignment.

On the next page is a list of the various behaviors, thoughts and mantras associated with each of the roles sited above. Circle thoughts, behaviors and mantras that seem to fit for you. Note that words that are highlighted by asterisk (*) below, will be fully discussed in the notations following the chart.

Role	Thought	Behavior	Mantra
Runaway	*That's stupid (to feel). *Let me out of this shit! *I'm not dealing with that! (someone else's feelings). *It's ridiculous to get so upset over this. *GET OVER IT! *I will show them! *I'll be somebody. *I am not like them. *I'm always either worse or better than others. *I'm always mentally comparing myself to others and falling short, unless I feel superior due to my numerous good deeds. *I may use my intellect as a weapon or as a method to rationalize my distancing behaviors, or as a method to avoid feelings altogether. *Shame on me if I do anything that even remotely resembles my origins.	*I move to Australia, Ethiopia, Russia, across the nation, etc. (geographical cure). *I never call family or I call them rarely. *I don't associate with anyone like my family. *I tell people, "You are being ridiculous, or GET OVET IT!" when they are sad or upset. *I emotionally distance from family and friends. *I have had many short-term relationships or none at all due to a deep-seated fear of commitment. *I often tell others how I succeeded from poor beginnings as a way of distancing my self from those beginnings. *If someone finds out about my family I may deny my connection to them. *I categorize people into different strata of prestige, all related to my fear of shame. *If I am not constantly successful in appearance, form, manner, and in finances, I am nobody and may, therefore, sabotage my successes. *If you look or act in anyway reminiscent of my family, I'll run from you and you may not ever know why.	*Don't go there (to feelings). * Hurry up and get over this! *Succeed at all costs! *Run from anything that looks, smells, tastes, acts like my family or the problem. *At the slightest difficulty in relationship: RUN! *This (feeling) shouldn't matter. *It's not that important. *GET OVER IT! *You should have dealt with this already. *Commitment means putting up with someone else's shit: why bother! *I'm somebody! *I won't ever tolerate one tiny reminder of my past. *I'm ashamed of my face because it reminds me of my family. *You wouldn't really want to know me. *Shame is synonymous with my past.

Role	Thought	Behavior	Mantra
Scapegoat (Priest)	*I am at fault. *I'm trying. (In answer to every internal demand to get better, there is this voice that says, I'm trying so hard, but I just can't get it.) *I'm sorry, I'm so sorry that I can't get it right. *If I could just get it right, you'd be alright. *I'm somehow responsible for all that happens in the lives of those I love. *I'm certain that if you are unhappy, I could do something about it if I just tried hard enough. *I am perpetually anxious about doing the wrong thing. If something goes wrong, my first thought is "what did I do?" *I might hurt your feelings if I tell you the truth. *It's always better to be nice!	*I'm always doing good deeds for others. *I tell others, no thank you through body language, words and behavior, anytime anyone wishes to do something for me. *I feel guilty about almost everything. *I apologize very frequently, even when no one is blaming me, even when I run into an object. *I cannot accept a compliment. *I often get in the middle of others' arguments, to provide justice, only to get blamed by both parties. *I sabotage my own success frequently. *I go through periods of feeling very guilty, even though I can't really explain why. *I never speak up to authority figures. *I may be very quiet, not allowing anyone to really know me. *I may seem obsequious to others, who see me as someone who will do anything for them. *I may find myself in relationships with others who use me. *I may find myself in relationships with others who give nothing to the relationship. *I find it extremely difficult to be honest about negative feelings toward others.	*I must make the sacrifice. *What if I get it wrong? *I must be right about everything. *If I am wrong people will suffer. *I'll never get it right. *I will sacrifice to make others feel good. *Sacrifice is the name of every endeavor. *You don't really want to know me. *If you really knew the truth about me, you'd run. *It is my job to make other's happy. *I don't deserve to be happy. *I have failed if I can't make everything right for everyone. *If you are unhappy, it must be because I haven't done a good enough job, or I've done something wrong. *I'm sorry, I'm sorry. *Oh, I'm so sorry. *I'm trying. I'm trying so hard, you just don't know how hard I'm trying.

Role	Thought	Behavior	Mantra
Scapegoat (Black Sheep)	*I'll show you. *You want to blame me, you say I'm bad? Fine, I'll just be bad. *You just don't understand me. Its fun to do the things I do. There's a thrill in getting away with it. *Sometimes, I think that there's a thrill in getting caught too. *I like living on the edge. *I'm a bad seed. *Nobody cares about me anyway. *People just use people. *There is no real love in the world. *Everybody's just in it for themselves. *I had to do it … I had no choice—they made me do it. *It's fun to outwit authority figures. *This is who I am … deal with it! *Why would I want to change, *I'm having a great time!	*I get in trouble at school. *I get fired often from work. *I get in trouble with the law. *I get involved in illicit activities such as drugs and alcohol. *I may become addicted. *I do things very differently from my family. *I mock custom, privilege, rank, title, authority. *I would never let anyone know that I have a compassionate or good feeling. *I do and say things for the shock value. *If you hurt me, I will take vengeance on you. *I find that though I have little to no faith in my own ability to change or improve my behavior, I put great stock in what you can do to get me to change … but then I resist you. *Other people have to be good even if I can't be. *I am certain that I will eventually betray you, if you don't betray me first.	*I'm a bad dude. *I'm just a bad dude. *That's all I've ever been, that's all I'll ever be. *I'm out of control. *I can't help it, i.e., it's your fault. *No one good could put up with me. *No one could ever really love me. *I don't know why I do the things I do. I just do. *That makes me bad to the bone. *There is no goodness in me. *If I can just be the badness they say I am, then I don't ever have to deal with finding my self-worth. *It's all a joke anyway. *Life is a joke. A big cosmic joke. *Don't trust anyone, anytime. *I am evil.

Role	Thought	Behavior	Mantra
Bully/Perpetrator*	*I'm always strategizing. *The other guy is always an enemy. *People are out to get their own. People will hurt you every chance they get. *They don't know. *They'll never find out about me. *I'll get away with it. *Feeling small is extremely embarrassing to me. *I wish I wasn't the way I am. *I hate myself. *You'll never get it, what I've been through. *I don't feel guilty ... they deserved it. *I feel great remorse deep down inside, but I will not allow myself to go there. *Deep down, I am terrified of being hurt again, and to compensate, I always try to look strong and brave. *They are always trying to piss me off, trick me or get something out of me. *If I tell you anything about myself, you will just use it against me. *If I don't manipulate, I'll just be a doormat. *I need to feel powerful to feel good about myself.	*I am sexually, physically, emotionally, verbally or mentally abusive** to others. * I can look you in the eye and lie to you. *My body is usually in the flight or fight mode. * I try hard not to feel. *I chose younger or more vulnerable people to hang out with. * I manipulate to get what I want. *I may be sexually addicted and/or addicted to relationship. *My addiction to abuse may keep me in a cycle of shame, in which I flip between trying to impress you and abusing you. *I shut down when confronted. *I play mind-games when confronted. *I anger easily. *I may explode frequently if this gives me a sense of power, or I may just seethe in silence. *I find it extremely difficult to be assertive. *I blame others frequently for things that go on in my life. *I am often very impulsive. *When I am not being abusive, I can often be intimidating through belligerence to get you scared of me.	*Put/keep your guard up. *Never let anyone inside/know you. *Life is shameful and disgusting. *I am evil. *You can't hurt me. *I'll always hurt you first. *There's no hope for me. * I'm way out of control and there is nothing anyone can do about it. *People would never understand me if I tried to tell them. *Watch out for me, I'm really a bad dude. *They don't want to mess with me, I'll hurt them. *Nobody/nothing scares me. *I'm tough. *I can handle anything. *I don't have to deal with this shit. *You can't trust people. *There is no way you will ever get to me. *It's all your fault. *You deserved it.

Role	Thought	Behavior	Mantra
Party Dude(tte)	*Life's a party. *Come on, lets just go have some fun. *Aw! Come on! Get over it. *Life was not meant for anything but having fun. *When people are sad, I always know how to make them laugh. *Once they are laughing, it is all over—I've done my job. *I don't need to know what I feel. *This whole thing about therapy is a joke. *Your kidding, right? *You don't really mean that people have to be sad sometimes. Jesus! I'll get drunk first. *I know, I know, I'm in debt, but a guy's/girl's gotta have some fun.	*I am always cracking jokes. *Some of my jokes are quite off-color. *Some of my jokes are sarcastic. *I say sarcastic things to people at times, and when they figure me out, *I just tell them that I'm joking. *I find it difficult to sit still when others are expressing negative feelings.*** *I get angry, if someone figures me out and pushes me to feel. *I have a hard time with committed relationships, because I know that eventually it's going to get heavy. *If I ever get sad or experience any negative feeling and you ask me what I'm feeling, my answer will almost always be I don't know. *I may have trouble staying employed at one job. *I can become very dependent on others to take care of me.	*Don't cry. *Don't worry. *Be happy. *Make others laugh. *It's a waste of time to feel any negative feelings.*** *My life is all about making everybody laugh. *If they're laughing they can't be crying, right? *Don't tell anybody, but I really feel very empty. *Listen, there is no need to take everything so seriously. *You want me to what? Marry you? See ya! *Children are really great, because they know how to be cool. *I won't grow up!

Role	Thought	Behavior	Mantra
Superhero	*I must feel needed in order to feel that my life has purpose. *I feel very righteous, or just self-confident, when I can be there for others. *I feel in control when I am rescuing others. *I don't ever have to think about myself when I am rescuing others. *I always have an eye out for what I can do for others. *I consider myself to be a very compassionate and caring person. *I know little to nothing about myself or my motivations. *It is very important that people see me as good. *It is very important that I please others.	*I spend a great deal of time rescuing others. *I may take on jobs such as fireman, police officer, nurse, doctor, therapist or teacher. (Not that these roles always imply Superhero roles.) *I always know just the right thing to say, and the right thing to do to rescue you. *I often set up relationships with others who need my constant rescue. *I often perform great feats to rescue others and am considered by many to be a hero. *I may know every detail of my partner's life, psychoanalyzed down to the last nasal hair. *I behave in ways that please others. *I feel that this is helpful to them	*I live for others. *When others need me, I am certain of my role in life. *Chaos is my friend. *I'm a trouble-shooter. *Only when I am rescuing you, can I feel good about me. *My life seems to light up, when someone I know needs rescuing. *Sometimes, I may even set up a crisis, when life seems boring, just so that I can resolve it. *You need me. Don't you? *I feel lost and abandoned when there is no one to rescue. *If people are displeased with me, I have no intrinsic value. *I must be liked, even admired by anyone to whom I would like to relate.

Role	Thought	Behavior	Mantra
Superwoman (or Man)	*I don't know why, but I'm the one everyone always seems to call on for everything. *I must keep jumping higher, longer, faster than anyone else, even if my hands and feet are tied behind my back. *Everything always seems to be so disorganized without my help. *It must get done today. *I cannot live with things hanging over my head until tomorrow. *I feel a tremendous pressure of time. *I feel a tremendous responsibility to respond correctly to authority figures. *I do not understand people who can allow themselves things like sick leave and vacations. *I am certain that if I am not available, the world I've built will simply fall apart. *They need me. *They haven't a clue what they are doing. *I simply cannot fail. *I simply cannot deal with failure. *People who can't manage like I do are weak, inept, stupid or otherwise less than me. *I really enjoy what I do!	*People are always asking me to do more. *I quite often inform people of their laziness or ineptness. *I can do phenomenal things in short spans of time: paint a whole house in a few days; take on two full time jobs; take on three part-time jobs; take on multi-tasks at work and do all of them yesterday; take care of the kids, the spouse, the job and the parents, while attending school and never missing a beat; etc. *My children expect me to always be there for them. *My spouse expects me to take care of his/her every need. *When there is a problem everyone seems to think that it is my responsibility to intervene. *And I do and I usually solve the problem. *However, I find it very difficult to feel that same urgency about meeting my own needs. *I may develop physical symptoms such as: High blood pressure, arthritis, skin disorders, heart disorders, seizure disorders, or anything else to which I am genetically or otherwise prone. *In spite of physical symptoms, I may still find it very difficult to take care of myself. *If I ever delegate, I stand over the project micromanaging until they finally hand it back to me.	*If you want something done right, do it yourself! *No one else can do this job as good or as thoroughly as I. *If I stop for one second, the world of pain and betrayal will flood in on me and I won't know what to do. *Knowing what to do is vital. *I must always be on top of everything. *I must always, at least, appear to be certain. *People must not see any fear in me. *I can say anything to anyone, anytime, just let me at 'em! *If I complain, I'm just being a bitch. *I'm tough. *I can handle it. *Okay, I'll do it. *Repress. Repress. Repress. *Who am I? Who cares—let's just get the job done! *Failure is not an option! *If I fail I'm just as weak, inept, or stupid as they are!

Role	Thoughts	Behaviors	Mantra
Victim	*Life is very, very hard. *You are just like everyone else—I can't trust you. *You just want to use me. *No one can be trusted. *No one out there can ever understand how hard it is for me. *When I walk down the street, people know that there's something wrong with me. *I know what you are thinking; you are thinking I'm a dud. *It's never going to get any better. I know that. *All these people who keep insisting that it will get better, just don't know how hard it is. *Oh, I can play the game … but I'll always lose. *I can put on a happy face, but it won't change anything. *Sometimes I think God hates me. *I think that I am a total screw-up, the world would be better off without me. *I sometimes think, I'll show them, I'll hurt me. *I have suicidal thoughts. *Sometimes I make suicidal plans.	*I may find myself victimized by persons and circumstances repeatedly. *I may make friends and relationships with people who use, abuse and/or betray me. *I often express hopelessness and despair. *Others may spend significant time trying to rescue me. *I say "Yes, but …" quite often, in conversations in which people are offering advice as to how to get out of difficult situations. *I often try to mind-read what others are thinking about me, then turn what I've assumed into reaction. *I often misunderstand others' intent. *People often seem to give me unsolicited advice, then get frustrated with me and ultimately abandon me. *It seems to me that I am surrounded by people who have the upper hand. *I experience long bouts of depression. *I have difficulty with spirituality because I feel that God is against me. *I may have attempted suicide.	*People suffer, that's the way of the world. *You can't fight City Hall! *You'll never win. *You might as well give it up, there's no getting around it. *I can't. *I have no choice!!!! (Said quite often and often defensively.) *You just don't understand! *I don't know what I feel, what I think. *No one will ever understand. *It's hard (meaning, it's impossible.) *If you came from my background you might have a clue, but even then … *I'll never make it. *It's always going to be this way. *I'm cursed. *I'm damaged goods. *No one could ever possibly want me. *Everyone thinks they are better than me. *Say what you want, you have no clue how hard it is for me.

Ponderings: Let's talk about the Bully/Perpetrator for a moment (since it was highlighted above with an asterisk), because this role is one of the most difficult to understand simply because it causes such harm to others. It is essential to understand that the Bully/Perpetrator is simply living out another optional role in order to survive. Bully/Perpetrators, as noted above often feel a great deal of shame, but this shame is placed in an abuse cycle that harms and/or affects others deeply. In fact, Bully/Perpetrators have taken on the identity of their perpetrators. Therefore, the original perpetrator or bully remains guilt and shame-free, while the bullied, who dons the perpetrator costume, carries all the guilt and shame. What do they do with this shame and guilt? They act it out on others. If Bully/Perpetrators could ever once get it that this costume is not the real person inside, then they could be free to live a normal, healthy, authentic life.

Let's talk about acting out or reenactment. Children are great examples of this. Whatever they see their parents do, they do. No matter how many ways a parent says, don't do it, if the parent is doing it, the kid is going to try it. They act out what they see. Further, they act out what they don't see. Whatever unresolved issues are floating around in their homes are often absorbed by children as if they were sponges. These unresolved issues float around in the homes of family members (usually parents) who are resisting resolution. Their resistance allows them to project the problem outward, at which point it is available "in the air" so to speak, for others to absorb. At the point of absorption, the child begins the process of identifying with whatever unresolved issues were absorbed. So, children watch and do, and they walk around and absorb.

Children act this stuff out. They are walking, talking theatres in the round. They cannot or do not know how to tell you what they are feeling and thinking, but they will show you if you are watching. This is why children act out the drama of sexual abuse using anatomically correct dolls in play therapy rooms across the nation. This is why, if a child hears his father cursing his mother, he will curse a friend, typically a female, soon thereafter. This is why if mom or dad has unresolved and repressed rage laying dormant, "in the air" the child may pick it up as if it were her own and act it out. This is why when children are abused, some of them pick up the identity of abuser.

If a child sees Dad hit Mom, he does not go up to Daddy and say, "Hey, Dad, when you do that to my mother it disturbs me terribly, so I really wish that you would stop." No, they act out the drama in some way, through some role. Since we learned this acting out or reenacting ability so well when we were children, we still use it as adults. This is what Bully/Perpetrators are doing. They are acting out the drama of their own trauma(s) or drama(s) on others. The only difference is that no one has given the Bully/Perpetrator some anatomically correct dolls to act it out on. No, adults move their acting out behaviors into more adult-like themes, using other people as dolls. We all, when we are living out our roles, use some form of acting out with other adults. Bully/Perpetrators just do it in the form of abuse.

In the example of sexual abuse, for instance, Bully/Perpetrators may perform many acts of sexual molestation or rape or just a few. They may become involved in sadomasochistic ritual and/or become sexual addicted. Whatever the case, what is really unfolding is the trauma of their own sexual abuse, or the drama of whatever power/sexual issues were unresolved and floating around in their homes or actually projected onto them by their perpetrator(s). The secondary gain attached is this: If I am the Bully/Perpetrator I am now NOT the one who is victimized. This gives me a sense of power, which, because of the mix of power and sex in my mind, may be sexually arousing. Once, I was victimized by a perpetrator, but now, no more. Now, I am the one who is strong. Now I no longer have to abide that horrible feeling of powerlessness I had as a victim. Now, I can reenact my personal trauma on someone else. It is a form of vicarious revenge. My perpetrator is too big for me to seek my revenge on him, so I will take you, and unconsciously pretend to myself that I am taking vengeance on my perpetrator. Now, I carry the guilt and shame for my perpetrator (meaning that in my mind my perpetrator is just an innocent victim of his/her own impulses) and now I am as big as my perpetrator as well, rendering him/her, in my mind, harmless.

If I was not abused, though only a few identified sexual perpetrators deny this, I may have absorbed some unresolved sexual/power issue in my home. Perhaps I have been sexualized by a parent who was emotionally incestuous, and am rendered powerless by this sexualization. I may find that I am aroused by rendering others powerless. Or, perhaps my father or mother is addicted to sex and though they do not ever demonstrate this to me, they do talk about sex incessantly, and when they punish me it is often because they are threatened by my sexuality. I may pick this up in the air and begin to act it out by being aroused by punishing others. We could go on and on here, but the point is that I've begun to identify with some sexualized power issue, putting my I AM in front of it. This is how I survive. This is how I refuse to die of the drama in my life. The problem is, as it is with all of the roles, the role now begins to create its own dramas and traumas. As I grow up and begin to realize my life as an adolescent, young adult, adult, the role becomes more the problem than a cure. Of course, it is not only a problem for me, but I am harming others as I go.

**For the purposes of clarity, we are going to define the various kinds of abuse, noted under the Bully/Perpetrator role above. It is important that we clarify what is and is not abuse, so that you may get clear on whether you have been abused, or whether you have been abusive. The definitions follow:

<u>Sexual Abuse:</u> It is abuse anytime a sexual boundary is crossed. There are degrees of abuse, ranging from mild to severe. Nevertheless, our boundaries were always meant to be honored. The following is a list, which includes mild, moderate and severe forms of sexual abuse:

Touching inappropriately, as in:

- A parent slapping or rubbing a child on the butt frequently.
- An adult or older child using sexual touch on any part of the body of a child/adolescent.
- Adults or older children, or sometimes, even people of the same age, taking prolonged hugs on a frequent basis, especially when these are uncomfortable for the one hugged.
- An older child or adult touching or asking to touch the genitals or any other sexualized body part of a younger child.
- An older child or adult asking a child/adolescent to sit in his lap, over his genitals, mentally sexualizing that act, so that the child/adolescent gets that message.
- An adult or older child masturbating in the presence of a younger child/adolescent or persuading a child/adolescent to masturbate in the presence of the older child or adult.
- The perpetration of sex (oral, anal, or vaginal) when an adult has refused it (rape).
- The perpetration of sex (oral, anal, or vaginal) by an adult or older child on a child/adolescent.
- Parental bathing of a child/adolescent well after the child should know how to bath him/herself.
- Sexual explorations (touching for the purpose of looking or exploring) of a child by an adult or older child.
- "Accidentally" rubbing up against or touching someone in a sexual way (froterism).

Sexual verbalizations which are offensive:

- Constant sexually offensive jokes, especially when the listener is a child/adolescent, or when the offender has been asked to stop.
- Private information about an adult's sex life given to a child/adolescent.
- Intimate information about parent's love life (even if not explicitly sexual) given to a child/adolescent.

- Actual statements of "I'd like to ..." or "can I see ..." etc. of a sexual nature made to a child/adolescent or one with whom one is not in a sexual relationship.
- Constantly asking for hugs, when it is strongly suspected that the hugs give opportunity for sexual fantasy, or acting out.
- Asking sexual favors of children/adolescents or of strangers.
- Calling someone sexually inappropriate names.
- Referring to a child in sexual ways (slut, whore, sexy, etc.).

Use of offensive material:

- Showing children/adolescents pornographic pictures.
- Asking children or adolescents to pose for nude or sexually explicit pictures.
- Showing children/adolescents pictures of nude people frequently as a way of introducing them to further abuse. (Not the same as children seeing pictures of nude art, or anatomically correct pictures or dolls.)
- Internet pornography, or pornographic communications with children/adolescents (i.e., email, mail, pictures).
- Again, offensive jokes.
- Teaching children/adolescents about sex in ways that traumatize or offend them.

Emotional Incest:

- Adults relying upon children/adolescents for all emotional needs.
- Adults putting the child/adolescent in the "husband/wife" role, in terms of emotional responsibility.
- Adults telling children/adolescents about adult sexual situations.
- Adults telling children/adolescents about adult problems, particularly sexual ones.
- Sexualization of interactions between adults and children/adolescents, (i.e., frequent demonstrations of affection through touching or rubbing as one would a date or lover; sexual body movements or body language while talking to children/adolescents; flirtatious behavior with children/adolescents; or encouraging flirtatious or sexual behavior in children/adolescents).
- Teaching children/adolescents explicit sexual behavior, through the use of pornographic pictures.
- Teaching children/adolescents explicit sexual behavior well before a child/adolescent has asked for or can understand such.
- Telling children/adolescents how to "look pretty for Daddy," or "handsome for Mommy," very often continuing this imagery up into adulthood, as if the child's "look" should be one which pleases and stimulates the parent.

Visual sexualization:

- Peeping at a child/adolescent/adult while they are dressing, bathing or having sex.

- Constantly watching a child/adolescent/adult.
- Staring at a child/adolescent/adult.
- Gawking by a stranger.
- Exposing oneself (as in flashing, exposition or asking for permission to show genitals) to anyone with whom one is not dating or in primary relationship, particularly a child or adolescent.

Grooming:

- Any form of gently nudging a child/adolescent to trust the perpetrator, toward the end of child abuse. Some of the following could be considered to be good parenting, but each has, as its express purpose, the intent to sexually abuse the child/adolescent.
    o Buying things to attract the child/adolescent.
    o Spending extra time with the child/adolescent to talk or play.
    o Keeping a child up later than bedtime to talk.
    o Allowing a child/adolescent special privileges.
    o Allowing a child/adolescent to "get away" with breaking rules.
    o Taking the child/adolescent on special trips or outings.
    o Picking out a child/adolescent from among siblings as a favorite.
    o Picking out a favorite student or adolescent employee.
    o Online chats about the child/adolescents problems.
    o Gentle flirtations that flatter the child/adolescent.

It should be noted here that any one form of sexual abuse can and often does lead to others.

<u>Physical Abuse</u>: Slapping, hitting, pinching, choking, violent pushing, kicking. It also includes throwing things at a person, or intimidating a person by punching a hole in a wall in front of them, kicking, throwing or breaking things in front of them. Any form of physical intimidation is considered here to be a part of the "Assault Cycle."

An Assault Cycle looks like this: (This example uses the primary relationship model, but it can be the same in any relationship dynamic, whether parent/child, business partnership, friendships or employer/employee.)

-I meet you. We are attracted to each other.

-I am charming, and know exactly what to say to make you feel good.

-Over time, I begin to show you that I have a temper. It starts in small ways, like in traffic, or over something that someone said.

-More over time, I begin to show that my temper takes physical form at times. I may hit the dashboard, or demonstrate road rage, or hit the wall. (The unspoken and unconscious purpose of this is to intimidate. It says, "Don't mess with me, or I'll do the same to you." Usually, without a word, people get it.)

-One day, I will kick over the coffee table at the house (or some other physical demonstration), over something you said, or I will punch the wall and then leave for a day or two. You will "get it," that making me mad is dangerous to you, both physically and emotionally.

-Each time I do this though, I may apologize or just become really sweet, or just settle into a "good time" with you, after the episode to convince you that you are still loved and these things won't happen again.

-One day, I will push you. You will say to your self that it was just a push. Again, there will be apologies, sweetness or a "good time."

-Another day, I will actually hit you, again followed with the apology or "good time," and I'll go back to the initial stage of being charming and wooing you back.

-Another day, I will say threatening words, like, "I'll kill you if ..."

-Eventually the hits will get harder, the apologies less demonstrative, as I begin to believe in my own power to keep you with me. Eventually, there are no more apologies or "good times." (My purpose is to assure myself that you will never abandon me. I feel such inner shame that I cannot conceive of the possibility that someone would just love me and stay. I must *force* you to stay.)

-As the cycle increases over time, and I "get away with" more and more abuse, there is finally the imminent threat of death. Many die at this stage.

Mental Abuse: Mental abuse is deception that is pervasive and threatening to the fiber of trust between you. It is trickery with intent. An example of mental abuse is the gambler who takes money from the mutual bank account without informing the partner of his/her intent to gamble with that money. Another is the artful dodging of blame, by always focusing it back on another. Or, it is a constant diatribe of lies regarding personal character or history.

Mental abuse is also, telling people what they are thinking, or interpreting their behavior for them. The intent here is to control through information: "I know you better than you know yourself, and if you think you meant something different, then you are wrong, or, worse, you are lying." In other words, I'm tricking you into believing things about yourself that may or may not be true, simply because I misuse power and deception is my standard operating procedure.

Mental Abusers play mind games. When you confront them with a problem, they blame it on you or focus the conversation around your confrontation, rather than on their problem. When you hope that they will open up to you, they avoid self-revelation, by changing the subject, or even outright lying. Whatever the game deception is its name. Of course, mental abuse can lead to other forms of abuse as well.

Brainwashing is another form of mental abuse though it also includes emotional trickery, so we will discuss it under Emotional Abuse.

Emotional Abuse: Emotional abuse is further trickery, but with intent to trick you emotionally. It takes the form of emotional games, often referred to as "mind-games," but with an intent to abuse emotion not mind:

- "Come here, go away," is one of the classic games played here. It works like this. I love you, come here and let me show you. But if you get too close, (too close to knowing who I really am, too close to intimacy, too close to feeling like it is real, to commitment, etc.) you can just go away. The person who uses this game, runs hot and cold. One moment they are very warm and nurturing, receptive, and/or sexual and the next, without obvious warning or provocation, they become very cold, even icy.
- Deprivation of affection, touch, eye contact and/or sex. Such withholding is definitely manipulative in nature. The emotional abuser uses the same power needs that the rapist uses as motivation. Its intent is to control. (NOTE: This is not the same as the person who has a sexual dysfunction, which includes loss of interest in sex. Emotional abuse is actual withholding.)
- Confront the emotional abuser and you will have to deal with numerous smoke screens. Anything works, as long as it toys with your emotions in the name of keeping the focus off of me.
  o It's not my fault. (It must be yours.)
  o I can't help it. (Feel sorry for me!)
  o You gave me no choice. (It's really your fault.)
  o How can you talk to me that way (even when you are calm and factual)? (See what you are doing to me?)
  o You are always blaming me for everything. (I'm your victim.)
  o You are just trying to make me feel bad. (I'm your victim.)
  o You are trying to make me the bad guy. (Feel guilty for victimizing me.)
  o Well, I just got a kick to the head (stomach, chest, etc.) (Now, I'm REALLY your victim!)
  o You know you are a real piece of work! Here you are bringing this up right when I'm … (Involved in something, anything, but considering what you have to say.) (You are really the bad guy here)
  o You are the problem here, not me. ('nuff said.)
  o Intense hostility always works here too, as a message to stop confronting.
  o Every time I get close to you, you start this shit. (A message that if you don't stop confronting, I'll leave you, or continue to withhold affection.)
- Emotional abusers rarely apologize for anything, or only do so when they feel that it will make them look better for so doing.

- Emotional abusers are "crazy makers." They may sit back coldly, while continuing to do something which they know is a violation of your trust, or space, or person, or honor, or commitment, yet when you finally become totally enraged, they will say, "Look at you, you are acting crazy, what's the matter with you."
- Emotional abusers don't like therapy. They tend to shy away from it, because they know, on some level, that to go to therapy will mean changing their life patterns. One of these patterns is working well for them. It is the pattern of emotional abuse.
- If they do go to therapy, they tend to do so only when they feel that they can prove someone else wrong, or to "look good" to those who are watching. They frequently lie in therapy.
- Emotional abusers tend to live in chaos. When there is no chaos, they will go find some, and blame it on you.
- The only thing that finally gets to the emotional abuser and sends them to therapy is a new paradigm, relationship or circumstance in which they can no longer manipulate others. When this happens they tend to feel quite lost and don't know what to do.

Brainwashing works with both the mind and the emotions. What the abuser wants from brainwashing is for you to think, act or both, as if you belong completely to the abuser. Of course, it isn't true that we belong to anyone, but the abuser doesn't want to know this fact. The brainwasher uses tactics such as the following:

- I withhold any kind of affection from you, until you will do just about anything to get it, then I require something of you in order to deliver the goods.
- If you comply with my requirement, I will demonstrate affection to you, but only for a while, until I feel that you know how to meet my requirement.
- Then I will withhold again, and again make another requirement, until you comply.
- We do this again and again, until I believe that you believe you belong to me.
- Once I'm convinced of this, then you will be promoted up to a position of closeness to me, until I need to make another requirement of you in order to convince myself still further that you belong to me.
- The requirements that I make may be anything from you owning one of my beliefs to your giving me what I want sexually, or both.
- Of course, the more vulnerable you are, the easier it is to brainwash you. This is why it works best on children, or adults reduced to child-like emotions, such as hostages.
- Once you are completely brainwashed, you will think that I can do no wrong, and that anyone who says anything negative about me is not only wrong but almost evil.

We can see from this that it would be fairly simple for a parent to brainwash a child. But it is also true that when children are closed out emotionally at home, or are severely abused, they are susceptible to being brainwashed by other adults such as teachers, pastors, more distant relatives, or even older friends. Further, people who live for years under strict obedience to an abusive "master" such as a spouse or parent are very often reduced to child-like emotional responses so that they cannot make adult-like decisions to leave the person who is abusing them. They have been brainwashed.

This is also how Stockholm Syndrome works. If I lock you up in a closet and feed you through a pet door for months, you are going to be reduced to child-like emotional responses and are much more likely to do what I want when I let you out for short periods of time. Once I've got you doing what I want, I can start giving short bursts of affection, followed by long periods of rejection, until I've got you where I want you.

Verbal Abuse: Verbal abuse consists of the use of name-calling, and/or of the use of graphic, explicit, offensive material used in an argument. Often people have difficulty with the term verbal abuse, because when partners or friends raise their voices to us, we tend to *feel* abused. Yet, sometimes this isn't abuse. Verbal abuse is, however, the use of name calling when in the midst of an argument. Also, when persons use very offensive material to get their point across this is also considered to be verbally abusive. Screaming at someone, especially if this is the primary method of arguing, is moving into the realm of *physical* abuse, in that it is quite intimidating and often does precede physical acting out. Occasionally yelling at someone is *not* considered to be abusive, perhaps aggressive, but not abusive. Sometimes yelling is pure expressive release and cannot be considered to be either aggressive or abusive.

*** It is also important that we clarify what we mean by "negative feelings" sited above in the chart, in the Party Dude(tte) description. It is important because, in fact, there <u>are no</u> negative feelings. In truth, feelings tell us two things: 1) Authentic feelings are like taste buds. They tell us about what it is that we've just bitten off. Do we like it, a little, a lot, not at all? Is it bitter, sweet, sour, salty, spicy, or tasteless? The only way we will know is to feel our feelings. They can put us in touch with our responses to the realities of our lives. 2) They can tell us, if we look deep enough, what we are thinking and what we believe. Prior to many feelings there has been a thought, very often unconscious to us, that birthed the feeling. The thought is an interpretation of an external event or even an authentic feeling. This interpretation is based on a belief. These beliefs and their accompanying thoughts need to be examined to help us decide what is really true. Later we will do some exercises on this. For now, suffice it to say that without recognition, definition and a sorting out of our feelings, we cannot be clear of our direction. Therefore, they are extremely important to us in living authentically.

However, many times we think that we have to separate feelings into categories. We think that feelings are either negative, or they are positive. Typically we see anger, irritation, sadness, rage, fear, horror, guilt, anxiety and other like feelings as negative. And we see happiness, bliss, ecstasy, peace, confidence, joy, wonder, awe, contentment, and even numbness, as positive. So, therefore, when we have what we call a negative feeling, we not only have to go through the experience of having the feeling, but then we berate ourselves for having it. And since we are so busy berating ourselves for every negative feeling we have, we have little time or energy left for even feeling the positive ones. Obviously, this isn't working to make us happy.

What if we could eliminate the concepts of good and bad, at least, as they relate to feelings? What if there are no bad feelings and no good feelings? What if they are just feelings? What if, like taste buds, they are just telling us what life tastes like? What if, when they are not doing that, they are but reactions to our own thoughts, our interpretations of life? If these things were so, wouldn't this mean that we could just use our feelings as guideposts along the way to show us the next step?

The truth is that our feelings may not always be authentic, but they do lead us to the authentic self, if we use them as pathways. For example, I may have a *thought* that I made a terrible mistake yesterday, on which I focus (either consciously or unconsciously) all day. By the end of the day, I'll probably be *feeling* pretty bad, pretty ashamed, because of this thought. Those shameful feelings are not authentic. But if I look at the shameful feelings and ask for the source, I may find that I was thinking shame-inducing thoughts all day. Then I can look back at the events of yesterday and ask myself some legitimate questions about what occurred yesterday and come up with a more accurate picture, than the shame-inducing thoughts. Now I have arrived at something true, something more closely aligned with my authenticity. In this example, though the feelings did not spring directly from the authentic self, still I have used them to find my own authentic interpretation of yesterday's events.

Many other feelings spring up more directly from our authenticity. For example, I'm feeling harried and stressed. These feelings might be telling me something about how my role is keeping me stuck in repetitive patterns that build more and more stress into my life. The Authentic Self is using these feelings to communicate to me that what I'm doing is not working. Or, perhaps I'm feeling peaceful because I've connected deeply to my authenticity. Or, I'm feeling an intuition that tells me that something is amiss. If I attend to this intuition, sorting it out from fear or judgment, I'll find that it has led me to something real.

As we shall see as we go, sorting becomes a primary process of finding and living the authentic Self. Such sorting includes distinguishing between fear and intuition, judgment and intuition, thoughts and feelings, someone else's "stuff" and my "stuff." However, the sorting does NOT include sorting between negative and positive feelings, for feelings have no negative or positive value, they simply are.

Now that you have more clearly defined the role, or dual roles that you play, let's take a look at the self-talk that you listen to in your head all day, every day. Below, make a list of all of the thoughts and mantras you circled above. When you are done with the list, ask yourself this question: "Where have I heard this before." Write in your answer beside the mantra or thought. (Having heard something before may mean having seen it before, or known it as implication from someone before. It may even mean that you picked up the message from someone without their ever having said it.)

Thought/Mantra:	Where have I heard this before?

We can see from the above exercise that these thoughts and
mantras are not original. In other words, they are not our
own thoughts, but rather they have been incorporated from
our world. Further, they come from our belief systems about
ourselves which we often obtained by listening to our worlds.
Below, make a list of every time, situation, or relationship
dynamic in which you give yourself these messages.
(For example: When I start a task at work, I tell myself "if you want something
done right, do it yourself." Or, I tell myself "no one will ever really understand,"
when I think about sharing intimate information about myself with my spouse.

When this happens:	I tell myself:

Ponderings: "Self-talk" is the psychobabble term for it. Self-talk is our mantra. As the term is used in yoga or meditation, a mantra, as we've said, is a statement made over and over again to assist a person in developing a certain state, often a mind-altered state, such as in the trance-like state of meditation. But we use them all day everyday without knowing it. And we do put ourselves in a mind-altered state. One could say that we are hypnotizing ourselves daily with our mantra, or self-talk.

For example: As the Victim, I may continuously say to myself: "Life is hard." "This is just my cross to bear." "Well, you just have to expect to suffer." Sometimes, I don't even know that I'm saying these things to myself, so that I have to look under things a bit to notice that these are my basic, core beliefs. I seem to totally believe that life is very hard, that I must bear my crosses, and that I must expect to suffer. If you are looking at those phrases right now saying something akin to "No, duh!!" you may be hypnotizing yourself into a state of Victim-ness. Consider this: What if life is not hard, but we just make it hard by believing it to be so? What if there are no crosses to bear but those, which we create? What if suffering is not the expectation, but an aberration? If you have lived the Victim role, those considerations will seem very odd and even ridiculous to you. But what if they were true and the messages you give yourself are false? If that were so, would you be invested in trying out new mantras, or testing the limits of your current beliefs to see what is beyond them?

Don't worry, you don't have to decide right now. For now, just let that idea gel inside you. Do nothing at all with it; just let it roll around in your thoughts. If you have dreams during the time this thought is gelling, write them down—we'll talk about dreams later.

The main thing to get right now is that we all have a mantra, whether we put any stock in Eastern Religion or meditation, or hypnotherapy or not, we are constantly talking to ourselves. And what we say creates our perception of life, of ourselves and of our relationships. These perceptions become our view of all of life. They are a state of consciousness. We hypnotize ourselves into our particular view of life through the use of these mantras. When we do this, we see nothing but the perceptions we devised through the use of the mantras.

Thus we can see that *perception is everything*. Consider looking into the kaleidoscope that we talked about earlier. When we look into the kaleidoscope, we see certain colors in a certain design. We *perceive* a certain pattern. But if we turn the kaleidoscope even slightly, the pattern appears to change. Now we perceive something different from what we looked at before. Our mantra, our self-talk, our beliefs create our perceptions in much the same way. They sort of set the kaleidoscope on a specific frame, so that we are always looking at the same pattern. No matter what happens outside of that kaleidoscope, we are still looking at the same picture. So that, if the "life is hard" frame of the kaleidoscope is what we are looking at, then even if life is easy outside the kaleidoscope, we don't see it, because we are still looking at the pattern of the design we set on the kaleidoscope years ago. But if we could, *if we could* just turn that kaleidoscope ever so slightly, we might see the pattern change, and we might, just from that one experience, begin to change our beliefs, then our thoughts, then our mantras.

So years ago, we set our kaleidoscope on a certain perception of what was expected of us. As a result we put on a role and began to act out the part. The picture, the stage, the script is set. We just live it, over and over again, sometimes wondering how we get ourselves in the same fix again and again. And it remains that way even into the now.

Below is another exercise in awareness.

Below write out the script for two or three specific dynamics described above on the previous pages. (For example: On the previous pages, you have written "When I am talking to my employee, I tell myself that I cannot trust people to do anything right." Based on this self-talk you will say and do certain things with this employee. Write the script for that.)

_____
_____
_____
_____
_____
_____
_____
_____
_____
_____
_____
_____
_____
_____
_____
_____
_____
_____
_____
_____
_____
_____
_____
_____
_____
_____
_____
_____
_____
_____
_____
_____

Ponderings: You see, what we are doing, each time we give ourselves these messages, is returning home. Thomas Wolfe says we can't do it, but we do, every day, many times a day. We go back home. We mentally take on the same psychological essence we took on as a child. We believe the same things, we think the same thoughts, we often feel the same feelings and even dream dreams that come from this psychological space.

Our childhood home is what we therapists call our "family of origin." That's a very heavy, and power-laden term, which means that we originate our roles in our first family. This may not be a biological family, it may not be a classical family at all. But it does tend to be the basis of the origination of our roles. Families are very interesting interactive entities. For example, each family member has a different personality (as can be tested out on the Myers-Briggs test), yet often, family members try to hold the same opinions, keep the same time schedules, and express themselves in similar fashions. These families are often what we call, *enmeshed* families. The extreme form of enmeshment means that no family member is supported for any individual distinction. Each family member *should* be exactly like all of the others. And each family member who is exactly like all the others is rewarded with a deep and abiding connection to the others in the family. But what would happen if one family member had a totally different personality than all of the other family members? For example, what if all of the family members but one were engineer types, thinkers, logical, practical, down-to-earth folks, who rely very little on their emotions. But then there is one who is an artistic type, who lives on feeling and makes decisions from feelings rather than thoughts, who creates from a process rather than from a linear equation. What do you suppose will happen in this family? Well everyone in the family, including the artist type, will feel that there is something very wrong with the artist type.

Another example of enmeshment would be, when a family insists on loyalty to its subscribed opinions, and/or to its very dynamic, above and beyond loyalty to anyone or anything else. What happens then when the children grow up and marry? You can guess. The family will either feel very betrayed when the child marries, or the child will marry someone who fits very well into the family of origin, or they will marry someone different from the family of origin, but remain loyal first to the family of origin. In the latter case, this means that when the young married couple have children, they will be raised as one of the parent's family of origin would have it, in spite of what the partner says. Other issues in relationship, such as money, time, clothing, schooling, etc., would all be decided by loyalty to the family of origin—not to the spouse, or anything else.

Enmeshed families may seem, from all outward appearances, to be very healthy, because they demonstrate affection and are very attached to each other. However, there are underlying issues of abandonment always lurking around the corner. In other words, one of the reasons for such pronounced attachment is because there is such a pronounced fear that if a family member doesn't do exactly what is prescribed, there will be some form of abandonment. Often children in such families feel doubly bound: "I'm damned if I do and damned if I don't." If they follow their own hearts they fear betraying the family, if they don't they betray themselves. They will often err on the side of caution and follow the family. Issues such as competition, repressed rage, low self-esteem, depression, fearful and phobic reactions, obsessive/compulsiveness, and very low tolerance for change are common issues in members of families that are enmeshed.

Families can also exemplify the other polarized dynamic: *Detachment*. In a detached family, it's every (hu)man for himself. Each person in this system is totally independent, to a greater or lesser degree, based on how detached the family is. No one shares anything with anyone. No one expresses emotion. There are very few, if any, expressions of affection, or if there are they happen only at prescribed times, such as when someone is graduating or marrying. But even then the expressions are muted and awkward. One seemingly innocuous example of detachment at the highest or lowest socioeconomic strata is career. The parent(s) work, to the exclusion of anything else. All of the family is put on notice that this is how it will be, and no one expects it to be any different. Children may grow up with a great deal of resentment about this. Of course, the patterns are not really related to socioeconomics, but to the masks and costumes the parents are wearing.

Awkwardness is another issue in such families. Primary caretakers in this family send out the message, "Don't get close to me, because I don't know what to do with it." Other members of the family hear and respond to this message accordingly. They, in turn, learn to send out the same message. Of course, these messages are not spoken. However, they are heard loud and clear. In all cases, the bottom line is, we are not a close family. We may even present the illusion of being close to the community, but in truth, no one in this family knows anyone else in this family. We are all strangers living under the same roof.

There are all degrees of gradation between these two polarities, with the healthiest families standing right in the middle. In healthy families, family members are encouraged to be themselves, encouraged to follow their own dreams, and are unconditionally loved and appreciated by other family members. They have both freedom of movement, and deep, abiding love. But this love is unconditional, not based on the condition of family loyalty or similarity. Members of this healthy family may have their own opinions, their own lifestyles, their own methods of operation, without being unduly criticized by other family members. They are not bound by the values or religion of the family, but are encouraged to find their own inner truth. They feel supported and loved yet unfettered by expectations. So, you see it is the best of both ends of the continuum. They have the freedom of the detached family with none of the coldness, and the love of the enmeshed family with no strings attached.

As we consider the family of origin, we may notice varying degrees of either enmeshment or detachment. In either case, this was our home. It is the place with which we became most familiar. Our reactions, attitudes, opinions and even our lifestyle itself, may all spring from the messages we received from our families of origin and the role itself. These messages were the mirrors we looked into to find our identities. In truth, one could say that when one reacts to a situation, person, expectation, etc., in the manner prescribed by family, or by the role, one is "going back home." We "go back home" this way when we are afraid, when we have a choice or a decision to make, when we are rejected, when we are heartbroken. This seems logical, don't you think? We go back home when we need to feel like there is a home. But often our homes were chaotic or dysfunctional, so what we go home to, is more chaos and dysfunction. Therefore, our acting out the role is a way of "going back home."

As you are going through the next several days, you may want to let that concept just "gel" for a while. Consider your actions and reactions. Ask yourself if, when you act, think, talk in a certain way, you are going back home. Just relax into the process and consider, without self-judgment, as you go.

Distinctions:

The Role,

The Authentic Self

Ponderings: In spite of the fact that the role has been very active in our lives, often throughout our lives; the Authentic Self has also been very active all along. How do we know? Well, first we know because we are still alive. For many of us, perhaps even all of us, putting on the role was a survival technique that had everything to do with the reality of survival from a real abandonment, or even a death threat, or the danger of eminent death. The rest of us were attempting to survive a perceived threat of abandonment, which we thought would amount to a literal or emotional death for us. In either case, something deep inside us wanted to live. What was that?

What was it inside of us that said, "Stay alive?" It was the voice of the Authentic Self. It was the roots of the tree, telling the tree that even when the wind blows, there is still life to live for. It was an impulse, a deep desire to live. Sometimes that desire is hidden, as in the case of suicidal ideations. We may be thinking about dying, but we are still living. We may need to tell someone else about our desire to die, but we are still alive. We may even be frightened of our own suicidal thoughts, but that very fear speaks of a desire to live. When we call a Crisis Line and talk to staff there about our desire to die, what we are really saying is, "Can you help me find a way to live through this?" Such calls, such conversations, such fears, all speak of a deep desire to live. We may not be able to feel it, but it is in action already. The minute we tell someone that we are having suicidal ideations, we are saying we want to live. We didn't think it was in us, but it became an action, it talked to someone about our fear.

The Authentic Self may appear in many other ways as well. It may appear in a simple desire to paint my bedroom blue (a favorite color). It may appear in the form of a seeming mistake that turns out to be "the best mistake I ever made." It may appear in a laugh that seems to come up from some tiny spark of real joy deep inside of us. It may appear in the work that we do. We may find that we love our jobs passionately, but hate our relationships. We may find that there are specific things about the tasks of our jobs that we love, others that we despise. We may find ourselves falling in love with people who are very much like us. These things tell us who we are, if we are listening. The problem is that often, we are not. Often we relegate these things of the Authentic Self to the back burners, back bedrooms, even the closets of our lives. We may tell ourselves, "Yes, I love this, but I don't have time for it." Or, "Okay, this makes me happy, but no one else I know is happy, why should I be allowed to be happy." Or, "That's silly, or frivolous." Or, "Who gets to do and be what and who they want?" Or, "That's just what I desire, it's not what I need." Well, one thing we will get clear on through the working of this book: *Our desires <u>are</u> our needs.* We need to be doing and being as we desire, or we are not truly alive. Our desires are guideposts to the path of highest potential for us. Yet, we have been taught, for so many centuries that the have-to, got-to, need-to issues always come first. What this means is this: Do not attempt to be true to yourself. Do not try to turn the light on who you are and become this. We do not have time or energy for such frivolity. It's a waste. Get busy doing what you have to do and get this fantasy out of your mind. It isn't real. People just don't get to do what they want. After all, who do you think you are that you, and you alone get to do and be what you want?

I find it fascinating that we, the people, tell ourselves as a collective, that no one gets to really follow their dream, no one can really completely have what they want. And yet, while we are telling ourselves this, we are worshiping the people who *seem* to have it. Celebrity status comes about because of the worship of those who don't have what the celebrity has: the good life. Our magazines and TVs and newspapers all tell us about those who have what we don't seem to be able to have. And yet, they may not have it either. They just seem to. So, we split ourselves down the middle, with one half of us saying that no one gets what they really want, while the other half is worshipping those who do (or seem to).

So, what do we do? We go home. We go back home to the familiar. What is real inside of us, simply feels foreign to us. So, we go back home—to what seems to us to be "normal." We never stop to consider that if everyone were living authentically, it would be the norm. The norm is only created by what everyone is doing and that very often isn't "normal." Well, let's try something a little different now. Let's build a new home. Just for the hell of it. Dream a dream. Build your new home on the following page.

Below, draw a floor plan for your dream home. You know you have one. Everyone has one. At least a vague idea of one. Here we are going to get more specific. What has your dream home always looked like? How many bedrooms? What's the living room look like? The kitchen? Once the floor plan is done, don't forget the outside. Draw the yard and the landscaping if you want it. Really think about this. This is your dream home. The one you have always wanted to have. Where is it? On the beach, in the mountains, both? Then define the colors you'll use. Do you want carpet, hard wood, tile? Think of everything you can imagine and draw it, or write it in here.

Now let's go back to the familiar again for just a minute, for comparison's sake. Below we will do an exercise on what happens when we go back home. When we go back to the old home, we deteriorate, we diminish, we depress. We feel certain particular and familiar feelings, we think particular and familiar thoughts, we perform some particular behaviors related to our feeling or thought, we listen to one or two messages in the form of a mantra. When we go to the new home we feel certain feelings as well. What are these feelings and what happens when we feel them? So, what happens when:

I go home to guilt and shame: I go home to the Authentic Self:

I go home to self-ridicule: I go home to the Authentic Self:

I go home to abandonment   I go home to the Authentic Self:
(by others or self):

I go home to Superperson: I go home to the Authentic Self:

I go home to running away: I go home to the Authentic Self:

I go home to making the sacrifice: I go home to the Authentic Self:

Above are just a few examples of what happens when we go home, and how that makes us feel. You may feel free to draw your own chart of when I go home to.... Fill it in. And then **below, now, draw a picture of your old home**, the one filled with guilt and shame, the one filled with Superwoman, the home of running away, the home of the Victim, etc. Use all the colors and designs that seem appropriate. Make room for any emotions you need and pencil or draw them in. (For example: Perhaps the walls might be made of self-ridicule and painted with shame).

Now, let's do some prime factoring. Let's take some of the messages that you get while living in the old house (you may need to reference the mantras you circled earlier). Let's listen for the bottom-line. For example: "If I complain, I'm just being a bitch" is a mantra of Superwoman. We can start prime factoring by playing worst-case scenario. Suppose someone thinks that you are a bitch. What does this mean to you? You might come up with answers like, well that means that they don't think I'm a good person. Then ask again, "What does this mean to me?" You might answer, "I'm not a good person." What does this mean? "It means I'm bad, I'm worthless, I don't deserve anything good." When you get to the point that you cannot go any further, you've arrived at the bottom line, the prime-factor. Let's try it:

Message	It means	It means	It means	It means	Prime-Factor
1.					
2.					
3.					
4.					
5.					
6.					
7.					
8.					
9.					
10.					

Your prime-factor is your catch-phrase. It is the reason why we do what we do. It is the motivator. If I fear that I'm a worthless person under it all, then I might do everything I can think of to prove that I'm not. So, I might not ever say what I feel, for fear people will think I'm a bitch. Pause and reflect on this before moving to the next exercise.

You may need to do this exercise over and over again, in order for you to become comfortable with the process of prime factoring. It is a very important process that tells us both how we are interpreting things, and, most importantly, it tells us what motivates us to do what we do. Now we are not such a mystery to ourselves.

Below write a letter of response *from* the Authentic Self, *to* the Role regarding these messages. Here your Authentic Self is responding to the above exercise. Your Authentic Self has known all along what you are up to. But your Role has just figured it out. How does your Authentic Self feel about this? You may need to put the picture you drew of the Authentic Self in front of you in order to find access to that part of you, before writing the letter. One rule of thumb: If you find that you are telling the role what to do, shaming it, using the "should" or "ought" words, or comparing to others or otherwise trying to coerce the role into some kind of new image, you are *not* speaking from the Authentic Self. This is just more of the role, try again.

_____
_____
_____
_____
_____
_____
_____
_____
_____
_____
_____
_____
_____
_____
_____
_____
_____
_____
_____
_____
_____
_____
_____
_____
_____
_____

Now let's start an argument: Below is a chart for arguing. On one side of the page, you are to list any messages or mantras that your role gives to you. On the other side of the page, you will list a counter-message that originates in the Authentic Self. For example, the Superwoman's message may be, "Knowing what to do is vital." The Authentic Self may say, in response, "Knowing what to do, only makes you feel as if you are on top of it, so that you don't ever have to recognize how overwhelmed you really are all of the time. You know what? If you don't know something, then you can ask, and you'll really learn something new. That means you are growing." Try your own now.

Role's Message	Response from Authentic Self:

Ponderings: Can you see now that your Authentic Self is much wiser than you think? In truth, every answer you need is inside of you. That's why working with the Authentic Self is so very important. Did you have trouble? Okay, think of it this way. If you heard a little child give themselves the messages you give yourself from the role, what would you say to that child? Write that down as your response. Do you know why that works, and we can know that it is real? It is because _you_ came up with those responses to your child on your own. These responses, whether they are addressed to you or to a child, once you tap into your real compassion for this child, are still your own original responses. And though you might not yet be able to feel that you could speak to yourself this way, you just did. It isn't easy to move beyond the thinking that we have always had. It is a major challenge. So, if you have so challenged yourself, pat yourself on the back. It's a big deal.

Your truest Self, your soul really does have the answers to the statements that really amount to a question. The question we are asking with our statement or message is something like this: Could I ever really just be me and still be loved by you? The answer the role has been giving all along is "no." And so we adjusted, we became what we thought we needed to be in order to be loved by some significant other. The answer the Authentic Self gives is "I love you. I want to be inside you. I want to live with you and about you and for you. With me, you will never feel alone again. I am the most significant 'other' there is. Though, thus far you have relegated me to the realms of 'other-ness,' in truth, I am right here, inside of you and have been all along."

The next question we typically want to ask here is, "If I am really authentic, will it mean that I have to be alone for the rest of my life?" The question itself shows how black and white we have become with this issue: _If I love me, then you will go away. If I have you, then I have to go away (from myself)._ The truth is that it is, indeed, very possible to be yourself and still be deeply loved by others. In fact, this is the only real intimacy that there is. More on this later.

The exercise above was meant to clarify for us that we have a clear choice at any given moment, which of these messages we will listen to. Which message will be responded to in attitude, in action? It is always our choice. The truth is that we are not "out of control." We may believe that we are, but we are not. In fact, every moment of every day, we are making a choice as to what we will think, and feel and how we will act. We may say that someone makes us feel angry, but it isn't true. We are choosing to feel angry. People do not reach inside of us and make us feel anything. We choose our reactions and responses. Even if someone puts a gun to your head and says, "Do it or die," we still have a choice as to how we will respond. We can do it, fight, die, or stay undecided until we either do it, fight or die. We say that we "have to" go to work but the truth is that we don't. We could stay at home, go out dancing or whatever. We choose to go to work. Why do we make this choice? Often it is because we know that if we don't we won't get paid. In other words, we don't want to accept the consequences of not going to work, so we go. Okay, but we still made a choice.

When we believe that we are out of control of our choices, we are using something that we clinical people call "External locus of control." We are saying that the external world controls us. In truth what we are doing is choosing to locate the control outside of ourselves. The word "locus" is Latin for "location." When people have this external locus of control, they feel out of control. They seem to be helplessly watching themselves get angry, have outbursts, get quiet, become invisible, shutdown, act-out, and otherwise perform all manner of attitudes, thoughts and behaviors. They come into therapy and say, "This weekend I had this fight with my husband, but I just couldn't tell him how I felt. I don't know why I couldn't but I couldn't." Or, they say, "I put my fist through the wall. She made me so mad, I couldn't help it." Or, they say, "After dinner, I went out to the bar, picked up someone and woke up the next morning, angry. I had to kick him out." When we say things like this we are talking about ourselves as if in the third person, as if we are only talking about it, not experiencing it first-hand. The question to be asked here is, "Who is doing these things?" The answer is "we are." The truth is that we are choosing to do these things. Why? Well, now we are talking about something that we can deal with. Why? Because we were afraid *not* to do these things.

When "you make me so mad that I put my fist through the wall," it is often because I was afraid that you might have the advantage over me. I was afraid that you wouldn't stay if I didn't scare you. I think that I'm not lovable enough for you to just stay because you love me. I have to scare you into staying. When I can't speak up for myself, it is often because I am afraid that if I do, you will go away. You will stop loving me. You will reject me, either outright, or at least momentarily. In either case, it feels unbearable to me, so I just won't go there. When I go out at night to find someone to sleep with, it comes from that desperate feeling of being totally lost, totally out of touch with any sense of connection to anyone. Before I can be disconnected from others, I am disconnected from Self. I feel that if I cannot touch someone, there is no me.

So you see, though we may think that control is located outside of ourselves, it is really coming from within. In fact, we are reacting to a deep and often ancient fear. And it is often true that when we believe in that fear, we will react the same way every time. The more conscious we become that we are making choices, the more we are developing what we clinicians call, "Internal locus of control." In other words, now I know that I am choosing. I am locating my control within my person. Therefore, in truth, our control is actually always coming from within, but we have the power to project it outward and assume that it is coming from outside of us. It seems to us, at first, to be easier this way, but in fact, it is making our lives harder, because we would like to have control over our own behavior, but don't seem to be able to get it.

So, the truth is, we have control every moment of every day. Let's say that again. *We have control every moment of every day.* We may not be able to control what others do, but we have absolute control over what we do, say, think, and feel. We are in charge.

The ultimate "authority figure" is CHOICE. It is very interesting that we use the term "figure" right next to the term "authority." They seem like oxymorons, yet we use the terms together constantly: authority figure. A figure is a shape, a form, a symbol, a seeming. It isn't real. Authority is power, and it is very real. Put the words together and you get: A symbol of authority, or a seeming authority. And this is an accurate description of anyone in authority. They seem to have authority. Why? Because we give it to them. We choose to allow them to have authority over us. So what is the ultimate authority? *Our choice.*

For example: A police officer is sitting across the street from a stop sign waiting for me to run it. I see the officer. I stop. What have I done? I have chosen to avoid getting a ticket. Suppose I chose to run the stop sign in front of the officer. Well, two things, the officer now has a choice to either give me a ticket or keep drinking his coffee and ignore me; and I have another choice to just nervously hope he missed it, to try to outrun him, accept a ticket, or to fight with him when he tries to give me the ticket. So, now, is the police officer the authority or is it really my choice? This is what internal locus of control is all about. It is recognition that we are constantly choosing. And in that same vein, we have a choice every minute of every day as to which home we will dwell in, the old home, made of the emotions, thoughts, attitudes and actions of the role, or the new home, made by the Authentic Self.

So, now, let's pretend a minute. Let's pretend that you could actually move from the old house, into the new. And let's pretend that you are packing your belongings in the old house to move them to the new. What are you packing? What would you really like to take with you into the new house? What would you want to leave behind? Below, are some boxes for the items you are packing. What will you put in these boxes? Write down on the box itself, what you are putting in the boxes to take with you. What would you put in the boxes you intend to leave behind? You are being asked simply to define each attitude, thought, message, behavior in the boxes you've packed. Is it Authentic? Do you wish to take it with you to the new home? Please know that you are *not* being asked to throw out anything, unless that is what you are ready to do. *Simply recognize it.* Remember this is just pretend. This is not a ritual cleansing, unless you make it one.

Fig 12:

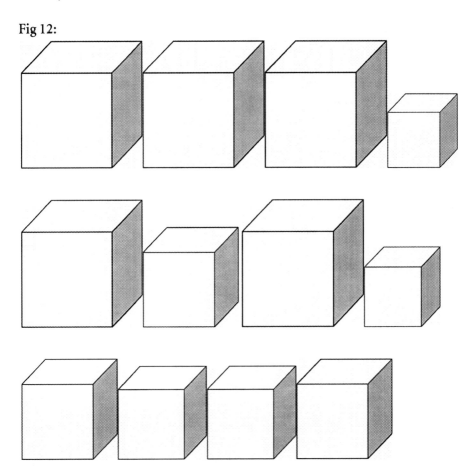

Ponderings: It is not what we say "no" to in life that makes the difference for us. It is those things to which we say "yes" that create real and lasting change. So, again, you are not being asked to say, "no" to any of the items in your boxes. You are simply being asked to know what you have packed. You may later choose to take some things with you to the new home. The other things that you do not choose to take with you to the new home, will stay in the old home. And you may go back and visit there anytime you choose. And you may stay for as long as you would like. The choice is entirely up to you.

So, let's say that you've done that. Let's say that you have taken the things that you want to take with you and you have moved them to the new house. What does this mean? Well basically, it means that you have begun to live by desire, rather than by design. By design, we live according to a structure, according to a list of strategies that we think will *work* in this crazy world. And we can look at our design if we see it clearly and we can say that, yes, for the most part it works. My Superwoman design works to keep me from having to ever feel vulnerable. My Victim design works to keep me from ever having to take responsibility for my life. My Bully/Perpetrator design helps me believe that I will never again feel powerless, or victimized. And on and on. But what if we could live by desire?

You desired your dream house and you drew the floor plan, painted the walls, landscaped the yard, and now, let's say, you've moved in. Now, you can begin to live there, everyday, all day. (Remember that you can still go back home anytime you choose, you are not trapped in an unfamiliar land.) But for now, let's just say that you could live there all the time. What would that be like? What is it like to live by desire?

Well, let's see.

Let's begin a "Desire Log." You are being asked to check in with yourself, several times a day, keeping this desire log, regarding the tasks and activities that you do. For each task or activity that you do, ask yourself this question: "Do I enjoy this task or activity?" Or, you may ask, "Am I having fun now?" You are encouraged to make a copy of this page and use it as many days as is needed to get a clear picture.

Desire Log

Task or Activity	Do I enjoy this task or activity?

It is the end of a week of filling in the Desire Log. What have you become clear about? What is still uncertain? Below you are challenged to perform or write out a role-play concerning your week. The Authentic Self is in one chair (you may need to actually place the picture of the Authentic Self in a chair) and the role is in the other chair (again, you may wish to place the picture you drew of the role in the other chair). If you are doing this in therapy, you are encouraged to perform the role-play. If at home, by yourself, you are challenged to write it down here. If you are performing, you will need to go and actually stand behind the chair of the role or the Authentic Self as each is speaking. You may begin by having the role speak. The role may ask the Authentic Self for opinions about living by desire. The role may feel conflicted about this whole thing, feeling that it is really impossible for people to live by desire. One of the questions often asked at this point is, "If I am the Authentic Self, does that mean I'm always playing nicey-nice?" Another one is, "How can the Authentic Self lead me in the direction of my truest desires?" Ask away. Then have the Authentic Self answer back. Again, the Authentic Self will not answer with shoulds or demands or oughts, or manipulations. These are all aspects of the role.

_____

_____

_____

_____

_____

_____

_____

_____

_____

_____

_____

_____

_____

_____

_____

_____

_____

_____

Role Play continued:

_____
_____
_____
_____
_____
_____
_____
_____
_____
_____
_____
_____
_____
_____
_____
_____
_____
_____
_____
_____
_____
_____
_____
_____
_____
_____
_____
_____
_____
_____
_____
_____

Below, write a poem from the role to the Authentic Self. (This is not a literary work, just write from your heart.)

_____
_____
_____
_____
_____
_____
_____
_____
_____
_____
_____
_____
_____
_____
_____
_____
_____
_____
_____
_____
_____
_____
_____
_____
_____
_____
_____
_____
_____
_____
_____
_____
_____
_____
_____

Below write a poem from the Authentic Self back to the role.

Every day for the next two weeks write a poem to and from the Authentic Self. Can you write a love poem from the Authentic Self? To the Authentic Self? (Copy this page as often as needed.)

_____

_____

_____

_____

_____

_____

_____

_____

_____

_____

_____

_____

_____

_____

_____

_____

_____

_____

_____

_____

_____

_____

_____

_____

_____

_____

_____

_____

_____

_____

Breaking Down
The
Barriers
To
Living
Authentically

Ponderings: Over the next several pages, we will begin to look at the barriers we present to living authentically. There are several of these barriers but none of these barriers exist at all in the Authentic Self. The Authentic Self is the roots of the tree. The Authentic Self is that place within where everything is just taking in energy and using it. Close your eyes for a moment and imagine that you are the tree above ground being stormed upon, with lightening, hail, and wind. Your branches are blowing wildly, so it would seem that you are holding on to planet earth for dear life. Now imagine that you are the roots, where there is no awareness of the storm, or if there is, it is just an awareness that there is need for more energy. Imagine that all you do, all day every day is take in delicious nutrients from the ground. You know how and where to seek them out and you know how to dig for water. Everything that you need to know, you already know. There are no shoulds here, there is only this very natural thing that you do, as natural as breathing or your heart's rhythm.

Some of you are considering living from that place as if it would be extremely peaceful and something you really desire. Others are looking at that place and saying, "That sounds pretty boring." But what if it isn't? Have you ever seen food on a plate that looked like it would taste terrible? Then you tasted it and found it to be really good? Well if you went as far as to taste it, you were willing to experiment with your perceptions. Our perception that it might be boring to live from the place of energy in our soul, is the perception that chaos is always better than nothing. It is black and white thinking and we will challenge that thinking here, if you are willing to experiment.

We often assume that without chaos there is nothing because we were raised in chaos. And so, when we go back home, we go back home to chaos. As children we did the magical thinking that we did in order to survive the chaos. We told ourselves, there was nothing but this chaos. And we believed ourselves. That was our coping mechanism. But it isn't true. It was the bunny we pulled out of the tattered hat. There is, indeed, something beyond chaos. It is creation. Once upon a time there was nothing but chaos, and out of that the earth and the solar system came to be. In the same way, we can create, from our original chaos, our dreams. And we can make them come true. In order to do that, however, we have to hurdle the barriers between us and our dreams.

The first barrier to authenticity is the F-word. That's right. **Fear** is one of the biggest barriers to authenticity. Fear of all manner of things. We may fear rejection, abandonment, the unfamiliar, boredom, the unknown, success, failure, intimacy, relationship, etc. We may fear all kinds of things. But when we act on our fear, we build it. When we avoid reacting to our fears, but simply recognize them, they become tools for creation of our lives.

Below, list a few of your greatest fears. Then take a few moments to play out the worst-case scenarios of these fears. Write the scenario down. What is the bottom line of this worst-case scenario? Prime-factor it. Ask this question, "If the scenario happened, what would it mean about me?" Write down the answer. Then ask, "If that were true about me, what would that mean?" Keep asking these two questions over and over until you've come to something that you think is the bottom-line of your fear.

_____

_____

_____

_____

_____

_____

_____

_____

_____

_____

_____

_____

_____

_____

_____

_____

_____

_____

_____

_____

_____

_____

_____

_____

_____

Below write a poem, story or letter about your fear. What would you look like, act like, how would others react to you, if your worst-case scenario were true? (If a poem, story or letter won't do it for you, draw a picture of the person you would look like if your worst-case scenario were true.)

_____

_____

_____

_____

_____

_____

_____

_____

_____

_____

_____

_____

_____

_____

_____

_____

_____

_____

_____

_____

_____

_____

_____

_____

_____

_____

_____

_____

_____

_____

_____

What do you imagine the Authentic Self is doing, while the role is reacting to your fear? Draw a picture (or write a poem, story or letter) about that.

Ponderings: What is the purpose of fear? If we are to use our feelings as tools with which to create our lives, then what purpose would the feeling of fear serve? Well, the first answer is clear. If you are standing in the middle of a street and a Mac truck is coming, your fear might be saying, "Move your ass, NOW!" If someone were to ask you, after it's all over and you're standing safely on the curb, how you felt when you saw that truck coming, you'd probably say "I was scared to death." This is the kind of fear we are aware of. It almost has to be terror before we notice it in many cases. On the other hand, there are others who are totally dominated by fear. But for most of us, fear is an unconscious motivator. This is because most of our fears are much more subtle and ingrained in us to the point that we react to them before we even know that they are there. For example: If I have a fear of rejection, then I may hide my true feelings from everyone, never telling anyone what I genuinely think of anything. However, I have so long established this style of reaction. I may have begun doing this as a child, when I was still largely preverbal. Perhaps then I only hid my feelings by not allowing them to appear on my face. The fear that originated this response is so long buried that I don't even know it is there. By now, I simply think that this way of responding is who I am. In other words, I no longer think that I am afraid. But I am. That is why we played out the worst-case scenarios above, so that we could become clear that we are, indeed, reacting to fear quite often.

Therefore, we can say that the purposes of fear are twofold: Protection and Over protection. I protect myself, when I jump out of the way of an oncoming Mac truck. But since most of us don't spend our days jumping out of the way of oncoming trucks, there are definitely other healthy uses for protective fear that we shall discuss shortly. I overprotect myself when I react to my fear by hiding my true feelings from others. Let's think about overprotection for a moment. When a parent overprotects a child, the child learns more fear. If the child goes out to play and the parent is always nearby saying, "Watch out for this or that," the child learns to be guarded. AND the child learns that only others, caretakers to be specific, can really protect him/her. Suppose the daughter tries to copy the parent in doing some chore, but the overprotective parent comes behind her and redoes the chore, or hovers over her with constant cautions and instructions. What does she learn? She learns that she can't really do it right; someone else does it better. But she can always trust the parent to do it right, because the parent watches out for her constantly and redoes everything she does. Overall, the daughter learns that she cannot trust herself with anything, but only the parent can be trusted. Therefore, she gives up on the self and learns to depend on others.

When our fears overprotect us, we are guarded and rigid, playing the overprotective parent to ourselves; or we are overly dependent on others because we have given up on ourselves. Sometimes we take on a weird mixture of these two by becoming dependent on pleasing others, while holding a firm and difficult line for ourselves. Guarded and rigid looks strong. It looks formidable. But it is based on fear. If you could remove all the rules, all the shoulds, oughts and have-tos from a guarded person, they would look scared and dependent. In fact, that guarded part of us looks formidable because it is afraid to look otherwise. For many, the guarded part of us is what we clinicians call, "hypervigilant." This is the "inner cowboy" who stays up all night to watch for thieves and killers. It is a steady, pervasive, "ready for fight or flight" stance toward all of life. It is overprotection, which assumes the worst before the worst is even considered by the world around us. Even when something good comes into our lives, we pick it to death, trying to find the evil intent behind it. And if something bad comes into our lives, well it is quickly reduced from bad to tragic. We are acting like the overprotective mother toward ourselves.

To work through this, one has to use the cowboy definition for courage. In the cowboy movies of the late 50's early 60's, it seems that there was always a little boy who would ask the lead "the question." The question was, "Ain't you sceert'?" And the lead, a cowboy, would always answer, "Well, yeah, I'm scared." The little boy would always be disappointed saying something like, "Y're yeller!" The cowboy would gently respond, "It's not having no fear that make's a man courageous, it's doing the thing, even when you are afraid." The little boy would always be impressed, the cowboy would take care of business and the audience would feel good.

Well that's the way it is. In order to deal with overprotective fear, we must be willing to be afraid, but do the thing, or don't do the thing anyway. We must be willing to cross the bridges of our lives feeling our fear, but crossing the bridges anyway. Paula Cole has written and recorded one of my favorite songs, called, *Me (Cole, 1996)*. The lyrics to the song are written below.

Me

I'm not the person who is singing.
I am the silent one inside.
I am not the one who laughs at people's jokes,
I just pacify their egos.
I am not my house, my car, my songs,
They are only stops along my way.

I am like the winter,
I'm a dark, cold female,
With a golden ring of wisdom in my cave.

Chorus:
And it's me who is my enemy.
Me, who beats me up.
Me who makes the monsters.
Me who strips my confidence.
And its me who is too weak,
Its me who is too shy
to ask for the things I love.
But I love and I love and I love.
But I love and I love and I love.

I am standing on the bridge
And I'm over the water,
And I'm scared as hell,
But I know there's something better,
Yes I know there's something better,
Yes, I know, Yes I know.

In the song, she speaks of standing on a bridge. One gets the picture of her having stepped out onto a bridge, arrived at the middle of the bridge where she can see both ends, what is ahead and what is left behind. Will she go back, or will she keep going forward? S/he quivers, sweats, worries, shakes, and then decides to keep going on to the other side. That is what it is like to deal with fear.

People say to us that we must face and overcome our fears. Often they mean that we should put on some kind of false bravado that says we can accept the unacceptable and tolerate the intolerable. This is merely more of the role. I am talking about walking *through* our fears. In order to walk through a fear, one must first hear it. What is it saying? Is it saying, "Get out of the road there's a Mac truck coming?" If so, do it. NOW! Is it saying, "Life is very, very hard, too hard to do much about?" "If you want something done right, do it yourself?" "You have to do this, or s/he will be mad?" Is it saying that you must spend all your life guarding the camp? If so, then these are overprotective fears. These are the ones we need to walk *through*.

The truth of it is this: Many of us, far too many of us, have *already* survived the worst thing that will happen to us in this life. That's right. The chaos and dysfunction that crystallized our fear into identity has already happened. And in many, if not most cases, this was as bad as it can get for us. So, why do we keep our guard up? It is simply because that's what we have always done. And as AA (Alcoholics Anonymous) puts it, "If you always do what you've always done, you will always get what you always got." If that's what you want, then you can put this book down, unfinished. But if you want what is really yours; if you want what you have always missed and longed for; if you want the only thing that has ever really belonged to you, then continue this journey *through* your fear and you will find it. What you will find is *you*.

In order to walk through fear, we must have something to walk on. This is the bridge of which Paula Cole speaks. I say that this bridge is made up of protective fear. Protective fear is different from overprotective fear, in that protective fear is authentic. Protective fear is that fear we have that we will not fulfill our lives. Protective fear is that fear that says, stop living a dead-like existence. It says "Wake up!" "Be afraid, be very afraid of having a passionless life!" "Be afraid of the role and its deadly messages to you!"

Protective fear is the voice of recognition that comes up in our heads and hearts telling us to stop betraying ourselves. It is the little voice that says, "What are you doing? Why are you doing this?" when we are just repeating by rote some old frustratingly familiar pattern of behavior and thought. Protective fear is the little voice of recognition that says, "Why am I feeling guilty for having friends, when I've been putting up with his/her affairs for years?" Protective fear is the voice that says, "I'm so tired, so tired of having to do it all for everyone all the time." Protective fear is the awareness that body parts are aching and the brain is exhausted from always trying to do the "right thing." Protective fear has all the right questions to ask, if we are listening. But our protective fear is often buried under years of living the role, so that it is difficult to hear. But if we can begin to listen, it becomes a bridge to authentic life.

Below, write a short story about your bridge. What's on the side you are crossing from? What do you think is on the side you are crossing to? What protective fears make up the bridge you are standing on? What do your overprotective fears look, feel, act like? (That is, are they snakes in your story, flies, frogs, slippery logs?) What do you imagine it will be like to get to the other side? Tell your story.

_____
_____
_____
_____
_____
_____
_____
_____
_____
_____
_____
_____
_____
_____
_____
_____
_____
_____
_____
_____
_____
_____
_____
_____
_____
_____
_____
_____
_____
_____
_____
_____

Below write a poem, or letter to your overprotective fears from the Authentic Self.

_____
_____
_____
_____
_____
_____
_____
_____
_____
_____
_____
_____
_____
_____
_____
_____
_____
_____
_____
_____
_____
_____
_____
_____
_____
_____
_____
_____
_____
_____
_____
_____
_____
_____
_____

Ponderings: The next barrier to living authentically is something I call, "the good/evil complex." The picture of the good/evil complex looks like this: There is goodness and there is badness (evil) and there is nothing in-between. The drawing below illustrates it.

Fig. 13.

GOOD ⟸⟹ EVIL

Essentially, what the good/evil complex does to us is eliminate our options. Let's see how that works. **Below, finish this sentence with a list of responses:**

I am good if I.... _____

_____

_____

_____

_____

_____

_____

_____

_____

_____

_____

_____

_____

_____

_____

Now finish this sentence with a list of responses:

I am bad if I.... _____

_____

_____

_____

_____

_____
_____
_____
_____
_____
_____
_____
_____
_____
_____

Please note above that your list of ways of being bad is in direct contradiction to your list of ways of being good. That's all we know about the subject. If I'm not good, I'm bad. If I'm not bad, I'm good. For the sake of argument let's take one of your items on the list of ways to be good and work on it. Let's say that you said that it was good to "care for others." Now that's a little vague, but it will do. Suppose we care for others because we fear that if we don't, others will not care for us. Are we good, or bad? Or, suppose we care for others because we feel obligated to do so. We may find that we really resent these people we are caring for. Are we good or are we bad? **Try a few of yours below.**

_____
_____
_____
_____
_____
_____
_____
_____
_____
_____
_____
_____
_____
_____
_____

_____
_____
_____
_____
_____
_____
_____
_____
_____
_____
_____
_____
_____
_____
_____
_____
_____
_____
_____
_____
_____
_____
_____

Let's try that again. Let's take one of the items on your ways to be bad list. Let's say that you said it was bad to be "selfish." Okay, let's say I'm selfish. I refuse to come over to your house and baby-sit for your children. You know that I don't really have anything to do that night, and I didn't even make any excuses, I just said "no." So, I'm selfish, right? Well, let's look a little closer. Suppose, I've been putting off some important personal work (like, say, working on this book) and I have set aside tonight to deal with it. Then you call me and ask me to do this thing for you. I say "no." Am I bad or am I good? **Try a few from your list.**

_____
_____
_____
_____
_____

Ponderings: Let's start here with the word selfish. That word gets thrown around quite a bit. The truth is the word "selfish" is usually used by persons who wish for us to do something for them. I wanted you to baby-sit for me, and you didn't do it. Therefore, I call you selfish. Now, who is selfish? More than anything else, this word is an excellent manipulative tool. Beyond that, it has little to no meaning.

How is this possible? Try this. How can we put others first? Go back to our earlier discussion of putting others first. As we said, it is impossible to put anyone else before ourselves. Putting someone else before yourself implies that you are putting someone else in your place. You are substituting them for you. Therefore, you are operating in absentia. You are not present. This is impossible. Even when we are doing something for someone else, we are present and we are getting something out of it. We speak of "self-less" acts. How does one go about being "self-less?" Well, one puts on a role, and pretends the self into the closet. But is it gone, really gone? The fact is that there is some gain for us in every act we do. Even if the only gain is that I gain a knowledge that you are satisfied and my love for you is such that I truly want your satisfaction. It *is* possible to love so unconditionally that we desire, truly desire a positive outcome for that other person. We have often experienced such emotion, especially regarding our children. But we didn't disappear to be aware of our children's satisfied state. We were present, experiencing their receipt of our gift. Therefore, we gained something as well. Is there, then, any such thing as a truly self-less act?

It is also true that we often call our shoulds and oughts and have-tos love. We say we are being loving when, in fact, we are really just being obligated. This kind of "love" is what 1 Corinthians, chapter 13 calls "nothing," "a sounding brass, or a tinkling cymbal." It says:

> Though I bestow all my goods to feed the poor, and though I give my
> body to be burned, and have not love, it profits me nothing.

We might well say that a person who gives everything to the poor and their body to be burned was a Mother Teresa, a Saint. But, at least according to this book we so often quote when we want to defend our goodness, it is possible to do these things without love. Therefore, it would seem that it is possible to do these things from "selfish" intent. Perhaps one does it out of a duty or obligation (a should, an ought, or a have-to). Perhaps some people do it because it makes them look good or feel good about themselves, because they feel like bad people way down deep inside. Does this make them good? Am I implicating us all in some kind of selfishness? Well to the degree that we change the definition of the word, perhaps I am. Have you ever known anyone who looked or acted like an elf? I have a dear, deceased friend whom I used to call, "my elf," because he was so elfish. He looked like an elf, and he was wise as I imagine elves to be. He was elfish, because he brought elves to mind for me. In just the same way, we are only selfish, when we bring ourselves to mind. When we become mindful that we are present in whatever circumstance, we are being selfish. This is not a manipulative or negative use of the word. One could say that when I am selfish, I am acting like my self. Then it is a high compliment. One which we could strive to accomplish if we so choose.

Of course, this definition does not negate the possibility that one can be so identified with fear and woundedness that one becomes narcissistic. But selfishness is not the same as narcissism. Narcissism is an obsession with entitlement. We'll talk more about his later, but suffice it to say that *one is not in danger of narcissism when one attends to the fact that one is present in all of one's doings.*

So, now, what is goodness? What is evil? I have a dear pastor friend who says that evil is the word, l-i-v-e, spelled backwards. He says that the only true form of evil is living backwards. I think of living backwards as living unconsciously. Living unconsciously is a way of living that is out of touch with what is true inside of us. It is denying our authenticity while living out of a role. It is living with a lot of unknown emotions and mantras that manage us without our knowing it. We've given unconscious permission for these things to manage our lives, but we don't even know that. So, while we may be relaxing into our roles, telling ourselves that we are doing the right thing each time we respond to guilt or fear, we might need to think again. Isn't it true that you found that some of your ideas of "goodness" could be construed to be "badness" under certain circumstances? Isn't it true that some of your ideas of "badness" turned out to not be so bad after all? So, what is goodness and what is badness?

The truth is that we had these terms defined for us centuries ago, and we have never yet changed the definition. We are, therefore, still living out of an arcane concept of words that seem to manage our entire lives, yet we haven't a clue what they really mean. If that is not living backwards, I don't know what is.

Let me hasten to say that if you have religious views on this subject, you are no less challenged to consider and reconsider this. Our religious views often come to us from others with the same view. We never stopped to ask ourselves if we really believe these religious perspectives, we just accepted them carte blanche. If we have never considered them, how do we even know if we really believe them? The truth is, that many, many of us simply swallowed the beliefs that we were handed without question, and if we questioned, we were told there were serious and permanent consequences for not believing those beliefs we were handed. Therefore, if it wasn't just blind following, it was blind fear. Either way we are blind. What do we REALLY believe? If our beliefs are going to be held on to in an authentic life, they will have to be authenticated. It is my sincere hope that this workbook will launch you into a study of your own spirituality, in a way that helps you authenticate that very real and important part of yourself. Our spirituality is primary to our sense of ourselves. Therefore, you are, hereby, being challenged to read and study and ask questions and seek answers that soothe your soul. We will speak to this in more depth later, in Chapter 7.

The truth is that for many of us, the good/evil complex affects us in this way: We get on binges. For a while, I'm on a goodness binge. I'm doing everything right, thinking right, acting right. Then some desperation hits me and suddenly I wake up a few hours, a day, a week, a month, a year later having slipped into acting out behaviors I don't even understand. I then call myself bad and slip back into a goodness binge. So first we are on a goodness binge, then we are on a badness binge, then we are on a goodness binge again. In all of that time, we haven't even asked ourselves what is real for us. What am I really feeling, thinking, doing here? Those questions are the questions of the authentic search. They lead to awareness. And awareness, if we use it to make decisions to take really good care of ourselves, leads to authenticity. Let's try it.

What is the desperation that sends me into playing the role, through either "goodness" or "badness?" Below, write a letter from your desperation to the Authentic Self.

_____

_____

_____

_____

_____

_____

_____

_____

_____

_____

_____

_____

_____

_____

_____

_____

_____

_____

_____

_____

_____

_____

_____

_____

_____

_____

_____

_____

_____

_____

_____

_____

Now, respond to that letter from the Authentic Self.

What does acting "good," even when it isn't sincere, do for me? Write a poem or letter about that.

What does acting "bad," or as it is often called, acting out, do for me? Write a poem or letter about that.

_____
_____
_____
_____
_____
_____
_____
_____
_____
_____
_____
_____
_____
_____
_____
_____
_____
_____
_____
_____
_____
_____
_____
_____
_____
_____
_____
_____
_____
_____
_____
_____
_____
_____
_____
_____

As you wrote the poems or letters above did you become aware of any particular theme? For example, did you find that when you act "good," you are hoping others will like you? Or, when you act out, are you hoping that you can release some pent up rage, or pent up frustration about having to be "good" all the time? If any like-dynamic is true for you, isn't it also true that your goodness/badness stuff, is not at all about goodness or badness? Couldn't it be about something like feeling lonely, or feeling enraged, or like emotions?

If this is so, what authentic things can you do to help yourself feel better when you have these emotions? For example, if you are feeling lonely, or isolated from the world, rather than trying to be good by serving others, why not try an experiment to spend time with these people without serving them, or instead of trying to please them, just enjoy them, and be real with them. Or, if you are angry or frustrated, rather than act out, why not do something to take care of your anger. Paint a room in your house your favorite color, talk to the person you are angry with, hit a baseball, chop down a tree you've been meaning to get rid of, etc. **Make a list below of authentic things you can do to help yourself feel better when these emotions hit.**

Ponderings: Our fears, our good/evil polarizations, as well as some other triggers we've yet to discuss, tend to make us "flip in or out" of the role and the Authentic Self. For example, the Scapegoat role might polarize by assuming that the boss really hates me, (because I really feel guilty most of the time) if s/he corrects something I've done. The more weight one puts on this side of the polarity, by obsessing about it, the more possible it is to "flip out" of the Authentic Self, and "flip into" the role. In this way, our thoughts, the messages we give ourselves keep us stuck on the seesaw of living. It is important, at this point, that we stop and consider exactly how this happens. See Fig. 14 below:

Fig. 14:

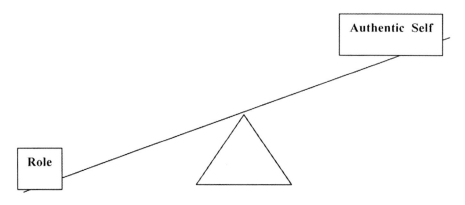

Above, write above the role side of the see-saw, some of the polarized thoughts, messages that you give yourself, which flip you either into or out of the Role. (Don't worry about working outside the lines.) Now write the messages that flip you back into the Authentic Self, above the box that says Authentic Self.

Ponderings: There is yet one more truth here. We can see, above that we can easily slip into the role by polarizing and by obsessing on the messages or mantras of the role. And we can see how changing our mantra to more self-aware, self-loving messages can flip us into the Authentic Self. However, sometimes there is another stimulus for flipping into the role again from the Authentic Self. Often, we flip back into the role because the Authentic Self is not familiar. It feels strange and, therefore, somewhat fake, at times. It is too good to be true at other times. It may even feel that "the other shoe must fall soon." We may, therefore, sabotage the Authentic Self, (until we get more used to it) by going back home to the more familiar role. So, if at any point in this journey, you find yourself feeling pretty good, fairly confident and doing the things that are real for you, you may also be aware that there may be another part of you, sneaking into the middle of the night to put a bomb in your airplane. This is your internal saboteur. S/he is sneaky.

Here's an example: You are feeling really good about yourself. You've talked to your boss about some recommendations you have for solutions to problems that had previously been eating at you, pushing you to flip into the Superwoman or Superhero role. You are trusting yourself more to speak up for what is true. You've been feeling attractive and not so afraid of being single. So, some Friday evening, you go to a party with friends. While you are there, you meet this wonderful person. S/he tells you how attractive you are, flatters you in all manner of ways and then invites you to go home with him/her. You do it. When you get there, you find that this person is very dangerous in some form and now you must find some way to escape.

That is a pretty drastic situation, but it does create the kind of sabotage we are speaking of. In fact, it may have even created a reenactment of your original trauma(s), taking you back to that old familiar place. Now you feel really terrible about yourself, feeling that you must start all over again. What happened? You were doing really well. This person flattered you, touched whatever unresolved issues you still have about loneliness and your own personal worth, and you dove down the slippery slide to the role.

Or, it doesn't have to be quite so drastic. Perhaps, it is just something that someone says that triggers your need to go back home. You've been doing really good, feeling good, acting according to the desires of the Authentic Self. But this morning, your co-worker said something about being overweight, getting on a diet, and mentioned something to you about joining her in an exercise program. Suddenly, you are very aware that you are still overweight. You begin to mentally beat yourself up, saying all manner of degrading things to yourself. Before you know it, you have slipped back into the role, can no longer manage to even notice the desires of the Authentic Self and are feeling very depressed.

At any of these points you may say to yourself, that the journey is not worth the trouble and you'd like to stop working on the Authentic Self. *Just remember that you have a choice. Know that during this journey, you may make several trips back to the role as you are deciding to live out of the Authentic Self.* But even if you go back, you can choose to say to yourself, "What does my Authentic Self want to do now?" Each time you go back home to the role, and return again to the Authentic Self, you bring a new box of supplies with you. Its just part of the process and it is okay. It's just another way of becoming very, very clear about which messages flip us backwards to the role. Once you are clear on all of those messages, then you will know exactly how to respond to each of them. At that point, you really will be dwelling in your new home. Then you will be able to hear the voice of the role calling you, but respond only to the Authentic Self; as opposed to, as it has been all of your life, hearing the voice of the Authentic Self calling you, but only responding to the rote power of the role. But that point can only be attained if you are willing to recognize and begin to deal with the messages you receive from the role.

Remember the argument assignment we did earlier? That's the same kind of argument you can have each and every time the role speaks to you, calling you back. And if you don't do it when you first hear the voice, even if you respond to the voice by going back home to the role, that's okay. Once you realize that you are back in the role, ask this question: "What does the Authentic Self desire now?" Whatever the Authentic Self's answer is, do it. Keep asking and answering the same way until you find that you have moved back into the Authentic Self. Then spend some time looking back and asking, "How did I get back into the role again?" Be very clear with yourself. Listen to the messages you gave yourself, (even if the message was simply: This is too good to be true, or it can't last, etc.) and write down the counter-message or argument from the Authentic Self, so that you can practice for the next time you get those same messages or hear their mantra. Then next time you get them, you are prepared with some ready-made responses that will put the old messages to rest.

One of the best things that can come out of revisiting the role is the fact that we have a renewed and deeper understanding of how the role affects us. We see again that it depresses us, makes us anxious, drives us to do things about which we are very ashamed, disrupts our relationships and even pushes us to suicidal ideations. And from that place, we can look back and see that only a few days before, we were feeling pretty good, no, we were feeling really good. And we felt confident about managing our lives. Then we can begin to ask, "How did I get here again?" Once we have really answered that question, we have now a method by which we can keep ourselves from sliding down the slippery slop again. It's kind of like drawing a map of a minefield. If you know where the mines are, you don't have to step on them and blow up your life.

Ponderings: The next barrier to living authentically is the area of difficult emotions. One of the most difficult things about difficult emotions is that we have somehow developed a belief that "if I'm having a difficult emotion, then I must act as if its message is very real." In other words, we begin to let our emotions (or the moods created by lingering in these emotions) control us. When you ask depressed persons why they didn't get up in the morning, they will often say, "Because I didn't feel like it." What they are saying is that my feelings, my mood took over every other aspect of my being. "I didn't feel like getting up," means I have stopped *thinking* like getting up, I have stopped *acting* like getting up. All I do is feel. This is not balanced living. In a balanced approach, we might say, "Oh, I don't feel like getting up, but I know that if I don't I'll feel worse today, I'll miss another day of work with no explanation, I'll suffer more, ultimately, I may lose my job, etc."

A feeling is just one aspect of our being. It is not the whole of us. What if we did the same thing with an emotion like anger? "I feel like punching your lights out!" Boom! Your lights are out! Road rage is like that. I feel like running you down, cutting you off, shooting at you—so I do. It is again, letting the feeling dominate. *But did you know that we have a choice about this?* When people are experiencing a difficult emotion that compels them to act, they often say, "I have no choice!" or, "I can't help it!" Actually, what they are saying is, "I have chosen to allow my mood, my feeling to dominate me. I have chosen to blind myself to any other option but acting out this emotion." And so they do. But it, like everything else we do, is simply a choice. The question then becomes, "Why do I choose to let my mood or feeling dominate?"

Often, with a difficult emotion such as anger, we say, "S/he provoked me!" Okay, and …? What we often mean when we say this is, "I had no choice but to act on my anger, I was provoked." Well, in actuality there are many ways to be angry without some external provocation. And provocation does not imply that we are compelled to react. We tell our children all of the time to ignore their provocateurs. So why do we, as adults, believe that we are compelled to react? It is because our belief systems tell us that a feeling becomes an action. This belief runs so deep that often we do not know we have a feeling until it becomes an action. We need to learn to develop thought boundaries between our actions and our feelings.

Another thing that we often say is, "I didn't mean it." Someone confronts us with some inappropriate response and we say, "I didn't mean it." What we are really saying is, "I chose to blind myself momentarily, so that I could do something I didn't like doing." *To any question about our behavior the answer is always, we have a choice.* In fact, there is no time in our lives, no instance, no circumstance in which we have no choice about our responses. Whether we like it or not, whether we know it or not, we are still, always in charge of our thoughts, feelings, words and actions. Everything we have done thus far has been a choice, and everything that we have yet to do will be a choice. *The biggest choice we have to make is whether we will choose consciously or unconsciously.* This is the whole purpose of this workbook, to help us learn how to choose consciously.

Note that we did not say that everything that I am is a choice. Who I am is a gift from whatever source created us. We did not choose the Authentic Self. It chose us. The very essence of who we are cannot be selected from the realm of the ego as we understand it. It must be selected or chosen by something bigger, higher, something more like soul. Here's an example: Many today still assume that gays and lesbians are operating out of a choice. But most of them will tell you, if you ask, that they did not choose to be gay. Some will even go so far as to say, "Who would choose a life in which you are rejected by almost everyone in the world?" Being gay or lesbian is simply another way of being authentic. We can be an authentic heterosexual or we can be authentically gay or lesbian. In that same way, we did not choose who we are. But we can choose what we will do, or say, or think.

Another truth is that we often get our circumstances mixed up with our responses. In some cases, we do not have any control over our circumstances. A tornado hits our home, a drunk driver hits us, our company closes down. These are certainly some circumstances over which we have no control. But we do have control over how we are going to respond to these circumstances. Yet we often believe that we don't. When we ask someone why he is depressed and he answers, "Because a tornado hit my home," he is not answering in truth. He is getting the event mixed up with his response to it. The truth is he has chosen the response of depression. In fact, he may think that since the tornado was beyond his control, and because this event was quite a shock, that he is *supposed* to be depressed. Well, of course, he is depressed, look what happened to him! That is what we might all say. But we have also met those people who took a devastating event and turned it into a life challenge, which brought out their true colors. Of course, this person may also have had some very difficult emotions. But here's the question, if the tornado created the depression, why doesn't it do that with everyone?

Our circumstances are not our emotions. They are two very different things. The biggest difference is that one is external and the other is internal. Circumstances are external. Emotions and other responses to circumstances are internal. *We often cannot control the external, but we are in charge of the internal.* Remember the tree, and the roots? The tree may be experiencing the wind, sleet, snow, hail, lightening, falling branches, etc., but the roots are only experiencing taking in energy and sending it up. We have a choice. We can be the tree blowing in the wind, or we can be the roots, taking in energy and giving it to ourselves. Or, to put it another way, when we are the tree blowing in the wind, we can choose to go to our roots and take in energy and give it to ourselves.

Okay, so what do we mean by control? Do we mean that we should not experience or express our emotions? Well, that's often what we hear, when someone says we have a choice, we hear, "Oh, they are telling me to repress my feelings again. I did that once and it got me to this place." No, it is not that black and white. We have many aspects of our being operating at the same time. We can have an emotion, and a thought and an action all at the same time, and they may not be similar at all. In fact, we can have a myriad of emotions active at any given moment. We can be feeling anger, sorrow, joy and peace all at the same time. Yes, it is true. We can feel anger and sorrow over a divorce yet feel joyous and peaceful for our newfound freedom and new life. And that is just one example. There are many others.

However, in our society, we have perpetuated the myth that we should experience only one thing at a time. How many times did we hear that from our parents: One thing at a time! Well, in some areas that is wise advice, but in others it works to our detriment. For example, what if a writer with writer's block gets an idea for a new chapter of a book, but right now, he is busy washing dishes. If he says, "No, one thing at a time. I'll finish the dishes first, then I'll go write," he may never lose his writer's block.

In truth it is possible for us to experience a shocking and very difficult circumstance and still live out of that place deep inside of us where everything is always okay. We say, "Yeah, right, maybe if I'm Buddha or Jesus or something!" But *every* tree has its roots. Every person has that place of authenticity deep inside, in which we are just, like the roots, sending up energy that says, "Live! Live fully, be alive," during every circumstance of our lives. The tree may have just lost a branch, but the roots are fine.

We've said what we don't mean by control; let's talk about what we do mean. The most effective measure of control we have in the realm of emotions, is to use our emotions as tools, to tell us something about what our next step might need to be. For example, if I'm feeling sad, I might need to know what the sadness is about so that I can address it in some way that helps me feel better. Suppose I'm feeling sad because I got left off the list of attendees at a party. I wasn't invited, I think. The message from the role might be, "See, I told you, you are not ever going to have any friends!" Okay, we hear that message and we say, "That's the message from the role, what would my Authentic Self say?" The Authentic Self quite often wishes to explore the feeling:

> Oh, you are feeling sad. What does this sadness tell you? It doesn't tell you simply that you were not invited, that was just the circumstance. It tells you that you need friends. Okay, let's get objective here and ask why were you left off the list? Was it because you are ugly, fat and stupid as your role says? Or was it because these people don't know you very well, may not know your address, phone number, etc. Or perhaps it is that these people really are not your type anyway. They are very different from you. You like to talk about all kinds of things that they find uninteresting. Perhaps the real truth is that you need friends with similar interests so that you will feel at home and will be affirmed in the things that interest you, etc.

The Authentic Self helps us know that our emotions are simply tools. Then they become the taste buds of life. They tell us about how something tastes to us. If we don't like it, we can do something about it. If we do, we can enjoy it.

But let's look at some typical patterns that keep us from exploring our emotions and using them for tools. Please note, in the following discussion "feelings" come first in the formulas. This does not mean that feelings actually always come first, though if they are authentic feelings they may come first. But, as we've said, feelings are very often triggered by a thought, an interpretation of an internal or external event. Yet even then feelings are often the first thing of which we are aware. And we become aware of the feelings through a second thought that either helps are harms. Keeping that in mind, here is the formula for being real:

Fig. 15:

Feelings   +   Thinking   +   Plans   +   Action   =   Being Real

Feelings which lead to thinking, which leads to planning, which leads to action, equals being real.

The problem is that we often do not operate this way. We operate in one of the following ways. Let's look first at the *passive* pattern:

Fig. 16:

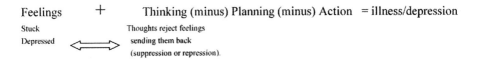

So, the passive pattern, says, my thoughts become aware of a feeling, but say, "That's a bad feeling, send it back!" When it gets back to the emotions, since I can't express it, or take action on it, I stuff it. And I stuff it again, and again, and again, each time it raises its ugly head, until finally I'm feeling stuck and depressed. Feelings must be expressed. But there is no way now for these feelings to be expressed. They've been left no outlet except to be taken into the spirit as depression or into the body as illness. Stress related diseases, like heart trouble, arthritis, skin disorders, fibromyalgia, etc. can result from such repression over a long term. Depression is the opposite of expression. Depression is a state in which several emotions are repressed. We'll discuss this in more depth later, but for now, suffice it to say that depression is NOT a feeling. It is a repressed state.

The *aggressive* pattern is just the opposite:

Fig. 17:

Feelings **(minus)** Thinking **(minus)** Planning = (Faulty) Action

I feel, therefore I act.

The aggressive pattern says, "I want to hit you, I hit you." "I want to marry you, we marry tonight." Whatever I feel comes up and comes out all over you. The aggressive pattern is one in which the aggressor quite often will say, "He made me do it," or, "He provoked me," or "if only you hadn't done that, I wouldn't have had to hurt you." For the aggressive person, there is no internal sense of responsibility. There is only an external locus of control.

The *Passive-Aggressive* pattern looks like this:

Fig. 18:

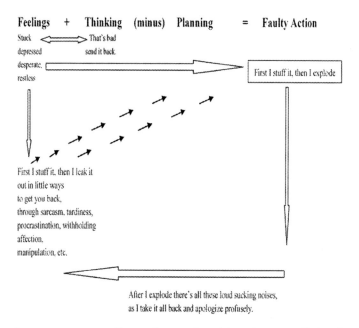

Feelings　+　Thinking　(minus)　Planning　=　Faulty Action

Stuck ⟷ That's bad
depressed send it back.
desperate,
restless

First I stuff it, then I explode

First I stuff it, then I leak it
out in little ways
to get you back,
through sarcasm, tardiness,
procrastination, withholding
affection,
manipulation, etc.

After I explode there's all these loud sucking noises,
as I take it all back and apologize profusely.

The Passive-aggressive pattern is the one with which most of us most easily identify. We try really, really hard to be "nice." We don't say what we feel or think, so that we will not offend anyone, or hurt anyone's feelings. We keep stuffing our anger until one day, we just blow. We say all the things we have always wanted to say. All those "you hurt me" stamps we've been collecting down in the cellars of our consciousness come flying out with expletives not deleted. For just a minute, it feels really good. Then we feel guilty and we take it all back with "I didn't mean it, I was just angry." When we say that, we are not only discounting our very legitimate feelings, but we have also stated very clearly that we feel that our anger is something we don't really mean. Have we solved any problems yet? The anger was meant to make us aware that there was a problem. Now, we have said the anger doesn't count, so the problem isn't real. But at least I get to keep the relationship, even if everything you do makes me angry, you are still here. I'm not alone. So we serve the breakfast in bed for a week, and apologize over and over again, swearing that it will never happen again (until the next time).

The other pattern of passive-aggressiveness shown in Fig. 18 is the one in which we leak out our feelings. Things don't go the way we like for them to, but we never say a word, until we choose to be sarcastic. Then if the other person notices it and comments, we can always say, "Oh, I didn't mean it that way!" or, "I was just kidding!" We can be late to the meeting set up by the boss, because we know it will embarrass him. We can be late every time to dinner, because we are mad that the spouse isn't more affectionate. We can procrastinate on a project we hated being assigned. We can manipulate by being pitiful, lying, playing mind games, throwing up smoke-screens, subtly sending out messages of what we want, talking about people behind their backs, etc.

All of these are passive-aggressive ploys. And we use them because we are afraid that if we don't, we won't get what we want, but we don't want anyone to really know we want anything. It's a way of feigning powerlessness, while gaining the edge on power subtly. For example, I'll put up and put up and put up with your behavior until one day I blow. You know that one day I'll blow, so your behavior never really gets any worse. Or perhaps I don't blow, but I stop having sex with you, or play mind games, or blame you. Though we never solve a single problem, the problem doesn't worsen. You fear my wrath or my manipulations, so you back down a little. In this way we can keep doing the same old dance.

Okay, now, let's get real:

Fig. 19:

Feelings	+	Thinking	+	Planning	+	Action	=	Being Real
I feel angry	+	I see the anger. What is the anger trying to tell me? Once I know what the anger is trying to tell me I can make a plan to deal with it.	+	I make a step-by-step plan to address the anger as if it matters, and in a way that makes my life better, or makes me feel better.	+	I stick to the plan. Even if someone dangles a distracting carrot in front of me, I stick to the plan.		

Being authentic does not mean never having a difficult feeling. It means that any feeling, whether difficult or easy, is meant to be a tool, to assist us in making our lives more real. We might even say that they are tools to help us build that new authentic home we are building. We begin to use all of our capacities to fulfill our desires, to make our lives complete.

First, let's talk about how this *doesn't* work. Authenticity doesn't work to get people to do things your way. I'm sorry. It is not meant for that. It doesn't make the world suddenly jump to your side of the fence, saying, "We're so sorry! You've been right all along. Wish we'd known it before, but, we were just too stupid." It doesn't make people change into the loving, whole people you always knew they could be if they just tried. It doesn't make all the bullies in your life come around and make wonderful, abundant amends to you. It doesn't make you rich, or beautiful or famous.

What it does, is it offers real solutions to real problems in a way that makes you feel confident that you can have an impact on your world. It keeps you authentic. Let's try an example and then we'll have you do one or two of your very own. Ann and John live together. They have a joint bank account. John spends tremendous amounts of money and never tells Ann when he is doing this. She writes a check to pay a bill and the check bounces. This has happened for the third time in a few months and she is angry. Here's what she does, if she is working the above formula:

1. She recognizes her anger. She names it anger.

2. She thinks about her anger, what she is angry about. She doesn't just blame John, rather, she reduces her anger to its lowest common denominator. She finds out what her anger is telling her about *her* life. Basically, her anger is telling her that she has very little say so, not only about money but about all kinds of things in her relationship.

3. As she thinks about this, she begins to realize that she has done very little to gain any control. She has not spoken up about her needs, she has, in fact, pretended that she didn't have any needs. She makes her plan accordingly. She plans to have a talk with John, and inform him that from now on she is going to speak up about her needs. She will tell him that she is not trying to disrupt their relationship in any way, but that she can no longer do it the way they have been doing it. She will say that she doesn't want to lose the relationship, but she does want to change some of the patterns. Her pattern, she will say, is one in which she devalues herself and does not speak up for what she wants and needs. Therefore, she will begin speaking up. She also will make some specific requests of John. Could they do at least, one of these three options:
    a. Separate their bank accounts so that she can pay bills from one account, while he uses the other account for his expenses.
    b. Keep the joint bank account, but John will tell her each time he spends money and exactly how much he spends so that she can account for this.
    c. Attend some money management seminars together.

4. She will stick to her plan. When John starts feeling blamed and gets angry, or starts saying "Yeah, but you...." she will say, "I hear that there are other things we need to talk about, but for now, can we just stick to this until I get through?" Whatever red herrings he throws out for her to chase, she will not do it, but will stick to her plan.

Has Ann guaranteed, by doing this, that John will agree with her? No, John may not agree with her. He may walk out and slam the door. But she has a *greater chance* of being heard if she says it calmly and with a plan. She has a *greater chance* of offering a solution and actually solving the problem. John may just come around. And even if John doesn't "get it," Ann can then go back to the drawing board and come up with a solution that doesn't involve John. Either way, she can solve the problem. Ann has practiced the art of authentic assertiveness, by taping into the Authentic Self and living, at least in this moment, in the Authentic Self. This confidence in the Authentic Self will build and build the more she uses these skills.

Now, it's your turn. Pick some difficult emotion that you have or have had recently, and work it through the above steps.

_____

_____

_____

_____

_____

_____

_____

_____

_____

_____

_____

_____

_____

_____

_____

_____

_____

_____

_____

_____

_____

_____

_____

_____

_____

_____

_____

_____

_____

_____

Do it again. Take some emotion you have felt recently, or even in the recent past, and take it through the above steps to being real.

_____
_____
_____
_____
_____
_____
_____
_____
_____
_____
_____
_____
_____
_____
_____
_____
_____
_____
_____
_____
_____
_____
_____
_____
_____
_____
_____
_____
_____
_____
_____
_____
_____

Let's try something else. But first let's ponder again: There is another purpose for difficult emotions. They are meant to assist us in seeing ourselves better. They, through the use of the technique below, assist us in seeing things about ourselves that we could see no other way. Let's see how it works. Let's take one of the more difficult emotions: anger. Suppose Joe is angry at Sam because Sam is so lazy at work. Sam never does anything. He totally resists accepting any responsibility for anything. He sits around on his duff all day long, chewing the fat on the phone, with his peers, even with the boss. And when the boss gets mad because the work is not done, Sam just blames his peers. He makes everyone else pick up the slack he leaves.

Well, this is clearly all about Sam, right? He really *is* the bad guy. Joe is doing his work, Sam is just not doing his. Well let's get out *the mirror*. The mirror we are using is that look at the external that is a reflection of our own internal. Why would we bother to do this? I mean after all, Joe is the good guy here and Sam is the bad guy. Well the problem with that logic is that it splits the whole thing off into the intellectual abstraction of "good" and "evil," whatever those mean. It means we can't solve the problem because we are so busy splitting our emotions off from our intellect. How is it that Joe is having such an internal reaction to this if there is nothing internal to be considered here? The reaction is coming from Joe's internal, not from the external Sam. Okay, so let's look in the mirror.

When Joe does this, he sees bits and pieces of himself that he is not aware of. Joe considers himself to be a hard worker. He seems to be at it all day, doing his work, turning it in on time, and trying to please the boss. Sam, on the other hand, is totally the opposite. Or so it seems. Let's look again. Sam is the mirror, and parts of him look just like Joe. How can that be? Well, if the truth be told, there have been several times lately when Joe slacked off on his work, played Solitaire on the computer, stayed away from his desk extra long, leaving others to take his orders. Well, Joe hadn't thought about that, forgot all about it, as a matter of fact.

But let's go one deeper. Joe hates this job. He'd like to have a low-pressure job where he could not have to be so driven just to make a buck. He's known this for a long time, but is just too settled in to try to do anything about it. Who ever gets to do what they want in this life anyway? Who gets to make dreams come true? That's for movie stars and fat cats. Not Joe. Sam, on the other hand, seems to be doing it. He's getting a paycheck, because every one else is doing his work for him. He's not pressured at all. He comes in, hangs out, does the least amount of work he can do, collects his money and goes home. Joe looks in the mirror, into Sam's reflection on him, and sees his own desire to find a low-pressure job. Now, Joe has found something really important: He can continue to be mad at Sam, or he can get busy working on his own life's desire.

Previously, Joe had believed all the negative messages he gave himself about the possibility of doing what he wants in his life. Now, he has to question that. Now, he has to ask himself if he has just been being lazy. Not the lazy of a few solitaire games but the lazy of not fulfilling his own authentic desires and dreams. Has he just been resisting taking responsibility for his own dreams? Well, that's just like Sam, isn't it?

Now, Joe is no longer angry. Now, he's on a mission to find just the right job, to make himself happy. And Sam, the man he hated, helped him get there. This is a very specific way of using our emotions as a tool. We get mad at other people, but those other people can be mirrors of things we don't know about ourselves. We can get very powerful messages about our lives and the things we are leaving out, or putting in that we might really desire to change, just by looking in the mirrors others present to us, through our own reactions to them.

So, let's try it. There is someone in your life about whom you have a very strong emotion or reaction. Try to pick someone with whom you are angry. But if you can't do anger, just choose another difficult emotion, like guilt for example. Write down the emotion and the reason why you feel it on the lines below: (Try to be brief but very clear about exactly what bothers you.)

_____
_____
_____
_____
_____
_____
_____
_____

Now, imagine that the person you feel the emotion toward offers you a mirror. Look at his/her features that aggravate, annoy, irritate, anger, or sadden you. How is each of these features a metaphorical trait of your own? Fill in the chart below accordingly:

Other person's feature:	Your matching trait/problem:

What have I learned from looking in the mirror presented to me by this other person? Is there something about my life that I can change now to make it more authentic?

_____
_____
_____
_____
_____

Ponderings: The truth about difficult emotions is that they tend to make us "assume the position" of the role. It is a knee-jerk reaction. We feel the emotion, on some unconscious level we choose to allow the emotion to take precedence over every other aspect of our being (including thoughts, plans, actions, even spiritual awareness) and we assume the position of the role. We allow ourselves to be scapegoated one more time, we play bully, we take on the Superwoman or Superhero job of the century, we run away, we make someone laugh, we do whatever we've always done, and it just gets us what we've always gotten, and somehow, we are surprised by this. The work of this workbook is to get us to the place where we can insert the Authentic Self, just before we assume the position of the role again.

Below, write a poem, or letter about how you assume the position:

_____
_____
_____
_____
_____
_____
_____
_____
_____
_____
_____
_____
_____
_____
_____
_____
_____
_____
_____
_____

Below write a "Once upon a time" story of a person who assumed the position over and over until one day s/he learned to be real. (Use as many pages as needed, or copy this page as many times as is needed.)

Once upon a time....

_____
_____
_____
_____
_____
_____
_____
_____
_____
_____
_____
_____
_____
_____
_____
_____
_____
_____
_____
_____
_____
_____
_____
_____
_____
_____
_____
_____
_____

The next barrier to living authentically is "if only" thinking.

If only thinking goes like this: "If only I hadn't wrecked that car my daddy bought me, I could have gotten more dates and been more popular. Then my self-esteem would have been better and I would have been able to hold down jobs better." "If only I'd never been molested, my life would be totally different." "If only I hadn't gone out that night so late, I never would have been raped." "If only my parents acted like they gave a damn, I would never have turned out this way." "If only I hadn't spilled that milk, my mother never would have abused me." "If only I'd locked my door at night, my father couldn't have gotten in to abuse me." "If only I were wealthy, my life would be so much better." "If only I had a better boss, I could do a better job and get promoted." "If only my husband hadn't left me, I'd be a whole person now."

I'm sure you know we could go on and on. And so we have. We have gone on and on throughout our lives, thinking "if only" thoughts that drive us mad, make us feel guilty and throw us catapulting right back into the role. How does this work? Well, it's like this. When I am doing "if only" thinking, I am not doing "How can I resolve this?" thinking. In other words, "if only's" keep us stuck in the past, repeating and repeating all the reasons why we are stuck. In essence, they keep us from being able to take responsibility for our present.

Self-blame is not the same as personal responsibility. Self-blame is just a form of denying personal responsibility. Self-blame keeps us wallowing in guilt, unable to feel the confidence to take responsibility and permanently resolve the issue. In fact, self-blame is a way of "assuming the position" of control. It is much easier for most of us to take on guilt than it is for us to admit that sometimes, terrible things happen that are beyond our control. Feeling that we can control our lives makes us take on the burden of things over which we literally have no control. Self-blame makes us responsible to other people, and events. There is little room left then, for taking real responsibility for our own lives. If I'm putting all of my energy into taking care of you or controlling some past event, how will I have any left for taking care of me? How will I even get clear on what is and isn't my responsibility if I'm busy taking responsibility for things over which I have no control?

Blaming others is also not the same as personal responsibility. The fact is that we can blame the other party forever. It feels good, it releases anger, it gives us the illusion of control through a judging vindication. We just don't want anyone to get away with it. We want them to suffer like we've suffered. And we will not take one single step toward making our lives any more meaningful, if all we are ever doing is blaming someone else. It's like we are waiting behind the curtains, for them to "get theirs," which means we are never getting out onto the stage of our lives to live out our desires. We are always only living vicariously, through the lives of our enemies! How is this helping us? In fact, it is just another way to avoid personal responsibility for creating the life we want.

And while we're at it here, we might as well, go ahead and talk about forgiveness.

Another F-word, actually. That one word is fraught with such legendary mythology, that we have a love/hate relationship with it. I've had people come to therapy with me after years of trying to forgive someone and say, "I just can't do it. I've tried so hard, but I can't forgive them. I guess I'll never get over this." What are they saying? They are saying, "I'll never get over this!" Without knowing it, they are saying, "I choose to stay stuck in this mire, by using forgiveness as my sticking power." They have the best intentions, but they just don't know that they are choosing to stay stuck.

Part of the reason for this is that we have been poorly educated with regard to the nature of forgiveness. Forgiveness, as we often use it, means absolution. It means this: "If I could just absolve you of your guilt for what you did, then I would have forgiven you. You will no longer be guilty and I will have peace." Based on this concept of absolution, we struggle and struggle for some form of clarity which will allow us to provide this person with the necessary protection from guilt. Yet, we also know that if we do provide them with this, we will forever be eating our own flesh because we don't really want them to be absolved of guilt. We want them to hang!! If only I could have justice, then I could forgive. If only I could forgive, then there would be no justice.

Forgiveness of this kind means that we can avoid taking responsibility for our lives. If I am stuck not being able to forgive you, then I am still your captive. You still have control of me. Worse yet, I am giving it to you. I am damned to continue to relive what you did, and cannot get absolution for myself because I cannot seem to forgive you. Further, even if I am able to convince myself that I have forgiven you, more often than not, what I have really done is simply repress my own feelings about what you did. I tell myself that I love you and I should forgive you, and so I say the words "I forgive you" to you or to myself about you. But really, I haven't done anything more than attempt magic through sending my true feelings away into unconsciousness. Then I come into therapy because I am depressed and don't know why. I've pretended to absolve you, and damned myself to live with the pain forever. We cannot take full personal responsibility for our lives if we are loaded down with this conflict between absolution and damnation. What a double-bind we put ourselves in! Our religions and spiritual beliefs never intended for us to be damned if we did and damned if we didn't, but this is exactly what this concept of forgiveness does to us. It puts us in a double-bind of eternal proportions. We live in hell because we cannot forgive someone else for putting us there!!

What if forgiveness isn't what we think it is? What if forgiveness really is just acceptance? And what is acceptance but the final stage of grief. You remember the stages of grief put forth for us by Kübler-Ross: 1) Denial, 2) Anger, 3) Bargaining, 4) Depression, and 5) Acceptance (Kübler-Ross, 1997). The fact is that self-blame, blaming others and forgiveness (as we know it) are all ways of bargaining. In other words, they keep us stuck reliving the traumas, or events over and over by having us bargain with reality, in the following ways:

- It's my fault: Therefore I must make some sacrifice of self to manage this. (I'm bargaining with my own self. I'll trade you my self, for the illusion of control.)
- It's your fault: Therefore, I must sacrifice peace of mind to hold on to my anger. (I'm bargaining with my peace of mind. I'll trade you my peace, if you just own what you did, or I get to watch you suffer, [which, of course, may never happen]).
- I'll forgive you: Therefore, I must sacrifice my heart, to the person who broke it. (I'm bargaining with my own heart. I'll trade you my heart, which I'll try to repress, so that I can absolve you.)

It is "if only" thinking that keeps us stuck in any of these three agendas. And then, if only this had never happened I wouldn't have to try any one of these agendas. The problem with this is that it did happen. And "if only" keeps us stuck in the bargaining stage of grief. I've seen many people literally stay stuck in bargaining for years, based on one of the above agendas. Bargaining says "If I.... Then you'll." Or, "If you.... Then I'll." Or, "If only...." But acceptance is very different. In order to discover what it is, we need to look back at the stages of grief one more time.

When Kübler-Ross came up with the stages of grief, she was *not* giving us the authentic path to acceptance, but was rather informing the clinical community of the stages *typically* experienced by those who were dying or grieving a death. It is, indeed, rather typical for us to experience depression, for example, in the midst of a grief experience. But if we are talking about moving through grief as an authentic pathway to acceptance, we must think of it very differently.

An authentic pathway to acceptance would look more like this: Denial, anger, bargaining, sorrow, acceptance. These "stages" would not happen in any order of appearance as listed above, but rather, and this is also fairly typical, they appear simultaneously and in any order. However, acceptance is the ultimate outcome, though persons may experience varying degrees of acceptance throughout the process along the way to the ultimate acceptance. On the authentic pathway to acceptance, denial is a gauzy state of disbelief in which we allow ourselves time to assimilate a difficult reality. It does not become a permanent coping pattern. On the authentic pathway to acceptance anger is the voice of our desires exposed. While it is true that we may become angry at God, at life, at a significant other, etc., during the anger phase, what we are looking for under the anger is the I AM. I am angry because I've attached myself to a position in life, a person, a thing, an event, a relationship and I believe that this position, person, thing, event or relationship makes my life complete. This discovery makes it possible to see beyond the attachment and into the Authentic Self, accepting its offering of peace. Rather than experiencing the depression, which is typical to grief, persons might authentically experience sorrow. They might need time alone to cry, to write, to ritualize their sorrow, but they don't repress emotions in such a way that they ultimately become depressed. Bargaining would still exist, but it would be recognized for what it is, an attempt at magic. We all wish for magic at times in our lives. Persons who are on an authentic pathway to acceptance recognize this wish, appreciate its fervent desires and where possible take responsibility to fulfill them. Where it is not possible to fulfill them, persons may need to pass through some more sorrow. Finally, acceptance comes. The blessed relief of knowing, way down deep, that this is how it is (was) and this is a reality with which we can live in peace. Acceptance says, "This has been my life, for better or for worse. It's how it was/is." Acceptance does not alter the present day reality by trying to repress, or change the facts of the past. Acceptance does not blame self or others, nor does it try to absolve guilt. Acceptance deals in reality, no double-binds, no double-messages, no blame, no shame, no games. It is in essence saying, "I accept my life on life's terms, rather than trying to get life to accept my terms."

In fact, acceptance is a form of personal responsibility. Here's how forgiveness as acceptance works. First, over time and process I begin to see what you did. I do not blind myself to it, or pretend it didn't happen. I see it. I see it clearly. I feel all of the nuances of feeling that it gave me. I name those feelings and explore them for their meaning in my life. I find the message behind these feelings, messages that will always have to do with how I take care of myself and my life. I will listen to and heed these messages, learning how to creatively respond to my own needs and desires. As I am doing this, I am letting go, more and more of what you did to me, and taking more and more responsibility for what I am doing to me or for me. I am holding you less and less accountable for my life and its goals as I am holding me more and more accountable to bring myself joy and peace. And then one day, I look back at what happened and find that it no longer matters to me, what you did; it only matters that I learned how to care for myself. I have learned personal responsibility. Now, I can look back on those events as things that happened, that helped me grow. This method allows me to take and use responsibility as a tool for building the life I want.

But responsibility is a big word. We resist responsibility because it carries all manner of difficult or impossible connotations. We think it means any of the following:

- Heinous duty
- Odious obligation
- Work
- Guilt
- Burden
- Taking up your cross
- Taking the blame
- Carrying the sword
- Swallowing it whole
- Accepting your punitive Karma
- Not crying over spilled milk
- Being tough
- Being strong
- Never letting anyone know you're hurting.

And on and on. The word has taken a difficult rap. But what if it really doesn't mean any of those things? What if it means only this: Response—Ability. Yup! That's it. It is simply the ability to respond. Most of us rarely respond to anything. Instead, we react. "They" act. We re-act. In other words, we are not putting feeling, thought, and planning into the scheme. We are simply acting based upon someone else's action. We re-act. Responding involves more. It is putting some pondering into the picture. Sometimes, it even means writing a whole new script. It means considering all the ramifications of my own feelings, thinking about them, coming up with a plan and then sticking to it. (See Figure 19, above).

Responsibility means that I have, *already have*, the ability to respond to my own emotions and thoughts. I feel something about my life events, or relationships, I think about it, I make a plan and I stick to it. This makes me personally responsible for what? Me. That's all. Just me. I'm not responsible for you or any part of your well-being. That is your job. When I say this to most people, they typically say, "Doesn't that make me selfish?" No, it makes you realistic. *The fact is that you can take responsibility for no one but yourself.* No matter how small or helpless a person is, they are still responsible for their own choices. Does that mean that we have no obligation to our children and elderly? Yes. It does. It means we are not obligated to anyone or anything. *However,* we do have the right to choose to be caring and careful about our children and elderly. That would be an authentic act, not an act without a feeling, thought or plan. Obligation responds only to the rules. One does not have to be authentic at all to know what society says one "should" do. Authenticity requires much, much more.

You see, for centuries we have believed that obligation was our only motivating onus for action. We did not trust authenticity to provide us with motivation, so we made up rules and told ourselves we had to obey them. This way we don't have to think much about what we are up to, we can just follow the rules, just say, "I do it because I have to." That makes it easy, doesn't it? But what is authentic about just doing something by rote that has no heart or mind in it. Remember the message we sited from 1st Corinthians, Chapter 13, regarding love? Well, it applies here too. Even if I give all my goods to the poor, *all my goods,* but do it without love, it is <u>*nothing*</u>! Nothing! So, remind me again of the point of obligation?

But our belief systems set up obligation as one of the finer points of existence. The word "duty" has taken on very noble connotations. But it is actually nothing more than obligation, i.e., a simple following of the rules. If we are obligated up to our ears, and if we can manage to be available to all of those obligations, *then* we are considered to be responsible people, and that means that we are good people. But the truth is, if it doesn't come from authentic love, it means *nothing.*

We have not trusted the heart. We have been taught to believe that it is full of evil and therefore cannot be trusted on its own. And the truth is that by itself, it is just a bunch of emotions. But put it together with spirited thought, plan, and action and you have a very handy system for managing your life.

The other thing that we have been taught is that we cannot know ourselves. We can know other people and "if only" we could get them all to do what we want them to do, we'd be fine. But that is exactly backwards. The truth is that we can know ourselves intimately, more intimately than we will ever know another single person on planet earth. We can know the deep inner recesses of our own internal processes on a moment by moment basis. We can actually know no one else that way. But we've been subtly and overtly taught that it is our job to know others in a way that makes them manipulatable, through all manner of schemes and strategies. If I can figure you out then I know how to please you so that I can stay in the Superwoman role. If I can figure you out then I'll know how to outsmart you in the Runaway role. If I can figure you out then I'll know what you expect of me and I can meet my obligations, in order to please you as Scapegoat/Priest or Superwoman. If I can figure you out then I can figure out how to outsmart you as the Bully/Perpetrator or Scapegoat/Black Sheep. If I can figure you out then I'll know exactly what to do to keep you in my life or keep you at a safe distance. I'll even know more about how to compete with you or win the next war against you. We've spent centuries putting our energies in exactly the wrong thing. If we'd spent half that time getting to know ourselves, we would have already ushered in a millennium of peace.

So, "if only" I knew myself and could follow my own inner direction, I could live in peace and feel as if my life were manageable. This is my only job: To know myself intimately and to follow my own internal direction. This is living authentically.

What are your "if only's"? Below write in your if only and its outcome. For example: If only I were rich, then I'd be happy.

If Only ….	Then I'd be ….

Taking personal responsibility: Below, fill in the column on the left with the same outcome (Then I'd be ...) listed above. Fill in the column on the right with your method, even if it's only a first step, of attaining the outcome listed to the left. For example, if you listed above, "If only I were wealthy, then I'd be happy," take the outcome of happiness and put in the 1st column below. Then devise a method, even a first step, for getting the kind of happiness you think you would have. You might need to examine this a bit. You might think that wealth is what you would have to obtain in order to be happy. But ask it another way: What kind of happiness would you have? Peace of mind? Joy? Security? Once you have answered that question, then you can proceed to make a plan for getting the object of your desire. If you think, for example, that wealth would give you security, but you feel that you cannot have wealth, therefore, you cannot have security, think again. Is there a way for you to make yourself feel more secure, right now, or in the near future? Be creative.

I'd have ...	If I ...

You have just taken at least some personal responsibility for accomplishing your own desires. How do you feel? Do you feel frightened, nervous or excited? These are normal emotions in response to changing our "if only" thoughts to responsible thoughts. We suddenly realize that we can give ourselves some of the things we have always wanted and it's a little overwhelming. Just sit and let this gel awhile, it will become more comfortable as you consider it.

The next barrier to living authentically is our Belief Systems, or as I've heard it so aptly put before, our B.S. Belief systems are just that, they are entire systems of thinking, feeling and acting based upon a network of interacting beliefs. Beliefs can be original, or they can be redundant copies of things we've heard others say and watched others do. When I was a little girl, I heard my highly opinionated mother declare over and over again, her hatred for George Wallace, then the Governor of Alabama. Now, I didn't know the slightest thing about George Wallace, but because she hated him, I hated him. As I grew up and learned more about him I realized that I totally disagreed with just about everything he stood for politically. Both of those two ways of digesting material had the same result, albeit the latter has a little less of a visceral quality to it; but they were arrived at in very different ways. In the first, I developed someone else's attitudes and beliefs, in the second, I developed my own objective viewpoint.

We can get our beliefs from anywhere: parents, siblings, friends, church, school, teachers, principals, TV, society in general. Or, we can decide what we believe by asking ourselves some serious questions about what makes us feel most authentic. Let's take, for example, the idea of being out of control. We may have acted silly, hyper, or we may have had tantrums when we were little, and our parents may have said, "You are just out of control!" Okay, what does this mean, if it becomes a belief system? It may mean that we have the capacity to lose control of ourselves. Well, that's pretty scary. What will that belief system allow me to do? Well, if I believe that I can be out of control and that, in fact, I *am* out of control when I act silly, or hyper or have a temper tantrum; then I will not investigate my motivations for these behaviors, I will just feel like they are beyond my power to change. It is interesting, I think, that mothers who say, "You are out of control!" to their children often follow it with something like, "If you don't stop that, I'm going to …!" Well, if they could stop it, they wouldn't be out of control, now would they? So that means mother has to take control. What happens to the kid then? He learns to depend on another's discipline to make him feel that he is in control. He learns that others have power that he lacks. Then mother wonders why it is that the kid seems to get worse and worse. She taught him how. And that's exactly what we do to and with ourselves when we develop similar belief systems.

It works like this: I believe that I can get out of control. When I am angry and violent, I am out of control. Someone must be able to say just the right words or give me just the right message or I will keep being violent. The person I'm usually depending on to make me stop being violent is the person toward whom I am being violent! And if that person can't say it, or do the thing that will make me stop, well, then I'll just have to hurt him/her. Or, if I'm angry when no one is around to stop me, well then, there will be no stopping me. This is how one belief becomes a whole system of thinking and acting.

As we've said, at all times, I have a choice. I can choose authenticity, or I can choose the role. Once we realize this, we can change our belief from one of "I can get out of control," to "I am always in control of my choices. I may even choose to become unconscious and irresponsible or even reckless so that I can appear to abandon control. Yet it is I who have chosen to abandon control, and it is I who have chosen to go unconscious while I allow myself to act out." This is just one example of a belief system and how it works within the roles we play. Let's look at some of your beliefs.

Let's look at your beliefs about the following topics. Then we will challenge you to consider new options. The topic is on the left, your belief about that topic is in column two, your behavior as a result of this belief is in column three, and a new challenging belief is in column four. Consult with your Authentic Self before filling in column four. You may turn back to your previous work on beliefs to give yourself some ideas about your beliefs.

Topic	I believe:	Which makes me:	Authentic Self says:
Life			
The World			
Mothers			
Fathers			
Men			
Women			
Parenting			
God (or spirituality)			
Career			
Relationships			

You have just begun the process of examining your beliefs for validity. You might aid yourself in this process by asking questions as you go through. You might ask do I like this belief? Who is the "I" who doesn't like the belief? Is it the Authentic Self, or is it the role? Why don't I like the belief? Does the reason sound more like the reasoning of the Authentic Self or the reasoning of the role? Or, you might say, "Does this belief keep me stuck in any way?" Or, you might ask, "Does this belief run counter to any other belief that I have?" If it is difficult for you to come up with a challenging or authentic belief, try imagining that you've just heard a small child whom you love deeply state your belief. What would you say to this child if s/he stated your belief? For example, let's say that you have a belief that "Life is hard." Imagine that you are sitting in a room next to a small child that you really like. You hear that child sigh deeply and say, "Life is hard." What would you say to him/her? Whatever you would find to say to that child that is loving and considerate of the child's well-being is what you can say to yourself now and this can become your new belief.

Some of our beliefs put us in a "double-bind." A double-bind is a message system that contradicts itself and paralyzes a person. It basically communicates, "You are damned if you do, and damned if you don't." Imagine riding down the street and seeing a sign that says, "Don't read this sign, under penalty of law." That is a double-bind. If you don't read a sign on the road, you might be violating a law or jeopardizing your safety. If you do read it, you are violating a law. Our belief systems can double-bind us so that we become totally ineffective. Here's an example of an external double-bind, which may help you see how our internal double-binds work.

Sarah loves her mother deeply. But Sarah's mother has played out the role of crazy-maker for Sarah. Sarah's mother is very abusive and constantly critical of Sarah. She tells Sarah that she disciplines her because she loves her, but her discipline is abusive. She tells Sarah that if Sarah would just cooperate with her mother, her mother wouldn't have to discipline (abuse) her. However, what Mom wants Sarah to cooperate with is very damning to Sarah. She wants Sarah to take care of all of her needs. Sarah is to keep up with the bills, keep the house clean, care for her younger siblings and be the perfect student. Sarah gives up her own childhood to strive to do all of these things exactly to her mother's specifications. But when she does, her mother abuses her anyway. Why? Because when she does these things so well, she makes the mother believe that she could have done them herself if she'd just tried. She is jealous of Sarah's ability to get these things done. Now, Sarah has done all of this to win her mother's favor, but she still doesn't have it. She's damned if she does and damned if she doesn't.

Our internal double-binds work the same way. An example of a belief system that double-binds follows. I may have a belief that I am "worth the trouble," that I can spend time, energy, money taking care of myself because I'm worth whatever trouble, or effort it takes to make me happy. However, I also have a belief that in order for me to be worthy, I must perform certain very difficult tasks. I will, therefore, become my own saboteur, so that I do not have to go to the trouble to assist myself through my current difficulties, because I haven't yet earned the privilege of being "worth the trouble." One belief contradicts the other. One belief says that I am worth it; the other says I am not.

Below is a chart which will help you sort out your doubly-binding beliefs. First, go back and reference the messages, behaviors and mantras you circled. Also reflect on the beliefs you've previously discovered thus far in your work here. Are there any contradicting beliefs? If you still don't see any, try this: ask yourself where you are stuck in your life. What are the belief systems you have that keep you stuck? Are there any contradicting beliefs here? Now work the chart below. (If you don't find any contradicting beliefs, this is great, move on to the next page. But do keep your mind open to this possibility.)

Belief #1:	Belief #2:	This keeps me stuck in:

How are you feeling right now? Write a paragraph below on your feelings about the exercise above.

_____
_____
_____
_____
_____
_____
_____
_____
_____
_____
_____
_____

When was the first time you can remember hearing each of the above beliefs said, or when was the first time you can recall believing your belief. Go back over the beliefs on the charts you worked earlier, and consider when you first picked up these beliefs. You did a similar exercise on thoughts and mantras in Chapter 2. You may wish to reference that as well. Write in the source of your belief below.

Belief:	Source:

You may see from the above that these beliefs are not YOUR beliefs. They really belong to someone else and you adopted them. More than likely, you adopted them because you were, in some sense, surrounded by them, or you felt that you must adopt them in order to fit in. Remember that fitting in is tantamount to survival when we are young, for we feel that abandonment would mean death in some form. You may also find some authentic beliefs in this mix. If so, the source will be your own original thoughts. If you find these you may wish to keep a running list of them as sources of comfort and authentic planning.

Now let's try something new regarding beliefs that double-bind us: Fill out the chart below with conflicting doubly-binding beliefs. Remember that if you cannot come up with an Authentic Belief just by checking in with yourself, you can use the technique of pretending that you are hearing a child, whom you love, state your belief out loud in your hearing. Respond, now to that child. However, you would respond to this child, is how *you* are responding authentically to these beliefs. (Feel free to tear out this page, or copy this page and place it somewhere in your home that you visit frequently. These Authentic Beliefs can now be used as affirmations.)

Belief #1:	Belief #2:	Authentic Belief:

Below, write a poem, or letter about your discoveries regarding your beliefs.

_____
_____
_____
_____
_____
_____
_____
_____
_____
_____
_____
_____
_____
_____
_____
_____
_____
_____
_____
_____

Now write a story of a person and his/her beliefs and their effects, and/or the effects of changing the beliefs. (Use as many pages as you would like, or copy this page as often as is needed.)

_____
_____
_____
_____
_____
_____
_____
_____
_____

Ponderings: We still have some very important work to do but before we do it, it is important to sum up this section of the book. On the preceding pages, you have worked through some of the barriers to living authentically. It is most important to note that you have *begun* the work of dealing with the barriers. It is certain that you can, and will—if you do the work—dissolve these barriers. You may, however, need to practice this work over and over for a while. Once you get into practice, it will become second nature. You will just start doing the work, every time a barrier presents itself. Eventually, there will be no more barriers. And you may be very surprised at how rapidly this can happen. It's just a turn of the kaleidoscope away. You just choose, at every juncture, to be authentic.

Fears may present at every juncture of moving closer to living authentically. The biggest fear of all *is* living authentically. As we have said, living authentically is new. It is not familiar. It seems so much easier for us to return to the familiar. The good/evil complex may present at any time, during work or play. But if we do the balancing work, we will move beyond it. Difficult emotions may present at any time, making us want to assume the position of the role. Yet we can begin to use these emotions as tools rather than as simply moods, which take us back to the old way of being. In so doing, we will build our new authentic home. Then our thinking can become a barrier as well through "if only" thoughts. But if we confront our thoughts at each junction and work on thinking more authentically, we will move past this as well. And our belief systems may present looming walls to hurdle, but if we go back and do the work on our BS, we can pass over this barrier too.

The exercises that you have done in this section can be done again and again. You may carry a notebook with you, so that you can sit down with pen and paper at any time and do the exercise for a few minutes before you confront a problem, while you are in the midst of a difficult moment, or even when you are just trying to decide how to prioritize your day. You can, at any time, write a letter to the Authentic Self from the role and receive a letter back from the Authentic Self. You can gain considerable clarity in an instant this way.

As with any significant life change, we must continue the adjustment until it is complete. If you stop doing the work, you may find a few days, weeks, months or even years later that you have slipped back into the old way and are getting the same old results. But even then, it is not too late to start over. Just pull out the workbook and get started.

Remember the Alcoholics Anonymous mantras:

It works if you work it.   &   If you always do what you always did, you always get what you always got.

Diagnosis

And
The

Authentic Self

Ponderings: While this chapter is meant mainly for those who have been diagnosed with one of the mental illnesses described below, it may also be very helpful for those readers who have not been so diagnosed. It is definitely true that one can live out the role, ascribing enormous life energy to it, without carrying the set of symptoms necessary to be diagnosed with one of these mental illnesses. So, it should in no way be thought that everyone who lives out of a role should carry a diagnosis. However, some readers have been so diagnosed, and can benefit from understanding how the role exacerbates the symptoms of their diagnosis. People are diagnosed with a mental illness because they demonstrate a particular set of symptoms that have rendered their lives dysfunctional or nonfunctional in the arenas of normal life, such as work, school, and relationship. For those of you who have not been so diagnosed, perhaps you are in relationship with someone who has. Or, perhaps you can glean even further information about the role and its impact on your life from the more extreme examples given in this chapter. If you feel that this chapter is not going to benefit you in any way, please feel free to skip it and move on to the next chapter.

Others of you have been diagnosed with some primary and/or secondary diagnosis. Be assured that the role plays into your diagnosis in some very important ways. In this section we will look at a few diagnoses, which are fairly common. Then we will do some work on how the role plays into these diagnoses and how the Authentic Self can help.

It should be noted that there are medications available for most of these disorders. This book in no way wishes to substitute for medications, used appropriately during the time when they are needed. If you are not using medications and find that the symptoms under specific diagnoses seem to fit you, and you are curious about how medications might help you, please contact a Psychiatrist to evaluate your need for medications. They may help you significantly. If you are already using medications, it might be helpful to think of your medication as a chemical foundation upon which to base the work of the Authentic Self. It is possible, however, that after doing the work of the Authentic Self, and after beginning to live quite happily, you will no longer need the medications. It is also possible that living quite happily will include continuing your medications. Consulting with your Authentic Self and your physician will help you resolve any questions about this. This is said so that the reader may know that any information written below does not cancel out the possibility that you might also need mediation.

The diagnostic criteria listed and discussed in clinical and lay terms below comes from the *Diagnostic and Statistical Manual of Mental Disorders, 4th Edition,* [DSM-IV] (American Psychiatric Association [APA], 1994), and will be sited with parenthetical page references. The discussions preceding and/or following the diagnostic criteria are the author's, in which the reader will find further explanation of the diagnosis from the author's perspective and discussion of the diagnosis as it relates to the authentic self and the role. This Chapter is not meant to be the definitive source of information about diagnostic criteria. Please consult the DSM-IV either online or in book form if you wish more specific information regarding a diagnosis. Your Psychiatrist may be able to assist you with this as well.

Depression: There are a few different kinds of depression. They are clarified below:

Major Depression. Major Depression is not a mild form of depression. One must be in this state of depression for a period of, at least, two weeks, prior to receiving this diagnosis. There may be a single episode of Major Depression or there may be repeated episodes. The following symptoms are typical to this diagnosis:

- Insomnia or hypersomnia almost every day.
- Decrease or increase in appetite (may include weight loss or gain of at least 5% of body weight in a month).
- Anhedonia (a marked decrease in pleasure).
- Suicidal ideations or plans and/or attempted suicide.
- Observable restlessness or slowing down.
- Feelings of worthlessness, or excessive or inappropriate guilt.
- Diminished ability to concentrate or think, or indecisiveness nearly every day.
- Marked shift in mood to sadness or melancholy that is pervasive (mood lasts and covers all areas of life).
- Decrease in functionality regarding work, school, social life, relationships, or any other area of basic living. (APA, 1994, 327).

Dysthymic Disorder: Dysthymia may last for many years, and must have lasted at least two years before one can be so diagnosed. One is depressed for most of every day, more days than not, for extended periods of time. The diagnosis does not include suicidality, and can, therefore, be considered a milder form of depression. However, it is possible for Dysthymia to erupt into a Major Depressive episode. Sometimes, when this happens, people originally diagnosed with Dysthymia, and being treated on an outpatient basis, get admitted to an inpatient unit and begin to look at the issues that started the dysthmyia in the first place. So, while they seem to be getting worse, they are actually getting better. The following symptoms are typical of Dysthymic Disorder:

- Low energy or fatigue.
- Melancholic mood.
- Hypo- or hypersomnia.
- Changes in appetite.
- Low self-esteem.
- Poor concentration.
- Difficulty making decisions.
- Feeling hopeless. (APA, 1994, 345-49).

Though there may be a chemical base to both disorders above, not living authentically can not only exacerbate the symptoms but have a causative effect. Depression is NOT an emotion. We constantly talk about depression as if it were an emotion. In fact, depression occurs because we are NOT using our emotions as the tools they were meant to be. More likely than not, we are repressing them. There are over 100 possible emotions persons can feel, and we can often feel several emotions at the same time, if we are paying attention. These emotions are tastebuds, meant to tell us the flavors of life. They tell us how we are doing in the business of making ourselves alive and joyful. They can tell us about whether our circumstances are those that we like or dislike. In these and other ways, emotions can be guideposts to authentic living. Emotions can also come from thoughts, messages, mantras and belief systems that are part and parcel to the role. We've seen how this can happen earlier in this book. But even these emotions are pathways to the Authentic Self if we use them as tools as described earlier. Overall, emotions give us messages about our lives. If we are not listening to these messages we are not living authentically. In fact, we are merely surviving, we are not living at all. Isn't this depressing?

Persons who are diagnosed with depression are very commonly living out the Scapegoat/Priest identity, the Superwoman identity, or the Victim identity. However, the Runaway, the Superhero and the Party Dude(tte) may discover, upon looking for the first time within, that they have also carried a long term Dysthymic response to life. The Scapegoat/Black Sheep will, more often then not, be more aware of anger than depression and may receive help only when and if s/he ends up in the penal system. However, the Scapegoat/Priest is depressed because s/he cannot seemingly ever be guilt free. Scapegoat/Priests will very often be so busy doing good for others, that they cannot see that they are part of the problem. Only when they begin to feel the pain of this awareness or some crisis in their lives do they begin to understand that part of their problem is this enormous sense of guilt for simply being alive. More often then not the Scapegoat/Priest role is Dysthymic.

Superwomen are depressed underneath all of the Superwoman bravado as a constant. This is Dysthymia. There may always be this melancholic response underneath it all, though they put on the smiling mask and leap another tall building in response. But Superwomen often do not realize that they have carried this depression with them for years, until they max out on being Super. Then they may develop a Major Depression. When they are no longer able to leap tall buildings because their bodies break down, or they are mentally exhausted, they get really depressed. Where before, they got up at the crack of dawn and worked till midnight, doing other people's jobs, now they can't get up at all. And they are often filled with remorse and shame because they have stopped being Super. Sometimes, at this point they launch into the Victim identity that may have been lurking under the super mask and costume all along. Those carrying the Victim role (whether or not the role comes out of an exhausted super complex) believe that life is very, very hard, that the walk is always a climb and the mountain on the other side is bigger than this one. They believe that the gods are conspiring against them to make sure that they are unhappy and miserable and that's just how it's going to be. Therefore, they are depressed.

Superheroes can also become depressed due to years of not aligning with their own emotions, but instead with the emotions of others. Eventually they "hit a wall," at which point they begin to realize that they cannot really change other's lives. At this point they begin telling themselves that they are worthless, because they cannot seem to make a difference in the world. In truth they have been carrying around a low-grade depression for years that is based on their refusal to access their own emotions and "rescue" themselves from the enslavement to the role.

Runaways may have been depressed for years, under the mask and costume, but they, like the Superhero and the Superwoman, don't realize it until they end up in some position in which they have to look at the family shame from which they have been running all along. Shame is one of the most devastating emotions we can feel. Runaways perceive either their family or their past as somehow shameful. They fear that this shame is something with which they must identify because it is somehow a part of their identity, by association. Therefore, when they can no longer run from this shame, it settles down over them like a shroud.

Party Dude(tte)s become depressed when they feel forced by life to grow up. They often believe that adult life is a huge, odious responsibility and they should not ever have to be accountable to anyone or anything. But something happens that causes them to have to commit to some adult challenge and they simply buckle under the enormity of it all. It should be noted, however, that this happens very rarely to Party Dude(tte)s, because they are so skilled at becoming involved with others who will carry the weight of life responsibility for them.

In order to relieve depression, Scapegoats must begin to understand that they absorb guilt seemingly from the air. They got into the habit of absorbing guilt in their families of origin, and they do it now, because that has become their way of living. They must understand this dynamic intimately. Then at each juncture at which they have a choice to accept or reject guilt, they must make connection with the Authentic Self and listen to its messages. The Authentic Self will be kind and loving to them. Contacts with the Authentic Self must be frequent, several times a day, and persons must be disciplined about making contact through letters to and from the Authentic Self, poetry, art, metaphor, story, dance, etc. Once they feel that peace of authenticity, guilt will never again have as much power.

Superwomen who have maxed-out must begin to understand that they could never have operated at that pace for a lifetime, unless it was a short one. Their exhaustion is a sign that it is time to slow down. In fact, the exhaustion is a message from the Authentic Self, though they do not see it that way. Instead, they often think that they were right to be so driven and wrong to be so tired. No, for years they have not listened to their bodies or emotions. Now, they cannot help but listen. What happened? The Authentic Self, through the body and emotions, said, "Enough already!! You won't listen any other way, so now I've got your attention!" The name of the game now is "start listening." So, when they feel like getting up and doing something, they should do it. When they feel like resting, they should do it. When they begin to honor their own authenticity, there will be no more need for exhaustion. The exhaustion and depression will be there as long as they refuse to honor the real, and will go away when they begin the journey of authenticity.

Superheroes must begin to access all of their feelings, not just their own empathy. As they do this, they quite often begin to recognize feelings of anger at those whom they have rescued again and again. People who have used them over and over again are recognized for what they have been doing. Actually, this form of anger is a message from the Authentic Self informing Superheroes of the I AM. This is the I AM that speaks clear and true about the needs and desires of the Self.

Victims must begin to recognize their own personal responsibility for their lives, rather than blaming life itself. The old adage recognized by Alcoholics Anonymous works here: Take life on life's terms, rather than expecting life to fit your terms. Everyone has negative experiences. It isn't the experience that makes or breaks our lives, but how we handle the experience. Taking on new mantras laid out by the voice of the Authentic Self is the most therapeutic endeavor for the Victim. Victims may find help in working and reworking the previous chapter on barriers to authenticity.

Runaways must begin to work with the shame messages that are deep down inside, hidden away under all of the running thoughts and behaviors. Is it true that if your family came from poverty that this is something about which one should feel shame? Is it true if your father was a criminal that you should feel shame? Further, what is shame but fear of what others are thinking of you, based upon a self-judgment that has to do with the good/evil complex? This is hard work, but it can be done. If you are a Runaway, take this book with you to therapy, and work and rework it until you are free of the shame that holds you to your past like glue.

Party Dude(tte)s might have a hard time even getting this far in this book, unless they are now depressed. But there is also a danger that Party Dude(tte)s might identify, once they become depressed, with the depression itself, because it means that they can continue to avoid taking responsibility for their lives. Whether or not this is true, if Party Dude(tte)s wish to have real happiness rather than just avoid responsibility, they must begin to rethink this entire objective. The problem, as we've said, is a mistaken view of responsibility itself. Again, responsibility is simply the ability to respond to my own authenticity. Authenticity, after all, is our pathway to real joy. So, what is the problem here? If you are the Party Dude(tte), work and rework the chapters of this book until you are free from the burden of the perpetual party, and are ready to receive real joy.

Anxiety: There are three different anxiety disorders we will mention here. Each has its own particular set of symptoms. They are as follows:

Generalized Anxiety Disorder: This is a pervasive anxious state. No one particular worry is the key, for there is just a general sense that all of life is something to be extremely careful about. Everything is frightening to some degree. One cannot seem to stop worrying and there is a great deal of paranoia present in the thinking. Persons diagnosed with GAD will have been excessively and uncontrollably anxious for at least six months, and at least three of the following symptoms will have created significant distress or impairment in functioning.

- Feeling stressed, restless, on edge.
- Easily fatigued.
- Difficulty concentrating.
- Irritability.
- Muscle tension.
- Difficulty falling or staying asleep, or restless unsatisfying sleep. (APA, 1994, 435-6).

Panic Disorder: With varying degrees of frequency and severity panic attacks may spontaneously erupt (with or without concomitant agoraphobia) often catching these people and those around them by surprise. (APA, 1994, 397). They may seem perfectly calm and capable at times, then erupt suddenly into panic. They can sometimes explain what made them panic after the event, but often don't realize that they are building up to panic until the panic attack is over. Within a 10 minute period of intense fear or discomfort, a panic attack will exhibit at least four of the following:

- A sense of impending doom.
- Heart palpitations.
- Profuse sweating.
- Body tremors.
- Sensations of shortness of breath or smothering.
- A feeling of choking.
- Numbness or tingling in body parts.
- Chest pain.
- Chills or hot flashes.
- Feeling dizzy, unsteady, lightheaded, or faint.
- Fear of losing control or going crazy.
- Fear of dying.

- Feelings of unreality, or feeling detached from oneself. (APA, 1994, 395).

Often, one attack is followed by a period of persistent concern about having additional attacks. The person is often worried about what the attack means, i.e., losing control, having a heart attack or "going nuts." It should be noted that panic attacks can be a part of agoraphobia (definition follows), and persons who have other disorders such as Posttraumatic Stress Disorder, Obsessive-Compulsive disorders, a specific phobia, or Social Phobia, often have occasional panic attacks. (APA, 397-8).

Obsessive/Compulsive Disorder: The DSM-IV tells us that the Obsessive/Compulsive Disorder includes two clear and distinct symptoms: The obsessions, and the compulsions. First, I am obsessed with something, then I am compelled to do something about my obsession. It is always hoped that in doing something about the obsession, the obsession will cease, but it rarely does. Sometimes it even worsens. An obsession is a thought, impulse or image that is experienced as intrusive and often inappropriate, and causes noticeable anxiety. Often a person who is so obsessed will attempt to ignore, suppress or neutralize the obsession with some other thought or action, such as, some mental aid to clear the mind, like focusing on spelling words or counting. People who are so obsessed do recognize that the obsession is coming from their own mind, not from some external source. A compulsion is an action that one feels compelled to carry out. It is repetitive and is aimed at preventing or reducing the stress created by the obsession. The action may be physical, such as hand washing, checking things, cleaning, etc., or the action may be mental, as in the case of repetitive prayer, counting, or saying words. (APA, 1994, 417-23).

For example, I may obsess that the bathroom isn't clean. I can't get my mind off of it and my thoughts are accompanied by a fear that bad things will happen in some way if the bathroom isn't cleaned up shortly. Therefore, I am compelled to go clean it up, even if it is 2 A.M. After I clean it up, I fear that I may have missed something, so I begin obsessing again that it isn't clean and bad things will happen if…. So then I am compelled to go and clean it again. This can repeat itself several times to the point of utter exhaustion; with a person returning again and again to clean the bathroom for fear that something was missed. OCD may take the form of being unable to purchase an item because it's not absolutely perfect, or if an "imperfect" item is selected, returning it to the store, only to buy another imperfect item which must be returned. The compulsive behaviors might include hand washing over and over, walking or eating a certain ritualistic way, cleaning, gambling, sex, drugs, etc. It does not matter what the compulsive behavior is, it is compulsive because one has obsessed about it and found themselves unable to stop the obsession until an action is taken. The anxiety one feels between the obsession and the compulsion is unbearable. Therefore, the compulsion must be carried out at all costs.

OCD may also take the form of mind control. I may be unconscious of the anxiety that compels me to seek such mind control, but I may become obsessed with intrusive thoughts of prayers, numbers, colors, or configurations and be compelled to continue to repeat them to the exclusion of other thoughts. This may mean that I am unable to function in my job, in the social arena or in school, because of the intrusive obsessions and the compulsion to repeat. This pattern may become a primary coping mechanism for any external stressor.

Often, at some point, adults who have this disorder realize that the obsessions or compulsions are excessive or unreasonable. This is easily identifiable to the adult because the obsessions or compulsions cause high anxiety and are quite time consuming. They may even significantly interfere with the performance of work or school, social activities or relationships. Given other diagnoses, such as eating disorders, substance dependence, hypochondriasis, depression, etc., the obsessions and compulsions take on the nature of the other disorder. For example, the substance dependent will obsess about his drug of choice and then be compelled to get high. (APA, 1994, 422-23). Though the DSM-IV does not stipulate to mild, moderate and severe cases of OCD, anecdotally, they do appear to exist in that strata, though this could be seen as the progression of the disease.

Agoraphobia: Though agoraphobia does not carry a diagnostic code, since it is diagnosed relative to panic, it is a pervasive phobic reaction. A phobic reaction in general is an extreme fear response to a *particular* stimulus. For example, persons may have a phobic reaction to snakes. Therefore, they will do all that they can do to avoid snakes, and will, if they see a snake, have an intense fear response. Agoraphobics respond this way to so many stimuli that it is difficult to assess a particular stimulus. They are terrified of everything that is beyond their own safe sanctuary, usually their home. As a result, over a period of time, Agoraphobics will go out less and less, until eventually, they cannot leave their homes at all. When they start to leave, they panic. The disorder originates from a fear of being in a place or situation from which there is no escape, or in which there is no help available. (APA, 1994, 396). Again, though the DSM-IV does not stipulate to a history of trauma for agoraphobics, anecdotally this has been observed.

The above mentioned anxiety disorders are all related to or complicated by the role and can be improved by living authentically. Often persons with these types of anxiety disorder live out one of the following roles:

- Generalized anxiety disorder correlates with the Runaway, the Scapegoat/Priest, the Victim, Superhero, Superwoman and the Party Dude(tte).
- Panic Disorder and Agoraphobia often correlate with the Victim, the Superwoman or the Scapegoat/Priest.
- Obsessive-Compulsive Disorder correlates with the Scapegoat/Priest or Scapegoat/Black Sheep.

GAD correlates with several roles because it is so general. Runaways are anxious and paranoid because they must always be on guard against anything that puts them back in touch with family-shame or with their own emotions. Scapegoat/Priests are anxious because they are carrying around enormous portions of guilt, which they cannot separate out and name. There is always this vague sense of guilt and an even deeper sense of needing to compensate for that guilt through sacrifice. Victims feel anxious because they know that bad things are always going to happen to them, so that they are always in a state of hyper-alertness waiting for the other shoe to fall. Superheroes are anxious because they are always worried about the person they are currently trying to rescue. Party Dude(tte)s are anxious because they are always on guard, making sure that they always have a joke at the ready, for any negative feeling that might arise. They are constantly repressing feelings, which creates a state of anxiety. Superwomen often carry a low-grade or unconscious anxiety around in their bodies, for they are always in a state of hyper-alertness, always on the ready to leap another tall building or run faster than a speeding bullet. However, Party Dude(tte)s, Superheros, Superwomen and Runaways might not ever seek treatment for anxiety, because this is an admission that there is a problem. If they do seek treatment it is when the anxiety has pushed them far over the edge in some way.

Persons with GAD often feel that they "should" be able to control circumstances. Worry provides them with the illusion of control. If I worry, they think, I'm at least doing something. Somehow they believe that if they think this thing through again and again, they will eventually hit on a strategy that will put them back in control. Under all of this worry is a deep-seated fear of being out of control. Part of living authentically is learning to take life on life's terms instead expecting life to meet our terms. We may have certain designs on our lives, and perhaps we will be able to accomplish these designs. But if we do not accomplish them, we may learn to be able to live with that. Persons with GAD often find anything other than their design on life, absolutely unacceptable. So worry becomes a coping mechanism, a form of magical thinking, in which they tell themselves that if I am worrying, then I'm going to keep the unacceptable from happening. If the unacceptable happens anyway, then I'll worry it to death until it sits upright.

In order to get beyond this, worriers or those with GAD will need to confront their own need to control reality. Life is going to be what we make it, regardless of the circumstances that we have been given as tools. When we see life's circumstances as enemies that must be fought against, we are not surrendered to the serenity, which recognizes what it can and cannot change. Remember the prayer?

> *God grant me the serenity*
> *To accept the things I cannot change,*
> *The courage to change the things I can,*
> *And the wisdom to know the difference.*

Essentially the worrier, or the person with GAD believes in magic. Worry is the hokas-pokas, the magic formula, the dance around the fire, which will accomplish the life I want. In fact, what is happening in most cases, is that I'm spending so much time worrying about the external circumstances, that I'm taking very little responsibility for my own choices and my own authenticity. If I can ever once start looking inside, I will find a whole world there that I have missed because I've been so busy working my agenda on the external world.

If you are a worrier or diagnosed with GAD, go back and rework the previous chapter on barriers to living authentically. Work the exercises again and again. Begin to see your worry as an extension of your role. Change some of your beliefs, work with your "if only" thinking and work and rework the section on fears. It is possible for you to learn to see life's circumstances as tools for building a life, rather than things that might destroy your life.

Panic Disordered persons are often playing out the Victim role. The mantra is basically: "Bad things *will* happen to me. I am out of control of my life. There are forces bigger than me that will always take over my life. I have no choice." When Panic Disordered persons play out the Superwoman, it is from the perspective that "I must be in control or bad things will happen." In this manner, they work themselves into a state of hyper-alertness that is very close to panic over specific triggers. Remember that on the flip side of Superwoman we often find the Victim. When Scapegoat/Priests have a panic attack it is because they do not wish to be held accountable for something, for they fear that they will not be able to stand the guilt.

When talking about their panic, panic disordered persons often sight the external trigger, instead of looking at the messages they give themselves. As they look at this trigger and that trigger, and the next trigger they begin to eliminate more and more triggers from their lives, until eventually they have excluded much of their lives. At this point they have become Agoraphobic. And, of course, for Agoraphobics, when anything makes them believe that they must move beyond their safe fortress, they have a panic episode.

Obviously, this is not working. The panic disordered person must begin to look at the internal messages, and stop looking at the external triggers. Looking at the internal messages does *not* mean looking at the message and saying something like: "You stupid idiot, why do you believe that? Stop this idiocy!!" No. In fact, looking at the internal messages is simply observing, listening, paying attention to the feeling that comes up when certain messages are given.

If you have been diagnosed with a Panic Disorder or Agoraphobia go back to the previous chapters. Reread your answers, rework and rework this until you have heard the messages and the mantras. Have an argument with yourself, do some prime factoring, check your beliefs, your double-binding beliefs. Do these exercises again and again until you have begun to understand that there is, indeed, another part of you who has much wisdom and heart, and has never been wounded. Continue to do this until you begin to see that you can always look inside for comfort from any fear.

The Scapegoat/Priest or Scapegoat/Black Sheep may be diagnosed with OCD. Scapegoats must pay a sacrifice. Something, someone must be sacrificed. For the Scapegoat/Black Sheep there is quite often an addiction of some type present that proves to the Black Sheep that s/he is indeed all the terrible things assumed. Addiction of any type has an obsessive/compulsive component to it. Further there is a ritual behavior to addiction. Even people who are addicted to nicotine perform certain rituals before they smoke that are all a part of the compulsive process. They pack down the cigarette pack again and again before lighting up. Or they may pack each individual cigarette. Some will hold the cigarette in the mouth for a while before lighting it. This same thing is true for any other addiction. Whether the person is addicted to cocaine, methamphetamines, alcohol or sex, the ritual quality brings in the good/evil complex in a "I'm so good at being bad" kind of way, in which the flip side is a strong urge to be perfect. This is why we sometimes see people in AA become addicted to the perfection of rigidity in sobriety. It's as if they are saying, "I was so good at being bad, now I've got to be perfect at being good." When these folks become sponsors in AA they can be extremely rigid with their sponsees, who may later have to untangle themselves from these rigid expectations in order to stay sober. Of course, this is not true of everyone who attends AA or sponsors others.

Scapegoat/Priests are trying hard to do everything right, because inside they feel wrong. The mantra becomes "I am evil, therefore, I must be good." With OCD, they become good to the point of exhaustion. It goes something like this: "I must choose perfectly, I must clean perfectly, I must buy perfectly, and I must be perfectly safe. There must be no imperfection. If there is, I will redo and redo until I either reach perfection or die of exhaustion trying." The Scapegoat/Priest is taking on the guilt of others, as in the case of sexual trauma, in which the Scapegoat/Priest holds him/herself somehow accountable for the deeds of the perpetrator. S/he gets the "If only's." If only I'd locked my door. If only I'd screamed. If only I'd told. If only I hadn't been such an innocent little child, this would never have happened. If only I'd done the impossible. And because I didn't, I'm really evil, and must sacrifice myself on the altar of some obsessive/compulsive ritual, such as hand-washing, to rid myself of the guilt.

Often, to compensate for the fact that they know, at least intellectually, that no matter how many times they redo, it will still not be done perfectly; they will make up a kind of magical perfection that they can live with. Therefore: "If I can check the door ten times, then I have reached the ultimate in perfection." Or, "If I can say the word 'delete' when I have a negative thought or feeling, then I have reached the ultimate in perfection." Or, "If I can count the letters in the specific words over and over until I am no longer sliding into some unconscious imperfection that I sense lurking behind the curtains, then I will have reached the ultimate in perfection." In other words, I am making up or providing myself with the illusion of perfection, so that I won't have to deal with the idea that no matter what I do, even if I clean the toilet all day, there will still be germs there somewhere. I have provided myself an escape hatch.

In truth the whole thing is an escape hatch. One theory about OCD is that both the obsession and the compulsions are distracting the person from some internal issue that they fear would, if considered, cause great pain or fear. One example would be the child or adult who secretly hates a parent s/he has been taught to worship. Suppose my mother and my extended family have taught me to believe that my mother is the most wonderful mother in the world, but deep down I know that she is extremely narcissistic and has manipulated her world into worshipping her. In fact, I know that her doting on me is merely an attempt to boost her own image in some way through me. As a child I may build elaborate, magical rituals around protecting my mother from my own rage. I may have to lock the doors to the house over and over in order to protect her from harm. I may be compelled to interfere with relationships she has that seem to take my place while believing that I am protecting her from danger. I may develop elaborate number/color schemes to mentally flirt with all day, so I don't have to recognize my anger.

For the OCD Scapegoat, these obsessions and compulsions are an attempt to rid oneself of shame and guilt. I don't have to feel shame and guilt if I can sacrifice myself to this obsession and compulsion. I don't have a life, but that's okay, I didn't deserve one anyway. Scapegoats with OCD end up sacrificing themselves still further to a life of slavery to their obsessions and compulsions. There is another way. If you are OCD reading this book, you can go back and work and rework Chapters Two, Three and Four again. What does your role say to you? What is your mantra? What messages do you give yourself regarding guilt, shame, responsibility? And what does the Authentic Self have to say about all of this? Would the Authentic Self really agree that you are to live this way, forever sacrificing your Self? What are your barriers to Authenticity?

It should also be noted here that there are a few medications (ask your Doctor about Anafranil or Clomipramine) being used today specifically for OCD. Please do check with your Psychiatrist about this. The combination of medication and therapy is often quite effective.

Posttraumatic Stress Disorder: There are two types of stress disorder: Acute Stress disorder and Posttraumatic Stress Disorder. The only difference between the two is the length of time between the actual trauma and the onset of and continuation of symptoms. Acute Stress Disorder symptoms occur within one month of the trauma, and last for a maximum of one month. With Posttraumatic Stress Disorder the symptoms may occur at the time of the trauma, they may occur several years later when a person begins to deal with the original trauma, or they may occur at the time of the trauma and last for up to several years, especially if untreated. Otherwise, the symptoms between Acute Stress Disorder and Posttraumatic Stress Disorder are the same and are as follows:

- A person is exposed to a traumatic event during which they experienced, witnessed or were confronted with an actual or threatened death or a threat to the physical integrity of self or others.
- Their response to this event is experienced as intense fear, helplessness, or horror, or, as in the case of children, expressed as disorganized or agitated behavior.
- The event is then re-experienced as:
    o Recurrent and intrusive distressing recollections. (In young children this may come out as repetitive play.)
    o Recurrent distressing dreams of the event. Again, in young children the dreams may not contain recognizable content.
    o Flashbacks (a sense of reliving the events as if they were currently happening). In young children this may take the form of trauma-specific reenactment.
    o Any internal or external reminders of the events cause significant distress.
    o Physiological reactions are often similar to those that occurred during the trauma.
- The person tries to avoid anything that reminds them of the trauma through:
    o Avoidance of thoughts, feelings or conversations about the trauma.
    o Avoidance of places or people that remind.
    o Inability to recall specific aspects of the trauma.
    o Marked disinterest in normal activities.
    o Feeling detached and estranged from others.
    o Inability to experience certain feelings.
    o Sense of shortened future, i.e., does not expect to grow up, get married, have children, establish a career, etc.
- Heightened arousal experienced as:
    o Difficulty falling or staying asleep.
    o Irritability or outbursts of anger.
    o Difficulty concentrating or racing thoughts.
    o Hypervigilance or a feeling of always having to be on guard.
    o Exaggerated startle response.

o   This disturbance causes impairment in social, occupational or other areas of functioning. (APA, 1994, 427-29).

Posttraumatic Stress Disorder (PTSD) is a disorder that directly results from having been traumatized. One does not choose to be traumatized, yet it does occur. So, one could say that this is something over which we had little to no control. Okay, but what does that mean about the rest of our lives? Persons with Acute Stress Disorder are simply adjusting to a traumatic experience in their lives. They go through an intense period in which they might experience the symptoms above, but these symptoms quickly resolve and the person moves back into a normal functionality. However, persons with PTSD are often living out the Victim identity, at least during the time of heightened symptoms. The belief systems go something like this: I avoid the places in which the traumas occurred because I am superstitiously certain that if I go there again, the same thing will happen. I am hypervigilant because I am certain that if I am not I will be victimized again. I relive the events because I am certain that they will always be with me—I am forever damaged by this.

PTSD may also characterize the Superwoman identity or the Superhero role. As Superwoman, I am hypervigilant in the highest order. Yes, I have nightmares and flashbacks but that's only because I'm not being hypervigilant enough. If I were stronger this would not be happening to me. I just need to get busy. As Superhero, I am constantly reliving the crisis I experienced, by living through other people's crises with them and attempting to rescue them. Therefore, I can never put my crisis to rest. It comes up in my nightmares, and daydreams. I refuse to revisit the site of my trauma, but I'll be revisiting yours all day long. Therefore, I will be hypervigilant to keep myself safe, vicariously, through rescuing you.

Believe it or not, we do have a choice about this. Go back and get the picture that you drew of the Authentic Self. Hang it over your bed at night. Talk to it, just before you go to sleep. Ask it to give you dreams that come from your authenticity rather than from the traumas. Then when you get a dream write it down. Ask yourself questions about each character, object or event in the dream. Who is this character? Is s/he real or imagined? Do you know him/her? If so what does this person represent to you? What do the objects or events in the dream represent to you? Write down your answers. You have just heard from the Authentic Self. *The Authentic Self uses dreams as riddles for your life.* When you answer the riddle, you get a deeper assurance of your authenticity. Dreams are the Authentic Self's observations about the identity. Why does it use riddles? Because we are so cut off from authenticity. The more directly involved we become with the Authentic Self, the more it will respond to us directly.

Dreams are very special messages. But when you are having traumatic nightmares, they are not telling you that the trauma is currently happening, or that you need to stay hypervigilant; they are telling you that you are still living *as if* the trauma were currently happening. In interpreting your dreams, you may need to seek therapy, or Jungian Psychoanalysis in which dream interpretation is the primary tool used. You may find books that assist you in interpreting your dreams. Whatever you do though, consult with your Authentic Self. No one else can tell you what your dreams mean to you. The role often has a very negative interpretation of your dreams. Listen to the Authentic Self. This is the correct interpretation.

Go back and rework the previous chapters again. Have arguments with your role, over and over again. Try to do some prime factoring. Re-discover your barriers to authenticity. Listen to the Authentic Self. You will find that there is no greater safety on earth than that provided by the Authentic Self. It is the place deep inside you to which you can go anytime at all. It is a place inside you that has never been wounded.

Substance Dependence: Briefly, the symptoms of dependence follow: (Three or more symptoms are required in order to be diagnosed as substance dependent).

- Recurrent substance use (can be binging for periods, followed by clean periods, or it can be up to daily use).
- The using pattern is life disruptive in that it renders some area(s) of the life dysfunctional or causes distress in one or more areas of life.
- The dependent builds a tolerance to the drug of choice. Tolerance means either a need for ever increasing amounts of the substance to achieve a high, or a noticeable diminished effect (no high) when using the same amount.
- The dependent may go into withdrawal without the use of the substance, dependent upon which drug s/he is using. S/he may take the same or like substance to avoid withdrawal symptoms.
- Often the dependent uses more of the substance than originally intended and uses over a longer period of time than intended.
- The dependent has a persistent desire and often unsuccessfully attempts to cut down or stop using.

- A great portion of time, energy and resources are spent trying to obtain the substance, use it, or recover from its effects.
- Many other important activities may be sacrificed in order to use substances.
- The dependent may develop consequences to health, home, relationships, jobs, etc., yet continue to use in spite of these consequences.

It should be noted that physiological dependence evidences tolerance or withdrawal, but it is possible to be dependent without physiological dependence. (APA, 1994, 176-181).

Dependence upon substances (alcohol, cocaine, benzodiazepines, opiates, narcotics, amphetamines, methamphetamines, etc.) is both a response to a chemical imbalance and a response to life. Persons who are addicted inherited a gene of dependency that is a set up for dependence in the same way that a person may be set up for a heart attack by inheriting the gene which potentiates it. One person, for example, who has not inherited the gene potentiating substance dependence, may drink, and may even, occasionally get drunk without becoming dependent. Another person, who has inherited the gene, may drink and start, thereafter, on a pattern of drinking which leads to alcoholism.

However, it is also possible for one who inherits the gene to consciously *refuse* to become dependent on substances. In the same way, it is possible for persons who inherit the gene for heart trouble to take such good care of themselves and to manage their stress in such a way that they never have that heart attack. Because this is so, we also know that there are often mitigating motivators in the environment, which lead to substance dependence. This is where the role comes into play. Typical roles for dependents range the gamut. They can play any of the roles. Getting into recovery, for the addict/alcoholic is tantamount to becoming authentic in many ways unless they use recovery as another form of the role. It is possible for persons to stay clean and sober and still live the role (the dry drunk), but it is awfully hard. Generally speaking moving away from the first three steps of the twelve-step program means moving back into the role, and eventually to relapse. The role is, in fact, a trigger for relapse.

For example, if I have played the Scapegoat role, prior to getting into recovery then once in recovery begin to feel guilty, this may trigger me moving back into full-blown Scapegoat identity. This means I will put back on the mask and costume of sacrifice and self-defeat or begin again living like the Black Sheep, which will definitely lead me right back to relapse. Often times, I hear people in recovery say, "I want to get back to where I was before I started using so heavily." My response to this is always, "If you go back to where you were, you'll just end up where you are." Addicts/alcoholics don't need to go back to where they were before drinking/using so heavily, that's what got them to drinking or using heavily in the first place. Instead, they need to be willing to identify with what is real inside.

Therefore, I recommend that recovering persons stay in touch with both the 12-Step approach and the Authentic Self. Being authentic while working the steps means working, for example, a real 4th step, not just listing resentments, but looking at what role put them in the place of resentment. In other words, if I resent you for making me feel guilty, or for the fact that I'm always having to rescue you, etc., then what role do I play in this drama? If I'm always partying like a good Party Dude(tte), or running from family and emotions, what is it that I'm running from and where have I run to? What is my payoff for taking on such a role? What do I get out of playing the role? Whatever that payoff is it is also a trigger for relapse. Work and rework this book, take it with you to therapy, discuss it with your sponsor. Don't stop until you are fully comfortable in your own authenticity.

Dissociative Identity Disorder: This used to be called Multiple Personality Disorder, and I'm very glad they changed the name. Multiple Personality Disorder sounds way out there. It evokes images of really spooky people, who others would like to avoid. Dissociative Identity Disorder (DID) exactly describes what is going on.

When trauma occurs, we often dissociate from it. Some say we have "out of body" experiences, in which we stand over to the side or up above, watching the trauma(s) occur. Many have experienced this phenomenon. If you have ever driven from one place to another and, upon arriving at your destination, can't remember how you got there, you have experienced a dissociation of sorts. You dissociated from your reality experience and went somewhere else in your head. Persons who have been traumatized do this quite frequently. Anytime there is any reminder of the trauma, they may simply go away. It is a protective devise, which eventually can become a barrier to experiencing life at its core, if we cannot ever learn to come back down to earth.

In the case of DID, persons dissociate beyond the general dissociation of the trauma survivor, all the way into another identity. In order to be diagnosed with DID, there must be at least two identities that recurrently take control of the behavior, and an inability to recall important personal information, which is too extensive to be explained by ordinary forgetfulness (APA, 1994, 487). Note that the DSM-IV does not say any longer that DIDs dissociate to another personality, but to another identity. Identity is what we have been talking about all along in this book. Identity is role, and role is identity. We identify with something that isn't who we really are, then we put on the mask and costume and wear it as if it *is* who we really are. Most of us have one role that we live out, or two roles that we combine in some fashion. The person with DID is much more extreme than this, dissociating into identities that are hardened into a predictable, personality-like state, each of which may vary from the others in terms of age, gender, language, personal history, name, knowledge and/or affect (APA, 1994, 484).

These identities become available to the person through a dissociation often related to fear. The identity that is called forth at a given moment is always the perfect identity to deal with the specific fear. This dissociative response becomes so practiced over time that the individual needs little awareness of the fear to evoke the identity. Further they are so practiced at it, that the identities used become hardened, so to speak, into a persona so clarified that it acts just like a personality all it's own. And because persons are in a dissociated state at the time of the identification, they do not remember what happened when the need for the identification has passed and they come back to themselves. The identities are often quite different, running the gamut from some taking the mask of young children in need of protection, to others taking a strong authoritarian role of protector. Some even act out sexually, while others are maternal and loving. All of the identities are in some form related to whatever trauma(s) called the need for dissociation up in the first place.

For DIDs, becoming authentic means *integrating* the various identities into one heterogeneous person. It means that the person has to come to terms with exactly what it is that a specific dissociative identity does for them, and begin to do that for themselves, without having to manufacture an identity. It means recognizing the various emotions that are both difficult and joyous and beginning to use them as messages from the Authentic Self, rather than as things to avoid through dissociation. I am always careful, in therapy, to say to a DID: "There are no should's here. If you want to do this work, you must know that it is the work of *integration*. If you are not ready for integration, perhaps I can refer you to another therapist now and, if you choose to, you can come back later when you are ready." I will not work with a DID who has not verbalized an intent to integrate. In the same way, you should know that this book is all about integration. If you have DID and are ready for that, then this work can be done and redone, with the help of a therapist, to authenticate your SELF. If you are not, then I recommend you seek therapy and come back to this book later.

Eating Disorders: These are characterized by severe disturbances in eating behavior, related to psychological factors. The eating disorders below do not include a diagnostic category for obesity, since the DSM-IV did not include obesity as an eating disorder. Yet, much has been written about "emotional eating" or "anxiety eating" which leads to obesity. Before we explore the other diagnoses, it should therefore be stated that obesity, for which there are now 12-Step groups called "Overeaters Anonymous," can also be addressed through becoming aware of and reliant upon the Authentic Self. When we address the Authentic Self in any form, we automatically calm down. We can look at our emotions as messages, we can ask them questions and become informed as to what is going on inside of us. And we can then be led to living more peacefully, much less out of compulsion and more out of trust in ourselves to be okay.

Bulimia: This is characterized by recurrent episodes of binge eating of huge amounts of food over a short period of time, and a feeling that one cannot control these episodes. Further, one so diagnosed tends to compensate for the binge episode through self-induced vomiting, misuse of laxatives, diuretics, enemas, or other medications; fasting or excessive exercise. This often occurs because one's self-assessments are unduly influenced by body shape or weight. (APA, 1994, 549-50).

Anorexia Nervosa: With this disorder, the individual refuses to maintain a minimally normal body weight. Persons with this disorder are intensely afraid of gaining weight and they exhibit an extreme perceptual disturbance regarding the size or shape of their bodies. It should be noted that the term "anorexia" implies loss of appetite, but no such phenomena occur with this disorder. In fact the individual may be quite hungry with a ravenous appetite all of the time. Or, they may have reached the point of starvation in which the thought of food becomes nauseating. Either way, they are, in fact, literally starving themselves to death. It should also be noted that anorectics can also purge. They may vomit or use laxatives to purge themselves of even small amounts of food, due to their intense fear of weight gain. It is common for anorectic postmenarchal females to become amenorrheic.

Often the anorectic exhibits physical symptoms, especially in the latter stages of the disease. It can affect most major organ systems and cause numerous physical problems including blood disorders and anemia, dehydration, heart problems, disturbances in brain fluid and resting energy expenditure. (APA, 1994, 544-45).

The Scapegoat identity, in both its forms (either Priest or Black Sheep, or both Priest and Black Sheep simultaneously), often correlates with eating disorders. For the Anorectic, the Priest is sacrificing Self for an image. In fact, it is an addiction to an illusive self, in which "I am my image," becomes the mantra. The belief is that I am ashamed to be me. "Me" has been critiqued and criticized, and mantled with expectations of perfection so much that I must become the image others need for me to be in order to deserve to live. And since we can never quite be that image good enough, some anorectics die trying.

The Bulimic may live out a Black Sheep (binge)/Priest (purge) cycle. I binge as the Black Sheep because, as the Priest, I am starving myself in some other area, either emotionally or psychologically. When I am binging I identify, most often unconsciously, with the idea that others know what is good and right for me. "They" want me to be perfect and I've tried really hard, but I must rebel against them now through a binge, because I really believe that deep down, I am evil. Now, because I am so evil, I must exorcise my demon identity, by purging.

If you have an eating disorder, and you are working this book it is highly recommended that you take this book with you to therapy and allow your therapist to see some of the material you are working. Then go back to the section on the good/evil complex and work and rework it, listening to the messages from the Authentic Self. Write letters to the Authentic Self, write letters back to the role from the Authentic Self. Draw pictures of the Authentic Self becoming active in your life. Write poetry to yourself from the Authentic Self. Work and rework the arguments, barriers and prime factoring exercises. Paint, color, dance, sing, until you know that you are real, and that your realness has a right to be here.

Personality Disorders: The DSM-IV explains this very well:

> *Personality traits* are enduring patterns of perceiving, relating to, and thinking about the environment and oneself that are exhibited in a wide range of social and personal contexts. Only when personality traits are inflexible and maladaptive and cause significant functional impairment or subjective distress do they constitute Personality Disorders. (APA, 1994, 630).

In order to be diagnosed with a personality disorder one must characterize an *enduring* pattern of inner experience and behavior that is significantly aberrant from typical cultural expectations and is manifested in thought, emotion, relationship and/or impulse control. The pattern is enduring and inflexible and is *pervasive* across a wide range of personal and social situations. The pattern leads to significant, diagnosable distress or impairment in social, occupational or other important areas of functioning. The pattern can usually be traced back to adolescence or early adulthood. The areas of inner experience and behavior that are significantly aberrant from normal cultural expectations fall into four categories, clarified below, using both the DSM language and clarifying lay language:

- Thought (or cognition):
  o Ways of perceiving
  o Ways of interpreting self, others or events
- Emotions (or affect):
  o Range of emotion (how high, how low?)
  o Intensity of emotions (Is it equal in proportion to the cause of the emotion?)
  o Lability of emotion (How many intense emotional responses can one have in a brief period of time?)
  o Appropriateness of emotion (Does a shameful thing make one laugh, or a funny thing make one cry? Is this a pervasive pattern?)
- Relationship (or interpersonal functioning):
  o Primary relationships are intensely affected.
  o Secondary relationships are often intensely affected.
  o Acquaintances are often pulled into the fray as well.
- Impulse control:
  o A pervasive "feeling" of being "out of control."
  o A pattern of action taken without thought or plan.
  o A pattern of action taken based on mood.
  o A pattern of action taken with no known motivator. (APA, 1994, 633).

For the purposes of this workbook, we will reference only the more commonly known personality disorders.

Antisocial Personality Disorder: Often this disorder is referred to as the "Sociopath" or the "Psychopath." The disorder is characterized by a pervasive pattern of disregard for, and violation of, the rights of others that begins in childhood or early adolescence and continues into adulthood. Deceit and manipulation are central features of this disorder often accompanied by reckless disregard for the safety of others. It is important to note that persons so diagnosed must have, as an adolescent, carried a diagnosis of Conduct Disorder (a disorder very similar to Antisocial Personality Disorder, but given to children and adolescents). Sometimes an adolescent was not diagnosed with Conduct Disorder, but one can look back at the history and know that such a diagnosis could have been given. At least three of the following symptoms must be present:

- Repeated unlawful acts.
- Deceitfulness:
    o Lying
    o The use of aliases,
    o Con games for profit or pleasure
- Impulsivity, or poor planning.
- Irritability, aggressiveness, fighting or assaults.
- Reckless disregard for the safety of self and/or others.
- Lack of remorse, indifference or rationalizations regarding hurting, mistreating or stealing from others.
- Consistent irresponsibility in the areas of work or finances. (APA, 1994, 649-50).

The role commonly plays into this disorder as the "Black sheep" under the Scapegoat category, particularly as the child develops into adolescence; and as the Bully/Perpetrator, particularly as the adolescent develops into an adult. The bottom line for Antisocials is that they tend to believe that they are "bad to the bone." Their entire belief system is set up around this one concept. Often we find that persons in jails are diagnosed or diagnosable with this disorder. Interestingly enough, these folks, once incarcerated, often tell others to watch out for them, as they see themselves as dangerous. At this point, they may not allow themselves to be caught doing something "nice," or "good" for others, actually sneaking around to perform their good deeds in the same way that others might sneak around to do something considered "bad."

However, prior to getting caught and incarcerated, they can be charming personified. They may buy gifts, even elaborate gifts, for people with whom they are involved, and they may act quite kind and giving, at least for periods of time. But it is all with manipulative intent. Their charm, is, in fact a game.

They like to toy with people. Sometimes, in extreme cases, this toying takes the effect of serial killing. Antisocials are commonly predatory in their thinking, living out the Bully/Perpetrator role with considerable aplomb. But when the charming-boy/girl mask drops, we see someone who is cruel, very often in the extreme, and someone who will blame you for his/her cruelty. In fact, they have been in a game of cat and mouse for quite a while; you just didn't know that you were the mouse.

As the Bully/Perpetrator, Antisocials can be abusive in any form, emotionally, mentally, physically, sexually and perhaps forms we have yet to discover. In fact, their very charming nature is a form of emotional abuse. They only give so that they can take and take so that they can take some more. The object of their game is not to have what you have to give, however, the object of their game is to toy with you. They feel that life is one big cosmic joke and that they have got to outsmart the gods in order to come out on top. Nothing makes them angrier than feeling that the joke is on them. They toy with you because they fear that if they are not toying with you, you are toying with them. In fact, the only emotion that Antisocials will allow themselves to really feel is anger. And it appears to go from zero to rage in an instant. In fact, it's been down in there in the operative mode all along. One might say that the reason for existence for the Antisocial is rage. Somebody is going to have to pay!

The Antisocial could also be the Party Dude(tte) in the extreme when avoidance of responsibility takes the form of stealing, or conning others. In this case there may be a combination of Black Sheep and/or Bullly/Perpetrator and Party Dude(tte) playing out here. The Party Dude(tte) does not, in and of itself, demonstrate the kind of deceit, manipulation and disregard for the safety of others that it takes to be diagnosed with this disorder. However, in combination with the Scapegoat/Black Sheep, or Bully/Perpetrator the roles can be deadly. However, generally speaking the Party Dude(tte)/Black Sheep combo will not evolve into the kind of Bully/Perpetrator in which people are physically harmed, unless the Party Dude(tte)/Black Sheep feels threatened. The object of the game for the Party Dude(tte)/Black Sheep is to make crime and disregard for rules and customs into a game. Therefore, rather than becoming the serial killer, as some Antisocials do, they might become the con-man or the illegal gambler, etc. This type may also, believe it or not, become the CEO of a large corporation, to toy with larger numbers of people. Unlike the idea that the CEO is the most responsible of responsible people, an idea that is odious to the Party Dude(tte), in this case the CEO is the ultimate gambler. It is quite interesting to watch an Antisocial CEO, use his corporation as his weapon of deceit and manipulation. Is there a law, a rule, a policy here? Let me see how many ways I can break it, without you finding out. Underneath it all is a fury to abuse and those who get in the way are more than likely to get abused through any means necessary.

There are many theories about the origins of Antisocial Personality Disorder, and often not much hope given for behavior change. Quite often this disorder is associated with early abandonment issues about which the individual, so diagnosed, is extremely enraged. However, there are many people angry and hurt over these same issues who do not become Antisocials. Further, there does seem to be a deep-seated identification with shame here as well. Therefore, the theory of this book is that Antisocials are completely identified as Black Sheep as very young children, even infants, carrying around immense portions of unconscious guilt and shame, and conscious compensation that comes in the form of acting-out behaviors. They picked up this guilt and shame from their environment when they were still so preverbal that they could not defend themselves. There was but a thin layer of gauze between their psyches and that of their parents or caregivers. Perhaps, for example, they had parents who did not want them, and demonstrated this in all manner of verbal and nonverbal ways. Or, perhaps they had parents who presented well to the outside world, but completely rejected the child as a messy appendage who interfered with the parents' image. Perhaps they were cruelly abused. In these cases and others, they grow up hating themselves and hating their parents for making them hate themselves. They grow angrier and angrier over time, devising more and more strategies for maliciously demonstrating their anger.

As they grow into adolescence and adulthood they spend considerable energy continuing this process of creating mountains of buried guilt in order to confirm the "badness" they believed in so much as a child. In so doing, they become the Bully/Perpetrator. They have confirmed their "badness," by adulthood, to such a degree that it is very difficult for them to move beyond that identity. They feel that to do so would mean forcing themselves to be "good," which would mean giving in to their, by now, globalized concept of "authority," which could only mean being rejected, abandoned and/or abused again. Of course, authenticity is not about being either bad or good. There are not only two categories for all of humankind. Authenticity is about being real.

Clearly identity work is the objective here. Therefore, if you are reading this book and think that this disorder fits you, please go back and work and rework the exercises on good and evil. Continue receiving letters from the Authentic Self, writing poems or letters to and from the Authentic Self, drawing pictures, writing story from the Authentic Self, until you are fully aware that the Authentic Self, the real you, isn't bad at all, nor is it good, but rather very wise, knowing your next best direction, having never been wounded at all. Perhaps you will also need some external constraints while you are working this book. Should you turn your self in to law enforcement? Are you on probation or house arrest? If your compulsions are dangerous to others, you will need to work this book in a confined environment, and with the assistance of a therapist.

Borderline Personality Disorder: This diagnosis is more commonly given to women then men. However, as the traditional roles for women and men change, these statistics may change as well. The Borderline Personality Disorder (BPD) has become more commonly known in America since the making of the film, *Fatal Attraction*. The lead female character, played by Glenn Close, in this movie is commonly known as a BPD. However, we should hasten to say that she also demonstrated quite a few characteristics of the Antisocial, above, and of the Narcissistic Personality Disorder, below. This is said to inform that *Fatal Attraction* is hardly the diagnostic manual for the BPD. In fact many BPD's demonstrate no violence at all, as opposed to Glenn Close's character who is violent in the extreme. However, the BPD does demonstrate a pervasive pattern of instability in relationship, self-image (identity), emotions, and impulsivity. The trigger for this pattern is a perception of impending separation, rejection, or abandonment, which creates profound changes in the image of the self (i.e., an implication that they are "bad"), in emotion or mood, in thought content or perception, and in behavior, inclusive of self-mutilation and suicidal behaviors. (APA, 1994, 650). Due to their demands or to their impulsive efforts to avoid abandonment, they often set up the very abandonment they fear.

Underlying all of this is an identity that shifts between being "bad" and being non-existent (when there is no sense of relatedness). Because they shift from a deep inner feeling of "badness" to another deep inner feeling of emptiness or nothingness, they often set up this conflict in their external world. They find people that they can put up on a pedestal as savior. Savior is the role that offers the most psychic distance while at the same time offering some sense of closeness. The BPD can keep the savior at arm's length with lies and manipulations, while imposing an intensity to the dynamic that assumes something akin to closeness. And, of course, since no one can perfectly save another, the savior will quickly be thrust off of the pedestal, now becoming demonized for not saving "good enough." In this way, they quite often set up "splits" in their external world, which match by proportion and intensity, the split in their own internal world.

In treatment facilities this is quite often seen when a BPD puts a particular staff member on a savior-pedestal, evidenced by statements like, "You are the only one here who understands me." This, of course, makes the staff member feel that s/he must be doing something right. A few days later, however, this person is taken off the pedestal and, in fact is considered to be a very poor staff member. At this point the BPD goes to another staff member, puts that one on the savior-pedestal and "tells on" the first staff member. The second staff member is then left to confront the first one. If the two staff members end up in a battle that the BPD can see, the BPD can then mentally play out the internal drama of "good/evil" vicariously, through the two fighting staff members. At least when BPDs are playing out this drama, they do not feel like "nothing." This quite often happens in their social worlds as well, with lovers and friends, so that they spend enormous amounts of energy creating splits between one person and the other in order to dramatize their own internal split. One method of doing this is to put one partner in a couple, whom the BPD has befriended, on a pedestal, while subtly or overtly maligning the other partner. This works very well when the first partner is already confused and hurt about something that his/her partner did. Very often, in this case, the BPD will end up having an affair with one or both partners.

At least five of the following symptoms, taken from the DSM-IV, must be present to be so diagnosed:

- Frantic efforts to avoid real or imagined abandonment.
- A pattern of unstable and intense interpersonal relationships characterized by alternating between extremes of idealization and devaluation.
- Persistently unstable image of the self, or of the sense of self.
- Self-damaging impulsivity in at least 2 of the following areas:
  o Spending,
  o Sex,
  o Substance abuse,
  o Reckless driving,
  o Binge eating.
- Recurrent suicidal behavior, gestures, or threats, or self-mutilating behavior.
- Instability of mood, marked reactivity of mood, lasting a few hours to a few days, in the form of intense, episodic:
  o Dysphoria,

      o Irritability,

      o Anxiety.

- Chronic feelings of emptiness.
- Inappropriate intense anger, or difficulty controlling anger.
- Transient, stress-related paranoid ideation or severe dissociative symptoms. (APA, 1994, 654).

The BPD is often deeply identified as Victim on the one side and Bully/Perpetrator on the other. The first step in the process of becoming BPD is an escape from the self. Whereas most of us have found someway to identify with something other than the Authentic Self, we still recognize the fact that there is a real self inside which gives us feelings we can at least recognize. The BPD is totally externally identified. This external identification keeps them from even recognizing anything internal at all, much less anything authentic. This external identification makes it easy for them to pick up on whatever drama is going on around them and wrap themselves up in it. This is also why they often carry a co-morbid diagnosis of conversion disorder, in which they adopt the illnesses of others. They cannot even imagine a real entity living deep inside of them, though for most of us this is a relatively simple concept. They fear abandonment by others because they have already completely abandoned themselves. This is why it is so easy for them to identify as Victim and Bully/Perpetrator. The only influence in their lives, as they see it, is external. Therefore, the external can easily victimize them, and they are therefore driven to punish that external through the Bully/Perpetrator.

    Their distorted cognitions often include a belief that somehow they are supposed to be taken care of by lovers, spouses, friends, in a way, which is far beyond normal expectations. When this does not readily and perfectly occur they often overreact, misconstruing content and meaning of any conversation regarding these unrealistic expectations. They distort any confrontation into outright abandonment, and will quite often set up an abandonment of their own, in order to go home to that familiar feeling of abandonment. At this point they can act out the Victim role and require someone else to take care of them. It amounts to, "Well, fine if you won't come over to my house and wash my dishes for me every night, then you don't really love me anyway and who needs you!" (I deliberately made the expectation humorous here, to demonstrate how distorted these ideas can be). Sometimes it comes down to, "If you are my lover, then you must be exactly like me. If you are not, then I am bad for not being just like you, (since I have you on a pedestal) so we shouldn't be together because soon you are going to abandon me anyway." Or, "if you are really very much like me then you must be bad, because I am bad. Therefore, I will mistreat you and make you want to leave, but then put you back on the pedestal and beg you to stay." This sets up an "I hate you, don't leave me!" see-saw that is extremely difficult for most persons in relationship with border-lines.

Borderlines often lack insight into this behavior. Why? Because they are often so identified with being the Victim that there must be a Bully/Perpetrator out there somewhere. This means that they will, as stated above, quite often feel paranoid, as if someone is out to get them, when this is no where near the truth. So, if someone tries to tell them that they are setting the whole thing up, they will quite often answer with "Yes, but …" or "You don't understand how hard it is for me…."

Often they will, take on a self-image of righteous avenger of perceived or real past mistreatment. This is how they move from Victim identity to Bully/Perpetrator identity. Or they can perceive that the world is really a very difficult place to live and life is always going to be hard for them, so if they are going down, they might as well take others with them. This is another way of getting quickly to the Bully/Perpetrator role. Remember that perpetration can be verbal, emotional, mental, or physical abuse, and/or even sexual abuse. Quite often, however, the abuse is emotional or mental, since these are often more subtle or difficult to pinpoint.

This shifting between the Victim and the Perpetrator identities is what cre-ates the suicidality and the threats of suicide or pseudo-suicidality so common for the BPD. We should discuss this, for it is an important aspect of coming to terms with the authentic self. For BPDs escaping contact with the authentic self is the name of the game. Staying external, rather than going internal is their *modis operandi*. The Victim/Perpetrator identity cycle is primarily an escape from authenticity. As we've said, the issue of abandonment comes about primarily because the BPD has abandoned the Self. Sometimes the BPD can completely escape the self through suicide, or at least come close to such abandonment through attempted suicide. Sometimes, however, their threats of suicide are a form of emotional abuse of another. The fear of abandonment thrusts them into a pseudo-suicidality with which they can manipulate others into staying, or at least not leaving or abandoning them. When the suicidality is real it is most often related to vengeance. They believe that the greatest harm they can do to another is to harm themselves. After all the self is a mere exten-sion of others. There is no real self anyway, so that their body becomes a weapon to use on others. Thus, the intent of their suicidality is to lurk behind the curtains on the stage of their drama and watch the suffering of those who survive their suicide. When it is pseudo-suicidality, it is not, as is classically thought, an attempt to get attention, per se, though that is one of the second-ary gains. Instead the intent is to manipulate others. In other words, again, they are using their own body/mind as a weapon against others. This is a dangerous game, however, as some accidentally commit suicide out of a pseudo-suicidal binge.

In order for the BPDs to heal they must work in three specific areas. First BPDs must begin to understand the nature of their own dynamic. This means that they must understand how the Victim identity gets triggered, how the Bully/Perpetrator gets triggered, and how one triggers the other. They can do this through listening to and becoming very acquainted with the mantras. Second, they must learn how to hear from and respond to the voice of the Authentic Self. In this way they will replace the mantras of the role with the messages of the Authentic Self. In this way they will learn to internalize rather than externalize their lives. Third, they must learn and relearn the constant: I am in control at all times; even when I *feel* out of control; I always have a choice. One does this work by working with the belief that one can actually get out of control. If you have this belief, go back and work and rework the exer-cises on beliefs. The concept that one has a choice at all times in all circum-stances basically turns the Victim and Bully/Perpetrator identities upside down immediately, for it puts one automatically in touch with authenticity. This is also how one can deal with the suicidality or pseudo-suicidality. The constant that one has a choice puts one in touch with the truism: We always have a choice about whether to live or die. All day, everyday, we are choosing to either live or die. The recognition that one has a choice when one is feeling sui-cidal puts one in touch with the fact that at least one part of the person wishes to live or one would be dead. It forces an inward glance. Choice gives us the responsibility for our lives. And choice cannot really be denied forever. Ultimately, even suicide is a choice, though many BPDs would deny this.

And with regard to every other aspect of borderline behaviors choice becomes a major intervention. One cannot be a Victim, if one has a choice about the circumstances one will tolerate. One cannot be a Bully/Perpetrator if one brings into conscious awareness the fact that no one else is responsible for one's life. One cannot use pseudo-suicidality as a weapon against others, if one is taking complete responsibility for one's own well-being.

Finally, working with the Authentic Self is the choice to be made. Saying, "yes" to authenticity means finding that one is not, nor ever can be empty. We have a self. The BPD is consistently projecting that self outward, feeling that if they cannot have relatedness then there is nothing. The first and most important relationship is the one we have or don't have with the Self. Everything else comes after that. It takes discipline to work daily on making contact and beginning to rely upon the Authentic Self, but it can be done. We just have to choose it. Get into therapy. Write to the Authentic Self and have her/him write back to you. Do this three times per day on any topic of concern. Work and rework the sections on the Victim and the Bully/Perpetrator. Work and rework the section on coming home. Work and rework the section on barriers to authenticity. Have your therapist work these with you. You will begin to notice your own internal wisdom, your own internal love and you will come to realize on an emotional, almost organic level that this place inside you has never been wounded.

Narcissistic Personality Disorder: This disorder is characterized by a pervasive pattern of grandiosity, need for admiration and lack of empathy that begins by early adulthood and is present in a variety of circumstance and relationship. Persons with this disorder are basically perceptually impaired. They have a perception of themselves that is inflated, and assume that others have the same perception of them. They are often surprised, shocked and/or angered when the rewards go to others instead of them. Quite often, they spend very little energy on achieving the rewards that they think that they deserve. Rather, they feel that they are entitled to these rewards, simply because they believe themselves to be superior.

A great deal of energy goes to their preoccupation with unlimited success, power, brilliance, beauty or ideal love. They fantasize about their "long overdue" admiration and/or privilege, and often compare themselves favorably with famous or privileged people. In fact, they will only associate with persons whom they believe to be superior and unique, as they themselves are, and further enhance their own self-esteem through these associations. However, their self-esteem is, in fact, quite fragile. Therefore, they will only form friendships or love relationships with persons who are likely to advance them in some way. They are often quite charming in order to be noticed, and expect admiration for simply walking in the door. They are puzzled, depressed or furious when they are not catered to. Their sense of entitlement, accompanied by a lack of sensitivity to the wants and needs of others, can result in an unconscious exploitation of others. They assume that others are totally consumed with them. Therefore, they may go on and on with inappropriate and lengthy detail about their own lives without ever referencing others as entities separate and distinct from them, who have wants and needs of their own. They often are unable to comprehend how another could be in a different mood, or have different desires from their own, and can become quite angry when they see that this is so. They are often contemptuous and impatient when others talk about their own lives, and are oblivious to the effect of their, often, caustic remarks on others. Snobbish, arrogant, patronizing, disdainful, haughty behaviors may characterize these persons in private, or to those who do not cater to them, though, as stated, they can also be quite charming. Five of the following symptoms must be present, according to the DSM-IV, in order for persons to be so diagnosed:

- A grandiose sense of self-importance. An exaggeration of achievements and talents, and an expectation that they will be recognized as superior without commensurate achievements.
- Preoccupation with fantasies of unlimited success, power, brilliance, beauty, or ideal love.
- A belief that s/he is "special" and unique and can only be understood by, and/or should associate with other special or high-status people or institutions.
- Requires excessive admiration.
- A sense of entitlement, or unreasonable expectation of especially favorable treatment or automatic compliance with his or her expectation.
- Interpersonally exploitive: takes advantage of others to achieve his/her own ends.
- A lack of empathy: is unwilling to recognize or identify with the feelings and needs of others.
- Often envious of others or believes that others are envious of him/her.
- Demonstrates arrogant or haughty attitudes or behaviors. (APA, 1994, 658-661).

If you have been diagnosed as Narcissistic Personality Disorder, you could be unconsciously living out a Scapegoat/Superwoman or Scapegoat/Superhero identity. The mix looks something like this. Somewhere along the way one picks up the negative messages of someone else, usually a parent who has extremely high expectations of the child. The child needs to be prettier, taller, brighter, superior in some way, or just plain different from what s/he is—in order to make the parent feel good about him/herself. This parent may also give double-bind, overt or covert messages such as: Become President of the U.

S. because if you do you will show me that I could have made it if I'd tried, instead of giving it up as I did; but don't be President of the U.S. because if you do, you'll show me that I should have tried. The child is then damned if s/he does and damned if s/he doesn't. This message is often given by a parent with whom the child is quite enmeshed, making the message all the more powerful.

The child grows up with an internal sense of being "less than," even while the parent is projecting "more than" onto the child. The child knows that s/he has not really earned this projection. This internal anxiety must be compensated through thought and action, ergo, the sense of entitlement. In fact, the child is being asked to sacrifice, through the Scapegoat identity, his/her internal sense of worth to the parent's needs. Simultaneously, the child is given the message that s/he must succeed at all costs, thus the Superwoman/Superhero identity. The super-identity takes the form of imagined success, because there can be not real success. Real success would be a betrayal of the parent, by ending the sacrifice of the Scapegoat. But lack of success is also a betrayal of the parent. The only way out of this double-bind is to believe or pretend, or assume the position of one who has achieved rewards one hasn't really achieved.

In fact the Narcissistic Personality Disorder is deeply wounded by the original rejection of his/her authenticity. Because they are often quite enmeshed with the parent who is also rejecting them, they will not allow themselves to feel their own woundedness, but instead create a fiction around it. The fiction is that they are deeply admired and esteemed by all. They therefore wear the mask and costume based on the rejection they felt from the parent they adored and the need to please that same parent.

In order to heal, this type of Narcissistic Personality must begin to go down below the wound to the place where they are not wounded. This is different from trying to stay above the wound by pretending. They must begin by seeing how and why they put on the mask and costume in the first place. They must begin to realize that they are reenacting their parent's rejection and demands on others. Then they will be able to see that there is a part of them that has not surfaced. This part is the Authentic Self. They can then begin to take the same amount of energy that they placed on getting admiration from others, on finding ways to make themselves personally happy. Once they realize that they are responsible for their own happiness and that their happiness has nothing to do with their parent's goals or rejections, they can really do it.

The Runaway identity may also correlate with the Narcissistic Personality Disorder. If I came from what I consider to be deplorable, shameful circumstances and I wish to be separated by time, space and identity from those circumstances, I may don the mask of arrogance in order to accomplish my Runaway feat. I may take this to the extreme, since the circumstances, people and/or past I am running from were extreme, and assume all manner of entitlements and privilege. My mantra is, "I am better than that and I, therefore, deserve better than that." In fact what I am doing is magical thinking. I'm imagining myself as entitled and assuming that I am in fact so entitled. Such assumption of entitlement carries with it all the accoutrements of position, power, prestige and relatedness. I may hang out with all the "right" people and don the charm and charisma of power. I may assume entitlement to money and power to such a degree that I would even take them from others. In relationship, I only relate to the "best" people and reject anyone who even somewhat resembles my past or those things from which I am running. I can become quite cruel in my rejections because how dare you assume that I could be with you who remind me of my past, or believe that you are allowed the same entitlements as I. As a parent, I may raise my children to have rank and superiority, because to have anything less reminds me of those things from which I am running. So, you see this type of Narcissistic Personality Disorder is the Runaway in the extreme.

Further, the Narcissistic Personality Disorder may live out the Victim/Bully/Perpetrator cycle. Woundedness is at the core of this disorder, no matter which role is played out, and woundedness is the primary issue for the Victim. The Narcissistic Personality Disorder can live out the Victim part of this cycle by telling others, at every juncture at which it might seem appropriate, that the Victim has been terribly wounded by life. They then deserve to be taken care of in exceptional ways because life owes them. Furthermore, you personally owe them and they will make you pay. Here, the Narcissistic Personality Disorder launches into the Bully/Perpetrator role, threatening harm to you and yours, or actually harming you for not providing for them in these exceptional ways. Because this person lives in a world made of fantasy castles and deep, dark dungeons, and built out of their woundedness, it is quite difficult for them to come into the real world of authenticity. But difficult is not the same as impossible. It can be done.

If you have been diagnosed with a Narcissistic Personality Disorder, or if you recognize yourself in this description, the first step is to get into therapy. Once there, ask your therapist to work and rework this workbook with you. You will need help in looking at your ideas with a great deal of objectivity. Your beliefs about yourself are not founded in reality, they are found in your role. But your authenticity is still there. And it does not reject you, rather it calls you to live it out freely.

There are several other diagnoses which are less common, but nevertheless common among the general population. Among these are bipolar disorder, a mood disorder that can have psychotic features, in which one moves from various kinds of mania into deep depression, in various degrees of rapidity; schizophrenia a psychotic disorder in which hallucinations and delusions are a chief component; social phobia an anxiety disorder in which the primary feature is fear of social situations; just to name a few. If you have a diagnosis that has not been discussed here, please note that your diagnosis is nevertheless significant. Further, please note that your role does play into your diagnosis, at the very least, exacerbating its symptoms. These diagnoses were discussed to give the reader the idea of how the role fits into the diagnosis. That, not your particular diagnosis, is the central theme here. If you have been diagnosed with any mental illness and are still concerned with its effects on you, go back and work the chapter on roles and barriers to authenticity. Work with your own mantra again and again. What are you telling yourself? Is it working for you? Are you happy yet? Write letters to and from the Authentic Self often and every time an issue arises. Take this book with you to therapy. Write, talk, dance, sing, do what is true for your own authenticity often enough to begin to feel its genuine peace.

Now that we have looked at several of the more common diagnoses and have been challenged to work with these diagnoses by finding the role within them, and the Authentic self below them, let's look at how you feel about your particular symptoms. You see, there are all kinds of messages we give ourselves. There are the original messages from the Authentic Self, there are messages from the role, and then there are messages about the messages. For example: You may receive a message from the Authentic Self that says, take care of yourself in a particular way. The role may respond to that message by saying, "Yeah, but I don't want to take care of myself; that takes effort and energy. Isn't someone else supposed to prove that they love me by doing this for me?" Then the role may have another double-bind message for that message, like: "Boy, you're a lazy-butt, and selfish too. What's the matter with you?" By this time you are not even listening to the Authentic Self anymore. Now you are arguing between the alternating voices of the role. But let's take the risk to listen now. Go back to the Authentic Self for a message about both messages. The Authentic Self might say something like:

Okay, so you've got some resistance to taking care of yourself based on the fact that no one else ever did it, and you resent this. That's a pretty common response. The only question is, if no one else is going to do it, and you're not going to do it either, doesn't that mean no one is doing it? Why don't we start with small steps? Suppose you begin allowing me to become more conscious to you, so that you can hear me saying "How 'bout a cup of tea and a break?" A long string of these little ways of taking care of yourself might just make it possible for you to believe that you can do it in other ways. But if you just beat yourself up for your resistance, you'll just keep sitting here repeating the pattern. Why don't we try something small right now?

Can you hear the difference in the responses? It's important to notice the difference. And it's also important to know that the first message you get back is not always the voice of the Authentic Self. So, let's try an exercise now.

Below is a Response Grid. Take one of the symptoms of your own diagnosis if you have one, and/or any issue of concern and write down the various internal responses to this, separate the responses out as to who the response comes from, the role or the Authentic Self.

	Message # 1	Message # 2	Message # 3
Role			
Authentic Self			
Role			
Authentic Self			
Role			
Authentic Self			
Role			
Authentic Self			
Role			
Authentic Self			

Ponderings: Okay, so now we have a handle on the idea that diagnoses are related to the role we've played. And we know that the Authentic Self is a real entity that can help. You may have, by this time experienced some emotional responses to the Authentic Self that feel pretty good. So, now, on an emotional level, you are aware that the Authentic Self exits and that it offers at least a modicum of peace. You may have even felt some sparks of joy. The whole thing of Self-discovery is a little like falling in love. The more we see the Self, the more we enjoy its company, the deeper we fall in love. Dan Fogelberg wrote and recorded a song entitled *Make Love Stay* (Fogelberg, 1974-1982), which begins like this:

> Now that we love,
> Now that the lonely nights are over,
> How do we make love stay?

And the next chapter helps us with this issue.

Relying
On
The
Authentic
Self

Ponderings: Just how much of your energy on a daily basis now, goes to being authentic? How much goes to living the role? Okay, be easy on yourself. You are in a new process, so there is no expectation that you be living 100% of the time out of your authenticity. But it is important to start getting a picture of just how much we are really putting our insights to work. The truth is that insight is not insight, which is not put into practice. Let me say that again: *Insight is not insight, which is not put into practice.*

The two biggest areas of our lives, as adults, are career and relationship. Relationship has always been a big one, as evidenced by the impact that our relationships have had on our lives. But as we get to be adults we get to start over in relationship. We get the opportunity to start a whole new family, in whatever shape or form we desire. However, if we are not living authentically, what we usually do, is create the same relationships we knew as children, all over again. We psychologically go back home again.

As children and adolescents we looked forward to our career, as something new and exciting. This was something we'd never had before. And we got to choose from thousands of options, as to exactly what we would do. But how narrow were our options, based upon the square box the role built for us to live in? Did we choose from our desires? Or did we think that these were out of the question and should therefore be ignored? Did we choose or did we just slide into a position and stay there? Also, what dynamics from our childhood, through the role, are we reliving in our work environments? What is your truth?

Let's look at career first. And let's start with the job itself and all of its tasks.

Below, create a list of all of your job tasks. Be very detailed, even including tasks like "interacting with my boss," or "interacting with my coworker." Try to list the tasks that your job description states as priorities, first. Then circle the appropriate number for each using the following criteria:

1: Yuk, I hate this! I'll postpone it as long as I can.
2: Okay, I'll do it, but don't ask me to like it.
3: This isn't so bad.
4: This is kind of fun.
5: Man! I can't wait to get my hands on this.

Task	Emotional Response
	1------------2------------3------------4------------5
	1------------2------------3------------4------------5
	1------------2------------3------------4------------5
	1------------2------------3------------4------------5
	1------------2------------3------------4------------5
	1------------2------------3------------4------------5
	1------------2------------3------------4------------5
	1------------2------------3------------4------------5
	1------------2------------3------------4------------5
	1------------2------------3------------4------------5
	1------------2------------3------------4------------5
	1------------2------------3------------4------------5
	1------------2------------3------------4------------5
	1------------2------------3------------4------------5
	1------------2------------3------------4------------5
	1------------2------------3------------4------------5
	1------------2------------3------------4------------5

How many 5's did you have? How many 1's? How many 2's and 3's? If you had a lot of 4's and 5's, you are definitely in the right job. Keep doing it, keep enjoying it. If you had more 1's, 2's and 3's, you might want to ask yourself why you chose this job. Or, put another way, if you could select any job in the world you would want to have, what would you do? Don't put any "Yeah, but, I'd have to go back to school," attached. And don't attach the amount of money you'd make or prestige you'd have. Just answer the question: If you could choose any job, strictly based on how much fun or deep satisfaction you'd have *doing the tasks of that job*, what would you choose? Let's play with that for a moment. Would it be an already established job, or do you have something in mind that is rather unique in the work world? **Below, write the answers to all of the above questions. Fill in the blank spaces with your own imaginings.**

_____

_____

_____

_____

_____

_____

_____

_____

_____

_____

_____

_____

_____

_____

_____

_____

_____

_____

_____

_____

_____

_____

_____

_____

_____

What if you basically like your job but there are some tasks that you really hate, and others that you could just do without? Should we just allow that to be so, with the common thought: Well, everybody has to do things they don't like? Well, suppose that's only been so because we've all believed it to be so. What if we didn't all have to do things we don't like? Or, what if we could at least reduce the number of things we don't like to a mere morsel of time? **Below, make another list of the tasks you didn't like above.** Beside the list, write in a method for delegating that task or connecting that task to another task that you really like.

Task	Method

If you find, over and over, that you cannot delegate or connect a task to something you love, then perhaps you are in the wrong job. Perhaps it is time to rethink.

But let's look closer still. What was your response when it came to the task of "interacting with my boss" and/or "interacting with my coworker?" If you didn't put in those tasks, do so now and respond to them. What was your response? **Answer the following questions with regard to your relationship with your boss?**

1. Do you like your boss? If so why? If not why not? (If you are tempted to answer, "Because he's an asshole!" think again. Be specific.)

_____
_____
_____
_____.

2. If you had to describe your internal reaction to your boss how would you describe it?

_____
_____
_____
_____.

3. Is there someone from your family of origin, or childhood, of whom your boss reminds you? Why?

_____
_____
_____
_____.

4. How does your role respond to your boss? What messages does the role give you about your relationship with your boss?

_____
_____
_____
_____.

5. What does the Authentic Self say to you about your relationship with your boss?

_____

_____

_____

_____.

6. Describe the perfect boss for you.

_____

_____

_____

_____.

7. What methods can you begin to use immediately, to start being this perfect boss to yourself?

_____

_____

_____

_____.

Let's try the same thing with the co-workers?

1. Do you like your co-workers? If so why? If not why not? (If you are tempted to answer, "Because he's an asshole!" think again. Be specific.)

_____
_____
_____
_____.

2. If you had to describe your internal reaction to your co-worker how would you describe it?

_____
_____
_____
_____.

3. Is there someone from your family of origin, or childhood, of which a co-worker reminds you? Why?

_____
_____
_____
_____.

4. How does your role respond to your co-worker? What messages does the role give you about your relationship with your co-worker?

_____
_____
_____
_____.

5. What does the Authentic Self say to you about your relationship with your co-worker?

_____
_____
_____
_____.

6. Describe the perfect co-worker for you.

_____

_____

_____

_____.

7. What methods can you begin to use immediately, to start being this perfect co-worker to yourself?

_____

_____

_____

_____.

How has this exercise helped you clarify your interactions with your boss and co-workers?

_____

_____

_____

_____.

Now, let's begin to explore. Below write the following story: **When I started this job, I was looking for....** Be sure to separate out feelings about bosses and co-workers from actual tasks of the job, unless, of course, when you started the job you were looking for relationships. Then move to the present. Do you have what you were looking for? Is it what you want now?

_____
_____
_____
_____
_____
_____
_____
_____
_____
_____
_____
_____
_____
_____
_____
_____
_____
_____
_____
_____
_____
_____
_____
_____
_____
_____
_____
_____
_____
_____
_____
_____
_____

Ponderings: Sometimes what we were looking for when we started a job is not what we really want in a job. But the truth is that the Authentic Self has a mission here on planet earth. The Authentic Self calls us to do something of high desire, and keen intent. We often, very often, ignore these callings and seek only to do that which is easy, available, or pays okay. In other words we are not original. Then we wonder why we are frustrated, overeating, overdrinking, overweight, over-the-hill people. Know why? Because we are not fulfilling our own deep-seated desires.

One of the worst mistakes we make as adults is to take the "whatever job" down the street, because at least in so doing we can bring home the bacon. We may hate the job, or dislike it, or mildly tolerate it, but we don't jump up in the mornings enthusiastically waiting for the opportunity to get there. Ever wonder why we have such a high accident rate on the job? Why Workman's Comp claims are so high? Why insurance benefits keep rising? Could be many, many of us are in the wrong jobs.

Many of us think of a "calling" as a duty, or a conviction. For the deeply religious, a calling might mean having a euphoric experience that includes a feeling of conviction or an audible voice of God. For others a calling is often more like a moral obligation, something we do, because we are either good at it or because it is good for others. Even when we feel stuck, we tell ourselves, "Well, I guess this is my calling, my cross to bear."

I'd like to redefine that word "calling." We are not on our mission or in our calling until we have fulfilled something deep inside of us. This something has everything to do with authentic desire and nothing whatsoever to do with pleasing others, or even being skilled at something. We can be skilled at something we no longer wish to do or, in fact, never enjoyed. After all, I know how to change a tire, but I wouldn't want to do it all day. You may provide all manner of counsel to your children, but you wouldn't want to be a therapist. And even if we think we have heard the voice of God calling us to do something we really don't want to do, maybe we should think again. Why would a God, any kind of God, want us to do something that does not fulfill us?

Think about this: If you could fulfill your highest and deepest desire by doing something everyday, what would it be? In other words, what is your mission? What did you come here to do? What did you come to give to planet earth? What one thing is more important to you than anything else in the world? You may not know the answer to these questions right off. You may have to list things and prioritize them. You may have to trim them down to one central idea. But stick to desire. Stay away from shoulds or pleasing others.

Strictly go by your own internal desire. What do you *want* to *do* all day every day?

Below, write your own mission statement. What would you do the most, if there were no one to ask what to do, or to tell you what to do? Don't just write any old thing. Think about it. And don't make the most righteous statement you can think of. Come from your heart, from the deepest inner yearning you can find. Think only of your most basic desire. Not what do you want to be when you grow up, but who are you in relation to your world or what would you like to be to planet earth? What do you *desire* more than anything to do while you're here? Key word here is desire, <u>not </u>SHOULD. What mark would you like to leave? It starts like this:

I am here on planet earth to….

_____
_____
_____
_____
_____
_____
_____
_____
_____
_____
_____
_____
_____
_____
_____
_____
_____
_____
_____
_____

Now, it's pretty clear that if you have decided that you are here on planet earth to make children happy or well, but you are driving a truck all day and never even see a child, that you are in the wrong job. But if you are here on planet earth to make children happy or well, and you are a kindergarten teacher who hates her job, perhaps you are just going about your job in a way that is not authentic to you. Or perhaps this particular job is too narrow. Perhaps you would like to expand what you are doing with children. Having said that, let's try something else. **Below, write a story of your fantasy job designed to help you fulfill your mission.** Remember that your fantasy may take the job you have and revise it along more authentic lines or it may be an entirely different scenario. Don't hold back, let the fantasy rip.

_____

_____

_____

_____

_____

_____

_____

_____

_____

_____

_____

_____

_____

_____

_____

_____

_____

_____

_____

_____

_____

_____

_____

_____

Ponderings: Okay, okay, so suppose you just came up with a job that is totally different from the one you are in. Now, you are really scared and you are thinking, "What have I gotten myself into? Now, not only do I hate my job, but I know that I am accountable for this!" I had a friend once who would sit momentarily with her fingers poised along the arm of a chair then begin drumming them rapidly in rhythm over and over on the chair. Once I asked her what she was doing with her fingers. She said, "That's my fingers saying, "Oh, my God, Oh, my God, Oh, my God, Oh, my God, Oh, my God!!!" In other words, she was allowing herself a mini-panic attack. Well, okay, have yourself a little attack and then let's talk.

Finding and beginning to live out of the Authentic Self inevitably produces change in some form. Remember that we said that working this book could be a life-changing experience. But the reward is that you get to be happy. You get to be fulfilled. You get to make your own dreams come true. So, okay, what do you do? You just found out you want to do something entirely different from what you are doing. What would it take to get you into the job that you described? Do you need to go back to school? Do you need to make a Web-Site? What do you need to do? **Below, make a list of ideas you have for what you need to do to bring this about.** After you have created the list, go back and prioritize it with which task needs to be done first, second, third.

_____

_____

_____

_____

_____

_____

_____

_____

_____

_____

_____

_____

_____

_____

_____

You may have just made a plan for how you could change your career, but what does one do in the interim, while one is still not in the job of one's dreams, but working toward it. Well first its important to remember that we are just thinking right now, there is nothing to say you should go do it all right now. Let the process unfold for you. Don't leap into should-ing on yourself with this information. Sometimes, just knowing you are working toward your dream is enough to ease off the frustration a bit so that you can focus on your current job in a way that, may not make you ecstatic, but makes your job a lot easier and less stressful. This, too, is taking care of yourself. **By tapping into the voice of the Authentic Self, describe below some steps you can take to make your current job less stressful and easier.**

_____

_____

_____

_____

_____

_____

_____

_____

_____

_____

_____

_____

_____

_____

_____

_____

_____

_____

_____

_____

_____

_____

_____

_____

What does the Authentic Self have to say to you about all of this change thinking? Write a poem or letter to yourself, from the Authentic Self regarding the work you have done above:

_____
_____
_____
_____
_____
_____
_____
_____
_____
_____
_____
_____
_____
_____
_____
_____
_____
_____
_____
_____
_____
_____
_____
_____
_____
_____
_____
_____
_____
_____
_____
_____
_____
_____

Write a letter from the Authentic Self to your role, about fear of change, the risk of living whole.

_____
_____
_____
_____
_____
_____
_____
_____
_____
_____
_____
_____
_____
_____
_____
_____
_____
_____
_____
_____
_____
_____
_____
_____
_____
_____
_____
_____
_____
_____
_____
_____
_____
_____
_____
_____
_____

What challenges have you uncovered while doing these exercises? What messages are you giving yourself about these challenges? Are they Authentic Self's messages, or the old messages of the role? Answer these questions below:

_____
_____
_____
_____
_____
_____
_____
_____
_____
_____
_____
_____
_____
_____
_____
_____
_____
_____
_____
_____
_____
_____
_____
_____
_____
_____
_____
_____
_____
_____

Ponderings: Let's look now at another arena of adult living: <u>Relationships.</u> Before we go one step further it should noted that people of all sexual orientations can equally work this section. Your sexual orientation is not the issue here. Relationship is the issue. If you are sure about your sexual orientation then just move forward. However, if you are confused about your sexual orientation, there is also an affirmative section of this chapter specifically written about such confusion, which is common to many persons, particularly in a society or culture that shames certain individuals and groups for their sexual orientation.

First let's talk about primary relationships. A primary relationship is a relationship that you consider to be your primary support. It is the one that is most important to you. Most often this is a spouse, lover or partner, but it could also be a parent, a sibling, or a friend if you are single. In other words, it doesn't have to be sexual in nature, though it most often is. We also have secondary relationships with a circle of people who are good friends. And then we have tertiary relationships (acquaintances) with people who we don't know well, who don't know us well, but with whom we work, or occasionally play. Each of these has a very important place in your life and each has a value all its very own. Often, the ones we are having trouble with are the ones that seem most primary at the time. But this is not always true. Primary relationships can become the most troubling because they are generally with the people with whom you intend to become intimate.

In order to understand that fact, we must first understand intimacy. Intimacy is not the same as wearing sexy undergarments to heighten your romance. Intimacy isn't defined by sex, though sex may be a part of intimacy. Intimacy occurs when you know someone very, very well, and they know you very, very well. This is not the same as knowing their address, phone number, their general behaviors and a few of the things they like. Intimacy is deep knowledge and support of the inner workings of another individual. Many of us think that we have an intimate relationship with whomever we have sex and say we love. It is very possible to have sex with, live with, and be in love with someone with whom you do not share intimacy. Intimacy is much riskier than just living with, having sex with and being in love with someone. Intimacy means opening up the doors of your own vulnerabilities and strengths, thoughts and feelings, securities and insecurities with another person whom you trust and who is willing to do the same with you. Primary relationships are meant to be intimate. Often they are not. But the authentic design for primary relationships is intimacy.

Since we often have sex with, live with and are in love with our primary relationships, when we don't have intimacy with these people, we generally experience intense pain. We misunderstand each other, we play games, we hide important information from each other, we draw conclusions from the significant other's behavior that may or may not have validity, we interpret looks and words in ways that may not be valid, i.e., we generally do not really know each other well enough to live peacefully having sex and being in love. In other words, in order to live peacefully with someone with whom we are in love and having sex, we probably should know them really well. In couples' therapy, I most often find that more than anything else that is "going wrong" in the relationship, there is a basic distrust between the parties because they simply do not know each other.

So, okay, since they are often laden with such anxt, let's work with primary relationships. First, for the purposes of clarity, though, as we said above, one can have a relationship with a parent that is primary, this section on primary relationships will deal mostly with committed sexual relationships, or partnerships. Second, in order to deal authentically with this issue, we have to look at what we have mutually created thus far in relationships. Often times, because we've been playing some role, we have become involved with someone who will play the counter-role. We attract someone who will support our role, so that we can maintain it. In so doing, we feel safe. Let's see how this works. Though there may be exceptions, the chart below gives the typical counter-role(s) for each role.

Role	Counter-role
Victim	Bully/Perpetrator or Superhero
Superhero	Victim
Scapegoat/Priest	Scapegoat/Black Sheep, Bully/Perpetrator, Runaway, or even Party Dude(tte)
Scapegoat/Black Sheep	Superhero, Superwoman or Scapegoat/Priest
Runaway	Scapegoat/Priest or Party Dude(tte)
Superwoman	Party Dude(tte), Runaway
Bully/Perpetrator	Victim or Scapegoat
Party Dude(tte)	Superwoman or Runaway

The Victim needs the Bully/Perpetrator in order to stay in the Victim role. This does NOT mean that the Victims consciously seek out Bully/Perpetrators, but that unconsciously, due to their own unfinished business, they will exhibit a pattern in which they "find themselves" in relationships with Bully/Perpetrators, quite often repeatedly. The Victim works well with the Superhero as well, because the Superhero needs to rescue the Victim, unconsciously reinforcing the Victim role. And, of course, this works in the reverse as well.

The Scapegoat/Priest will need to be associated with people who induce guilt or the sense of responsibility in order to stay in the role. Scapegoat/Black Sheep are pretty good at holding others accountable for their behavior, so they are going to look for someone who will accept the blame, i.e., the Scapegoat/Priest. Bully/Perpetrators rarely-to-never take responsibility for their behavior, so they are also going to be looking not only for someone to abuse (Victim), but also for someone to blame (Scapegoat/Priest). The Runaway runs from anything that looks like shame or blame and so often gets in relationship with those who will carry the responsibility (Scapegoat/Priest) or who can avoid responsibility with them (Party-Dude(ttes). And Party-Dude(tte) (as Peter Pan personified) are unwilling to take responsibility for anything or look at their own behavior in any way, and so will look for those who can carry this for them.

Scapegoat/Black Sheep need a Superhero to rescue them from their own choices. Superheros are the bail-payers, the places to live, the people to use. The Scapegoat/Black Sheep wants the Scapegoat/Priest to pay the sacrifice for the Black Sheep's "sins." And Scapegoat/Black Sheep need Superwomen to take care of responsibility so that they can run their game, committing crimes, drinking, drugging whatever it is that they do that keeps them feeling like a bad dude(tte). Runaways need the Scapegoat/Priest to carry all of their guilt, make sacrifices for their lack of feelings by feeling everything for them, etc. Runaways also often run with Party Dude(tte)s, feeling, in fact, like they have an awful lot in common. The Party is often a good place to run to. And where you find a Party Dude(tte) you will most probably find a Superwoman (or in some cases Superman) nearby. Superwoman is picking up all the trash on the floor after the party, taking care of business, working two jobs to make sure the bills are paid and being ever so responsible, so that the Party Dude(tte) doesn't have to be. Bully/Perpetrators, of course, need someone to bully, so that they can stay in the Perpetrator identity; otherwise they do not feel safe at all. So, they pick out a Victim or a Scapegoat/Priest to bully. Victims can be bullied in a multitude of ways, and the Scapegoat/Priest can be bullied through the manipulative tool of guilt.

In our primary relationships, we are seeking something called homeostasis, which means "balance." We want things to stay the same, so that we can feel safe, and we want to feel that we have achieved some form of balance. These counter-roles make us feel a sense of balance. Why? Because they play out the other side, the other pole of the polarity. They hold the other seat on the see-saw. The most interesting feature of this see-saw is that we forget to consider how our own weight affects the balance. *Often long after we've figured out that we are repeatedly attracted to Mr./Ms. Wrong, we continue the pattern.* Why is this? Is it because there is some deep, dark, sick, perverse side of us that is sucking us into its ever-widening vortex of pain and humiliation? This is what we often think. But this is not it. The reason that we continue this pattern is that in the discovery process of figuring out that we are attracted to the same pattern over and over again, we forgot to look at our own part in that pattern. We forgot to look at our role. There is only one way for us to change the pattern and that is to get out of the role.

You see, there is only one dance that the role knows. Every time the role meets someone, it is going to start doing that same dance. If the other person is going to relate to us at all, it will be based on two things: 1) His or her role, and 2) The dance they see us doing. In fact, we simply will not allow someone to join us at all, unless they know how to be the partner in the dance we are doing. When we step forward, therefore, they are supposed to step back. When they put their hand up to spin us, we are supposed to spin. That's the dance. And only the people who can dance that dance get to dance with us. Their role allows them know our dance. Why? Because their role needs our role, and our role needs theirs. Thus we have established homeostasis. We can dance without stepping on each other's toes or falling over each other. Not that the dance we are dancing is pretty or healthy, but it is our dance. We know it.

The truth is this: *If we want to attract a new kind of partner, we have to change the dance we are doing.* And the same thing is true of working with our current partner. We can develop a new homeostasis, if we both learn a new dance. Changing the dance is what we've been doing in this workbook. But how does one change the dance one is doing in relationship? One begins by being authentic at every juncture where there is an opportunity to dance the old dance of the role.

We have a choice. We can keep dancing the same old dance, or learn a new one that is more authentic. Either way, it starts from the very beginning of the process. If I am single, and working on being authentic, and someone asks me for a date, when I go on the date, I don't assume anything. The fact is that I don't know this person very well and the purpose of the date is to get to know him/her and to allow him/her to know me. So, let's see, we go out and I tell him every intimate detail of my life and then that night we have sex, right? Well, there is no wrong or right here, no judgment. The only question is, is this authentic? For the answer to this, you have to tune in. You have to ask the Authentic Self what it wants. We'll practice in a little bit, but for now, this is all we need to know. If we consult with the Authentic Self, it will tell us what to do and guide us along an authentic path. So, if I have typically played the Victim role, a way to get victimized again is to expose myself, and the vulnerable parts of my underbelly to someone I hardly know, then sleep with him or her, all in one swoop. In this case then, the Authentic Self may guide us to take our time.

If you are single, the first step is to look at *your* previous dating behaviors. What did you do in the past? What were the results? What were you blind to, now that you are looking back, that you wish you had noticed? How could you have paid better attention? What did you say and do that was your dance, the role? The next step is: Do it different this time. Of course, the most effective way of doing it different is to speak and act from the Authentic Self. But even if you slip up and don't do that all the time, just doing it different is better than doing the same old dance.

A date is a kind of interview. Not that the person you are dating is going to get the interrogation, but that you are watching, listening, paying attention. When you get home from that date, you can jot down some notes about things that you liked, things that hit you "funny," yellow flags and red flags that you think you saw. Generally, this kind of observation means that you are not going to jump in the sack on the first date, but the choices are all yours. If you take your time, however, and pay attention, you might find that this time, you end up in a relationship with someone with whom you can really relate.

The problem for some of us is that we take the first date, to mean we are in a long-term relationship, especially if we've had sex. It's kind of like this: Okay, you kissed me, you're attracted to me, we had sex, this means now that I'm committed to you and you to me. In other words, we get the words commitment and attraction mixed up. I *can* be attracted to someone I don't know very well. It happens every day. It *is* possible to fall in love at first sight. But even falling in love is not the same as commitment. Commitment is something else entirely.

Falling in love with someone is a heightened state of elation that comes up directly from the unconscious. Falling in love is not a conscious act. We do not sit down one morning and say, "Today, I'm going to fall in love." No, rather it is something that seems to be happening *to* us. It seems to be choosing us. Anytime something comes into our awareness from the unconscious, the door to the unconscious has been opened. That means that whatever else is in there may come out attached to that new awareness. Therefore, if I have unresolved issues about my abusive father pushed back into my unconscious, then when I fall in love, I may just fall in love with someone just like dear old Dad. Falling in love then can be compared to dipping one's spoon into a bowl of vegetable soup. When we do this we don't usually come up only with a piece of beef, or a carrot. We come up with a spoonful of assorted vegetables, some beef and the broth. In that same way, when we dip the spoon into the unconscious by falling in love, we may come back with a spoonful of the old unresolved issues that were still in there. In this way, we find that the psyche's very natural urge toward wholeness is operating. How do we know this? Because we are attracted to persons who will push us to resolve old unresolved issues. In fact, falling in love is, at least in part, an attempt, on the part of the psyche to bring unconscious material UP into our awareness. Issues such as these may come up to be resolved (just to name a few):

- Fear of abandonment
- Fear of intimacy
- Possessiveness
- Dependency
- Old unresolved agendas, misconceptions or issues from childhood.

Therefore, it is most important to recognize that relationships can be our teacher, for they can teach us about ourselves. In fact, our relationships are mirrors for us, if we will use them this way.

At the risk of hearing you say, "Oh you are taking all of the fun out of it!" I must say this: *When we fall in love with someone, we are falling in love with an aspect of ourselves.* The question then is, is the aspect an aspect of the role, or an aspect of the Authentic Self. People fall in and out of love all of the time. Some people fall in love with people they can never have, like, say, movie stars. Some people fall in love with people who will abuse them. Some people fall in love only with married people. Some people fall in love only with alcoholics. Are we having fun yet? Yet, when, as a therapist, I talk to clients who are in very negative, even abusive relationships they often will say, "But I love him/her!" as if that is the reason to stay and tolerate the negativity and/or abuse. We must be careful not to get chaos and passion mixed up. It is clear, when we look at it from this perspective, that we must not allow ourselves to be deluded by the idea that falling in love is the only ingredient necessary to making a good relationship.

If we look at it this way then, it seems fairly clear that just because we have fallen in love, this does not mean that we should automatically commit. Most of us were taught just the opposite. When we asked our parents, "How will I know when I'm in love?" if they answered at all they said, "Oh, you'll know." And if they taught us about relationship at all, we learned these things:

- You have to compromise.
- You have to sacrifice.
- Love is all you need.
- If you love someone, that is almost like God calling you to be with them.

We will discuss the first three myths a bit more later, but for now, we should recognize that the last one is utterly false. We are not being called to commit when we fall in love. When we fall in love we are being called to learn.

In fact, when we fall in love, it is time to get very closely allied with the Authentic Self and listen and listen and listen. In so doing we not only get to know ourselves better, but we may protect ourselves from getting involved again with someone with whom we will only regret becoming involved. Further, we may begin to open ourselves more and more to the internal healing of the wounds that created the split, which created the role, and the ensuing negative attractions in the first place. When we do this we open up to the possibility of finding someone with whom we will not regret our involvement and with whom we may commit for that long-term, happy relationship we've been dreaming of. *The fun comes when we have grown to the point that we are almost always living authentically, and we get attracted to someone who can do the same and who encourages our continued growth.* So let's try an exercise on the next page. We will start with the beginning of relationship, the date.

You are preparing to go out on a date. You are really excited because this person is someone you find to be very attractive. Before you get ready to go though, you are going to look back at your *previous dating behaviors.* Answer the following questions on the questionnaire below as honestly as possible, with regard to how you acted on dates **in the past.** Remember, don't answer as to how you think you ought to act now, but answer as to how you acted in the past:

1. When s/he asks what restaurant you want to go to, you:
    a. Say, "Whatever you want."
    b. Say, "What are the options?" but when s/he starts to list them, you listen for hints of what s/he wants so that you can respond to that one.
    c. Say, "What are the options?" listening to his/her list and then adding a few of your own, hoping that the two of you will come to an agreement.
    d. Say, "I'd like to go to _____."

2. When s/he starts telling his/her story about the day or the lifetime, do you:
    a. Listen carefully so that you can pretend to be just like him/her?
    b. Listen off and on, but mostly to the sound of his/her voice?
    c. Listen for his/her story, to find out more about him or her and how s/he lives and thinks?
    d. Rub your foot against his/hers under the table, lost in reverie about what's going to happen after the meal?

3. S/he makes a sexual comment, with hints that s/he would like to finish up the meal quickly and get on to desert. You feel a bit uncomfortable. You:
    a. Laugh awkwardly and ignore his/her statement, hoping that when s/he puts the moves on you later you can find a way out of it.
    b. Look him/her straight in the eye and say, "That was a very inappropriate comment. You must think you are all that and then some!"
    c. Tell him/her that you are flattered by his/her remarks, but that you'd rather just spend some time getting to know him/her and enjoying the evening together.

d. Ignore your feelings, knowing that if you don't do what s/he wants you'll lose him/her for sure.

4. S/he mentions that s/he has always hated his/her mother and anyone, or anything that reminds of her. What does this mean?
    a. S/he is a poor risk and you cannot ever date him/her again.
    b. You need to listen and ask questions about this, paying attention to how his/her statements affect you?
    c. You need to tell him/her that the date is over and that you will not waste one more minute of your time with such a screwed-up person?
    d. You should feel sorry for him/her because s/he had such a terrible childhood, and try to help him/her as much as you can?

5. As you are eating, you begin to realize that s/he is drinking the alcoholic beverage, rapidly and that by the time your appetizers have come, s/he has already had two drinks and is starting on a third. You:
    a. See this as a red flag, telling yourself that anyone who would drink this much on the first date will probably drink even more on any other date.
    b. Notice that s/he is drinking a lot, decide this must be the plan for tonight and join him/her in drinking.
    c. Tell him/her that s/he must be an alcoholic and you will have nothing to do with him/her after this, hailing a taxi home?
    d. Pretend nothing is happening.

6. When you near home that night, s/he makes several comments about coming up to your room, getting more and more manipulative and/or insistent each time. You:
    a. Ignore his/her comments entirely as they make you extremely uncomfortable, and hope that s/he will just go away when the time comes.
    b. Tell him/her that you really do mean it when you say that you would like to spend some time getting to know him/her and therefore, s/he will not be coming in.
    c. As s/he continues to insist, you say, "It seems pretty clear what you want tonight, but I need to let you know that your insistence is making me very uncomfortable and I would like for you to stop."

d. As s/he continues to insist, you give in.

7. Your date is over. The next day s/he calls several times wanting to stay on the phone for long periods of time, finally asking to see you again tonight. You feel very uncomfortable with this, feeling that it is moving way too fast. You:

a. Talk to him/her the first time, but check the caller-ID and refuse to answer the phone again after that, dreading your next interaction with him/her.

b. Feel that this means that s/he is really very attracted to you and that even though you are uncomfortable, you should talk to him/her and allow him/her to come over that night.

c. Tell him/her in no uncertain terms that you need for this to go slowly and that you have plans for today and tonight.

d. Feel quite conflicted since you feel that s/he must need you, but you have things to do and feel uncomfortable with the whole situation. Still it is not nice to.... So, you just talk to him/her and let him/her come over tonight.

8. It is your third date. Everything has been going well until s/he tells you that s/he is still very confused about his/her feelings about an ex-lover. You:

a. Tell him/her that you'd like to continue your relationship as friends, but that you are unwilling to date him/her if s/he is still having feelings for someone else.

b. Be very understanding and sensitive to his/her needs, as you continue to date him/her knowing that if you are sensitive and patient you will win him/her over.

c. Recognize that since this is only the third date and there is no commitment, s/he is free to discuss whatever. You tell him/her that you appreciate his/her honesty and you are willing to listen anytime, but that this also means that you definitely need to take it slow.

d. Begin to tease him/her sexually, feeling that if s/he just makes love to you, you'll win him/her over.

9. After you have been dating for some time, s/he calls you to tell you that s/he would like to bring his/her ex-lover, who is in town visiting, on the

next date with you. You agree since s/he has told you that they are just good friends now, but at the dinner that night you begin to notice that they are obviously flirting with each other. You:

 a. Find a way to talk to the ex alone, telling him/her "Keep your hands off!"

 b. Interrupt their flirtations with, "Well, it seems that you guys can handle this date by yourselves!" and walk out feeling rejected, belittled and ashamed.

 c. Find a way to get alone with your date and say, "You know, I'm getting really uncomfortable here. It seems that the two of you are still interested in each other and I'd really like to go home now."

 d. Ignore it. Of course they are going to flirt, they used to be lovers. As soon as s/he is gone, you'll have him/her all to yourself again.

10. After you have dated 6 or 7 times, you are having a deep discussion with your date. S/he tells you that in his/her previous relationships there have been several physical fights in which s/he hit the partner. You:

 a. Tell him/her that you understand because you have had that same problem.

 b. Tell him/her, "Well, of course you hit him/her, look how s/he was acting!"

 c. Tell him/her in no uncertain terms that you do not believe that physical fights are ever necessary or acceptable in a relationship and you in no way tolerate anything that even looks like its moving toward physicality. Therefore, given his/her history, you will not date him/her again.

 d. Tell yourself, it's okay, s/he would never treat *you* that way.

Scoring:
1. a=0, b=0, c=4, d=4

2. a=0, b=0, c=4, d=0

3. a=0, b=1, c=4, d=0

4. a=2, b=4, c=1, d=0

5. a=4, b=0, c=2, d=0

6. a=0, b=4, c=4, 4=0

7. a=3, b=0, c=4, d=2

8. a=2, b=0, c=4, d=0

9. a=1, b=2, c=4, d=0

10. a=0, b=0, c=4, d=0.

> If you scored 36 to 40 you were very authentic on this quiz. This means that you prob-
> ably know how to be authentic on a date. It doesn't mean you always are authentic,
> just that you know how to be. If you scored between 15 and 36, you may need to work
> hard on authenticity in dating. However, you are somewhat aware of your feelings in
> this regard, even if sometimes you react instead of respond. Becoming aware of your
> feelings is the first step. If you scored between 0 and 15, you really need to work in this
> area. You may be likely to put yourself in harm's way, either emotionally or physically,
> maybe even sexually.

If you noticed, the answers that scored with zeros often used the word "ignore,"
or imply that you are ignoring what is going on. Ignoring your own feelings
and needs is asking for trouble in the dating world. The answers that scored 1,
2 or 3, at least showed some awareness of feelings. Perhaps there was a reactive,
rather than a proactive, response; some were aggressive or used poor problem
solving, but you were at least aware. The answers that scored 4, were the most
likely authentic responses given the situation and the set up feeling about it.

    If it turns out that you scored low on this test, don't be alarmed. Dating is
one of those areas in which we were taught a lot of "stuff" that just isn't true.
The old "play hard to get" adage, is just as false as the new, "Lay 'em and own
'em" adage. What no one bothered to teach us about attracting a partner is that
the more authentic we are the more potential we have of attracting an authentic partner. Go back and re-work the chapter on barriers to authenticity only
this time, work it as if you were working on yourself in terms of how you
relate.

    As a therapist, I very often hear the question, "Well, if I start living authen-
tically, will there be anyone else out there that I can relate to?" The answer is
that real attracts real. The answer also is that role attracts role. It is, indeed, a

very interesting phenomenon, this whole business of attraction. We are only now beginning to understand how much of attraction comes from the subtle undercurrents flying through the air around us. How we send out these undercurrents that others pick up on and respond to is somewhat of a mystery still. But that we do, in fact, send out these undercurrents as message is obvious, if for no other scientific reason than the fact that we've managed to attract the same kinds of people over and over without knowing how or why. For example, if I am living the Victim role, I am sending out subtle messages that tell people this. They, in turn are picking up that message and sending me a message back. This is rarely done in an actual discussion, but certainly, as we can tell from the quiz above, there are many verbal cues given out, which if we are paying attention, can be read and renounced or handled.

The truth is that if I am living authentically, I will not, after a while, find myself attracted to persons who cannot offer me some degree of authenticity. Persons who are living a role will begin to be less and less attractive as we are more and more quickly able to spot them. Further, while we are attracting more authentic people, we are repelling people who play old roles. Those who play the old roles are not attracted to authenticity; they are attracted to their counter-role. And the beautiful part about it is that when we are living authentically, we may not even have to go looking for a partner. We may find that as we are just going through our days, we attract, both as friends and lovers, persons who are very attracted to real. And as we find that these persons are attracted to us, we have all the time in the world to find out more and more about them.

To be sure, many persons on the journey to authenticity, as we shall see below, have to go through a period, usually not terribly long in duration, in which they find that the persons with whom they had previously formed friendships and even primary relationships aren't working the way they used to. What is happening is that we've begun to step on each other's toes in the dance, because one of us has changed his/her step. At this point adjustments will need to be made in the relationships and/or decisions made which relinquish these relationships. This period may seem a little dark and discouraging. But we may know with certainty that on the other side of such a period is the option of seeking and finding new more valid and authentic relationships or living in much improved old relationships. At this point it is a good idea to begin making a long list of what kinds of things you want in an authentic relationship or partner. You will need to work this list and rework it as you are experiencing more and more of the Authentic Self. This list is useful as a reminder not to settle for less.

Okay, now suppose you are already in a relationship with someone. What do you do? How do you authenticate a relationship that started out as an attraction between two roles? Do you remember the family roles illustration we did, in which we said, if one member of the family jumps off the ruler, the ruler tilts and all the people left on the ruler start bumping into each other? (Fig. 11) This bumping around becomes very uncomfortable. And, because of this discomfort, it gives everyone else on the ruler the same opportunity you have had, the opportunity to become authentic. Of course, as we said, before they get around to this, they may, at first, try to get you to get back up on the ruler. But if you continue being authentic, out of their own discomfort they are presented a choice: Get real, or find someone else to fill the role.

That's the way it works. If you are in a relationship, you are not obligated to finish the relationship out as the role. Relationships are meant to evolve and grow. They are not meant to form an alliance and thereby become stagnant. A relationship that can survive your authenticity is a relationship worth keeping. A relationship that cannot survive your authenticity is a relationship that will pull you backward into misery instead of helping you move forward into joy. YOU have the first choice. You can choose to become authentic in every area of your life but this one. You may choose not to become authentic at all. Or, you may choose to become authentic in all the areas of your life. We already know the consequences of choosing to remain in the role, and now that we've had a taste of being authentic, it becomes harder and harder to maintain the role. It should also be noted that the consequences for choosing one area of our lives in which we will maintain the role is that this eventually becomes impossible. We will either block out authenticity in several ways, not just the one, or we will find that the one area in which we have chosen to maintain the role becomes more and more dissatisfying.

It is a risk to become authentic in relationships. It is possible that you will see that your partner has no intention of relating to you authentically. However, the truth is that it is more of a risk to stay stuck in the role. Still, the choice is absolutely yours. If you chose to become authentic in relationships it means looking squarely at the ways in which *you* are playing the role in the relationship. That means getting really honest about something we have already referenced, called "secondary gain."

When we dance the dance we have danced as the role, we do so, in relationship, because there is some gain in it for us. This gain is often one of the main reasons we put on the role in the first place and then often, the reason why we got into the relationship we are in. For example: The Party Dude(tte) may choose to marry the Superwoman because this is how s/he manages to avoid responsibility. The deal is, then, that if I stop being Party Dude(tte) no one will take care of me anymore and I'll have to start taking care of myself. That will probably feel like a loss. And it will probably be, at first, quite frightening. That's just one scenario, let's try a few. If you are willing to be brave enough to look at this closely, it may change your life.

Below, fill in the chart with your secondary gains: What are your secondary gains in continuing to relate from the role? If you are someone who has used a *dual role*, such as Victim/Perpetrator, be sure to fill out the secondary gain for each role.

Role:	Secondary Gain:
Runaway	
Scapegoat/Black Sheep	
Scapegoat/Priest	
Party Dude(tte)	
Victim	
Superwoman	
Superhero	
Bully/Perpetrator	

Okay, now that we know the secondary gains we have been looking for in continuing to relate from the role, we can address these secondary gains as real needs and attempt to meet them in legitimate ways. For example: Suppose that my Scapegoat/Priest role serves me well by offering me a secondary gain of a sense of goodness, rightness, or being okay. Well, then I can work and re-work the section on the good/evil complex to get a feel for my particular complex. Once I have done this, I can begin to seek out authentic methods, conscious authentic methods of doing things that make me "feel good." Or, suppose I have a need for attention. Well then I can find direct ways of getting attention consciously. I can ask for hugs from my spouse, I can take up acting to get applause, etc. This is called re-working. We are re-working secondary gain by turning it into primary gain. No more secrets. I want this thing, and I will find a way to get it directly.

In the chart below, re-work your secondary gains.

Secondary Gain:	Re-working:

As we work with our own secondary gains, we begin to change our patterns of behavior. Whereas, once as the Runaway you might have told your partner,

"Oh, get over it!" for the secondary gain of mastery over your own vulnerabilities; now you might say, "This scares me, but I'm willing to hear your pain." This happens because you are now willing to seek safety for your vulnerabilities. You acknowledged your fears and your beliefs that, in some cases, may have set up these fears, and you took responsibility for devising plans to make yourself feel safer. Then, because now you are meeting your own needs in some very clear ways, you are not so dependent on your partner to help you dance the dance that gets you the secondary gain.

All of that said and done, we still must understand that there is another person in this picture, with a will of his/her own. The skills that we are learning don't "work," in the sense that once you learn them, suddenly your partner changes his/her patterns as well. These skills "work" in that they help us to get in touch with and begin to rely upon the Authentic Self. Everything comes under that heading. Therefore, we must know that our partners may like being Superheroes, or rescuers, for example, so much that when we no longer need rescuing, they may also experience a loss and want us to be the Victim again, or refuse to see that we are not the Victim anymore. Or, they may decide with us that this Superhero role is not working for them anymore either. *The absolute truth here is that our partners have all the same options we do.* Therefore, they may opt to not engage the Authentic Self at all. They may opt to stay stuck in their roles. They may even opt to find someone else who will fill the role better than you are doing, now that you are becoming authentic.

In other words, we have to know that, when we start into this authenticity stuff in our relationships, we may offer healing to the relationship, but we may also lose it. But as we've said, the relationships that can hold together through authentic change are the valid relationships. *The ones that can not were never authentically valid anyway, at least not for the long-haul.* Remember again, that this book offers a life-changing experience. Growth is always a risk. Some things may change a little, others may change entirely. Nevertheless, I assert to you today, that *living authentically offers more joy in a single day than living the role can offer in a lifetime.* The choice, however, is always yours.

Okay, so how does one begin to discuss these things with a partner? Well, we begin with the truth. The fairest thing that we can do with our significant others is to tell them, that we are changing and growing in certain specific ways, which may mean that we will start responding to them differently. One very effective way of setting this up is to design a special appointed time to talk, by saying something like, "I have some very important things to talk with you about, I wonder if we could talk tomorrow night after dinner?"

Another very important feature of these conversations is the classic "I" statement. Your only job in these conversations is to inform of *your* new way of looking at *your* own life, and *your* new way of behaving. So often, we get into these conversations with an agenda. We will tell ourselves that we want to tell them how we are changing, but in reality, what we are really doing is telling them to change. But in this example, all you are doing is informing of *your own* changes:

> I wanted to talk to you about this because the changes I'm making, and will continue to make, will have an impact on you. As you know, I've been working on being more authentic or real and in doing so I've begun to realize that I've been playing a very specific role with you. My role has been the Superwoman role. That means I take on loads and loads of responsibility for things that really need to be handled by others. This has had an effect on me over the years in the following ways.... I think it has also affected our relationship in these ways.... Therefore, in order for me to keep working on myself, I've decided that from now on I'll be responding differently, in order to be more authentic. I know about some specific situations to which I'll be responding differently, and I'll tell you those in a minute, but first I want to tell you that this may not be easy for you. You may even be uncomfortable with it at first, but I hope that you can adjust with me, because I love you and our relationship is very important to me. I want you to know that I believe that if you join me in this, our relationship will be much healthier and more satisfying to both of us. It is important that you know that I'm very clear on this and will not, if I am conscious of it, return to playing the role anymore. But I am willing to talk to you, anytime you need to, about how these things are affecting you. Specifically, I am already aware that I will be changing how I respond to you when....

What you have done with this example is inform that changes are coming, that they are inevitable and irreversible, and that you intend to work with your partner in adjusting to these changes, because of your love for him/her and your respect for your relationship. Now, your partner has a heads-up that this is going to happen. S/he may not like it, and may not even be willing to really take you seriously, but there it is. It is important to note here, however, that your partner may be very relieved to know what the problem is and how to solve it, and may, therefore, be very willing to adjust and adapt. This too, may be frightening, but again the risk has a reward. In any case, now, when you actually do respond as you said you would, s/he will not be surprised, thinking, "What is going on here?" This is as fair as it gets.

Now the hard part comes. Now, you must respond as you said you would. So, let's suppose that this Superwoman is talking to her Victim/Party Dude husband. It is important to note at this point that this does not have to be a husband/wife scenario, it could be any primary relationship. It is also important to be reminded that the partner, who ever it is, may have been sitting on ready for quite some time to make changes and just didn't know how, so is quite ready to join you. However, just so that we can learn how to deal with the hard stuff, we've chosen a hard example. The wife has already had the above talk with her husband, including the specific that he can no longer assume that she will be available to take him to work without some advance notice. Now the first opportunity to make good on it arises. He begins telling her that he can't get to work on his own because he's just too shaky to drive. He's been up again all night, he says, working on the project for the boss (though she knows he's really been drinking and gambling online) and he's really tired. He needs her to take him again, he says. She gulps hard, knowing that this is one of those things that she's been doing for him that he must do for himself. She says, "This is one of those times when, as hard as it is for me to say it, I must tell you 'no.' I'm not sure what you'll do, and this is also hard for me, but I'm going to have to leave it to you to work out."

Notice, if you will, how this ex-Superwoman, includes her honest statements about her concern for him while she is asserting that she will not be available to assist him in this. This is one way of letting people you care about know that though you are changing what you will do, this doesn't mean that you no longer care. She has also relayed her own concern for herself that she knows that she may worry about him once she says "no." Nevertheless, she sticks to her guns. However, we must also remember that this man may now be quite angry. He's done this same thing hundreds of times, and he's always counted on her to take care of it for him. It is true that, since she has already informed him that things like this would be changing, he could have gone to her the night before and asked, "If I stay up again all night, will you be able to take me to work in the morning?" But he didn't. He made the assumption that she would do this, without his asking (a fairly typical assumption for those associated with Superwomen). The assumption, "Oh, Superwoman, (or Superhero) will handle it," is very common.

Before, we go to how she can handle him and his responses, let's look at this: How does she know that this is something she no longer wishes to do for her husband? She listens to her own feelings about it. A long time ago, when she first started considering the changes she wanted to make, she began to look inside her self to see how she felt about this. Now, when he says his spiel about her taking him, she looks inside again. There's that grinding feeling in her chest again, like this sense of impending crunch. There are thoughts of, "Well then how will I get to the things I need to do?" There's anger. There's resentment. There's a feeling of being used. Any or all of these will do to tell her that this is definitely not an authentic task.

It is important that we understand how she came to know that this was not authentic for her, because when he presses her to change her mind, she will have an awareness of exactly why it is that this behavior does not work for her. So, okay, let's say that he is very angry and uses his anger to attempt to manipulate her into changing her mind. He may say, "How can you say that? You know I've been up all night!" Or, "Don't act like you care about me while you are showing me you don't!" Or, "Is this one of those things your new guru taught you to do?" Or, he may even go for the below the belt punch: "Okay, I just won't go to work today. They'll probably fire me because I don't have the project in there for the meeting today, but, hey, that's okay, you'll still be working, right?" (Notice how quickly the Victim has now become the Bully through manipulations that come to the edge of emotional abuse, even crossing the line with the below the belt punch.)

Any and all of these responses are designed with unconscious or conscious intent to get the Authentic Self out of the way and to put Superwoman back into the relationship. Why? Because Superwoman is familiar. We already know how this familiarity works internally to pull *us* back in, or send us back home. Well, it works the same way for those to whom we are related. This man may feel as if the rug has just been pulled out from under him. It's frightening to suddenly be cast into a new role with little to no assistance as to how to respond. If we keep this in mind while we are thinking of our next response we might come across with a little more compassion and actually manage to work through it. But it is often quite difficult for us to think in these intense moments of what to say next. Therefore, we often lapse back into the role, giving in, or arguing to justify our stance, or trying to "fix it" for them by teaching or cajoling. That is why planning in advance how you might respond in these cases is so helpful. The more you "rehearse," either on paper or just by playing out the scenarios in your mind, the more you will be ready for whatever gets thrown at you. Several things are important to remember.

- Make "I" statements (i.e., "I need," "I have decided," "I'm uncomfortable with," "I'm unwilling to," "I'm willing to," etc.) Any time you lapse into "You statements (i.e., "you are just trying to," "you are so selfish," "you always think you have to have your way," "you are just trying to get me to play the role again," etc.) *you* are trying to justify, placate, teach, accuse or cajole your partner. This simply throws you back into the role.

- Avoid anything that smacks of "fixing it."
- Remember what made you make this decision in the first place.
- Remember to honor yourself and your own feelings.
- Allow the other person to have feelings and reactions of their own without trying to talk them out of these feelings or fix it for them by giving in.

"Fixing it" for others is a form of vicariously fixing it for ourselves. I'll make you feel better so that I don't feel so uncomfortable. In the midst of these difficult communications, it is very easy for us to assume the needs of the other person, simply so that we no longer feel uncomfortable. "Okay, okay, I'll do it," is the most obvious example of this, but it comes in other forms as well. Trying to teach them how they should respond is one such way of fixing it. Trying to tell them how they should be feeling is another. One such comment that I heard, which I thought was so ingenious, was "You should be grateful that I'm working so hard on our relationship. It's sure more than you've ever done!" Well, that all may be true, but what a great Superhero come-back, with tinges of the martyr thrown in for good measure. We do not solve anything by slipping back into the role. We simply repeat the same old pattern. *It is a test of our willingness to stay focused on the Authentic Self, to stay out of our partner's business.* Our partners' responses, even if ungrounded, frightened, uncertain and manipulative are entirely up to them. Giving them the right to their own responses, allows them the necessary room they need to grow.

Below we will make a plan for your responses in the heated

moments: Try to get very clear on exactly what the scenario is, what you need and how you will state your need. (You may go back and work and re-work this page as many times as is needed.)

Scenario #1:

_____
_____
_____
_____.

When s/he says:

_____
_____.

My Authentic Self will say:

_____
_____.

Scenario #2:

_____
_____
_____
_____.

When s/he says:

_____
_____.

My Authentic Self will say:

_____
_____.

Scenario #3:

_____
_____
_____
_____.

When s/he says:

_____
_____.

My Authentic Self will say:

_____

_____.

Scenario #4:

_____

_____

_____

_____.

When s/he says:

_____

_____.

My Authentic Self will say:

_____

_____.

Scenario # 5:

_____

_____

_____

_____.

When s/he says:

_____

_____.

My Authentic Self will say:

_____

_____.

Ponderings: There's one other thing that should be added. We all, sometimes, act like three year olds. And sometimes our partners will do this to us. When they hear us saying, "No, I'm not going to do it the way I've always done it," they may attack us with a whole barrage of manipulations. You may see them jump from "You're guilty, how can you do this to me?" to, "I'm guilty and pitiful, won't you please take care of me." If this is happening, you can choose to launch into something called the "broken record technique." Based on the story above, of Superwoman taking her husband to work, it could go something like this: (M stands for manipulative statement, R, for the response)

> M: "You are unbelievable! How can you leave me stranded like this?"
> R: "I know this is hard for you. We're both adjusting to this new way. I'm going to let go and let you find a way to work this out for yourself."
> M: "You've always done this for me, how can you pull out now, just when I need you the most."
> R: "I know this is hard for you. We're both adjusting to this new way. I'm going to let go and let you find a way to work this out for yourself."
> M: Don't ever say you love me again. You could not love me and do a thing like this."
> R: "I know this is hard for you. We're both adjusting to this new way. I'm going to let go and let you find a way to work this out for yourself."
> M: "Listen to you, you sound like a damn robot! Can't you see how unfair you are being?"
> R: (Silence).
> M: "Okay, fine. You just wait till you need me sometime. I'm gonna pull this crap on you, too."
> R: "I know this is hard for you. We're both adjusting to this new way. I'm going to let go and let you find a way to work this out for yourself."
> M: "I can't believe you are doing this. Okay, here's the deal, I just won't go into work today. I'm sure that Phil will fire me, but I just can't drive."
> R: "I know this is hard for you. We're both adjusting to this new way. I'm going to let go and let you find a way to work this out for yourself."

You get the picture. Basically, what you are doing is staying calm and focused. You are not biting, when s/he throws in the baited hook. It's a clear way of staying focused on the Authentic Self regardless of the manipulations going on around you. Now depending on the person you are dealing with, their responses to this can be anything from eventually finding a way to get themselves to work, to literally "upping the ante" by staying home that day. If you are with someone who will continue to up the ante at each juncture in which you are trying to assert your authenticity, it may be time to reconsider the value of this relationship. People who do this are saboteurs. They have no intention of joining you in making your relationship more real. Until and unless they are willing to join you in making your relationship real, your relationship will not improve. You may still become authentic, by speaking and acting your truth in relationship, but the path will be covered with booby-traps. If you choose to stay in this relationship, you will need to be very aware of the booby-traps, and become quite skilled in dealing with them, if you are to become authentic, in-spite of your saboteur partner. Therefore, you may need to work and re-work, and re-work the above response plan in order to stay focused.

It is also possible that your primary relationship is abusive. Often manipulations take the form of verbal, mental, or emotional abuse. If this is true, and you can look back to Chapter Two, Defining the Role, for definitions of the various forms of abuse, then you may have to make very clear boundaries. NOTE: At this juncture we are speaking only of verbal, mental or emotional abuse. We will speak to physical and sexual abuse momentarily. If you are being _verbally, mentally or emotionally abused_, it is very important that you begin today to take care of yourself by honoring your own authenticity. Here's an example of one possible way to begin talking to your partner about this: (Note that before you start such a statement, you should have his/her undivided attention, and s/he should agree not to interrupt. If the partner cannot agree to avoid interrupting, perhaps you two should have this talk with a therapist present).

> You know that I've been working really hard on becoming more real, so I really need to talk with you about some things that are very difficult for me. In the process of this work I'm doing on myself, I've come to understand that certain things that you are doing (or "I am doing," if you have been living the Bully/Perpetrator role) are abusive. I'm going to tell you what I mean by this in a minute, but first, before I go any further, I need to let you know that these things are no longer going to be acceptable to me. I'm going to work very hard to have peace in my life, and I will do whatever I have to do to get that.
>
> Here are the things that I have learned are abusive. When you (or I) say … these things are abusive and I need to let you know that I can no longer accept this behavior on your (my) part. I am willing to go to therapy with you, in order for us to unlearn these behaviors together, but I am not willing to allow abuse to continue in this relationship. I want you to know that when it happens I will call it "abuse" and I will make certain

very definite decisions to take care of myself, even up to leaving you, if it continues. Further, I am fairly certain that you and I will not be able to work through this without some professional help, so I guess I'm letting you know that if you are unwilling to go to therapy with me, I'm going to assume that you are not willing to put much effort into this and whatever you try will ultimately fail. In that event, I will be forced to leave you. That is not what I want. I want this relationship to work. But it cannot go on this way. Some changes will have to be made.

Notice that the statement: 1) includes a recognition of the work you are doing, 2) clarifies exactly what you are calling abuse and 3) declares that these behaviors are no longer acceptable. It is a very clear statement of change. Therefore, however you word this statement, it should contain these three ingredients. I am making very definitive statements about this, with some clear boundaries attached, because, just to put it bluntly, there is really no way to stay authentic while you are tolerating mental, verbal and emotional abuse. *To tolerate abuse is to betray the Authentic Self.* There is simply no way around it. You may be trying to decide *if* you will live authentically while you are tolerating abuse, but you cannot live authentically and tolerate abuse at the same time.

As to physical or sexual abuse, the first order of business, if you are going to live authentically, is to create a safe place for yourself. Denial is not a safe place. Denial is often the first line of defense for us when we find that we have landed in a physically or sexually abusive relationship as adults. And the first words of the denial package are usually, "but I love him/her." This is definitely a case where love is not enough. You may count on this: *If your partner has hurt you in an aggressive outburst, s/he will hurt you again and each time that s/he does it will be worse by degree than the last time s/he did it.* Yes, s/he will go through cycles in which there is no abuse, even times when it seems very romantic and idyllic. Still, the abuse will return, each time worse than the last, until eventually your life is in danger. See the Assault Cycle discussed in Chapter Two, Defining the Role.

If you are being sexually abused in a relationship, it also will get worse over time, and may also begin to include physical abuse, or physical abuse may begin to include sexual abuse. In either case the abuse worsens, rather than lessens. The problem for most of us, in staying in these relationships is that we tell ourselves it will get better over time. We do this for so long, that by the time that we realize that it won't ever get better, in fact it will get worse, it is too late; we are so trapped that death is often imminent.

The best-case scenario for these situations is to get out of the relationship at the first hint that it will become abusive. Many of us skip right over that scenario, so the next best is to get out early, before the assault cycle has reached the deadly stage. Many can go live temporarily with family at this stage. But, since many of us skip over this one as well, the final best scenario is to slip out to a safe-house right now. Be sure it is a safe time to leave without getting hurt, take the clothes on your back, your children, this book *AND GO!*

Now, I want to hasten to say that if you have remained in an abusive situation this does not make you a "sick masochistic" person. It simply means that you have played out the Victim role to its bitter end. It is all you ever knew. What else would you have done? Nevertheless, it is not too late. You can leave today!

I'll never forget how disappointed I felt, during the O.J. Simpson trials, at the number of articles I saw that said, "Why didn't she leave!" I saw not one article written during that time that said, "Why don't abusers stop abusing!" This is such an interesting and damning philosophy, which is still running rampant through our society. We so often still believe that a woman is responsible for a man's behavior, or that the abused is somehow responsible for the abuser's behavior.

This whole philosophy started out in the heterosexual, patriarchal world, in which the man was considered to be a helpless Victim of his libido, and should not be held accountable for its ramblings. If a woman was dressed in less than total body covering, she was being seductive and should, therefore, be held accountable for the man's behavior if he raped her, or otherwise molested her. This may be why, in the 16th and 17th centuries, men wore tight pants that showed off their genitals, and women wore long dresses that covered their ankles, and high collars that didn't even allow a view of the neck. In spite of the sexual revolution of the last century, we still hold, unconsciously and sometimes quite consciously, to this philosophy.

Therefore, we still have a pervasive belief that if the husband cheats, it's because the wife wasn't good in bed. This is even true in the gay and lesbian relationships that I have treated in therapy. They often believe that if their partner cheats, they must not be good enough in bed or that they are somehow missing something that someone else can give their partner. We often blame the "other woman" (whether it is really a literal woman or not) rather than looking our partner's square in the face and saying, "Why did you choose an affair instead of honest communication with me?" Even if the honest communication says, "I don't love you anymore," still it offers a clean ending without betrayal.

Likewise, we still often hold to the arcane belief that if a woman is raped it is because she was out too late, or dressed too scantily. I can't even number the clients who have come into therapy with me, who tell me that they cannot tell their husbands, or even their gay lovers that they were raped, because they will be perceived as somehow having asked for it. They fear that their partners will be angry with *them* instead of angry with the perpetrator.

In that same way, we have consciously or unconsciously held to the belief that if someone is abused, they have somehow asked for it. And the abusers are more than happy to support that belief, by saying things like, "if s/he hadn't provoked me I wouldn't have had to hit him/her." Many people even still believe in the "masochism" theory, that people who are abused enjoy it. Again, this has its origins in the old belief that the man could hold his wife as property, so of course, he could not be blamed for abusing her. Still, we should know that in passing this idea along, we are giving the Bully/Perpetrator an excuse to keep abusing.

We have translated that philosophy into all manner of relationships regardless of sexual orientation or gender. But it simply is not true. If a man abuses a woman it is because he has unresolved issues of his own. And in those more rare incidences when a woman abuses a man, it is still because she has unresolved issues of her own. If a woman abuses a woman it is because she has unresolved issues of her own. If a man abuses a man it is because he has unresolved issues of his own. People who bully or perpetrate, especially in a pattern, are living out of the Bully/Perpetrator identity. The Bully/Perpetrator identity is based on fear and shame. I fear that I am so unworthy of love that I must force people to love me by scaring them into staying. Further, I fear being abused, therefore, I must abuse first. *None of this, absolutely none of this, has its origin in the abused.* My soapbox on this has always been and will always be: When we start putting our money into specific and effective treatment for abusers, which addresses the Bully/Perpetrator identity, we will no longer have to put it into safe-houses, or treatment for the abused. And we will no longer ask, "Why did she stay?"

Whatever else being authentic is to you, it cannot possibly tolerate abuse. Therefore, the decision for those of you who are currently in abusive situations, be it mental, emotional, verbal, physical or sexual abuse, is "Will I take the risk to live authentically, or will I stay in this abusive situation?"

We said earlier that we would talk in-depth about the other three myths of relationship:

- You have to compromise.
- You have to sacrifice.
- Love is all you need.

The problem with the first two is that we think that the terms compromise and sacrifice are synonymous. They are not. When I ask people what they mean when they use the term compromise, they will often say: It means I give up something and s/he gives up something and we're both feeling more loved. Let me sum up my response to that in one word: NOT! Compromise is not giving up anything. Compromise is recognition of the rights of others to choose according to their own needs, wants, desires, perceptions, etc. Compromise simply says: I'm going to be me, so you be you and we'll see what happens.

While it is true that sometimes in a primary relationship, partners may agree that tonight we'll go to the restaurant I like and next week we'll go to the one you like, what we are talking about here is restaurants not personalities and basic human need. When our parents taught us that we'd have to compromise, what they often meant was you give up everything for relationship. And that lesson learned must be unlearned later in life when we've gotten the second divorce because we kept giving up everything for relationship.

The challenge in relationship is to stay in the authentic self while we relate to another human being. We have, for so many centuries believed in all the old wives' tales and the old arcane archetypes of giving up the self for relationship, that we somehow feel that we are betraying society or all the old wives, or something, in order to become authentic. But the truth is, that unless we are in authentic relationships *we* are not in relationship. If all you are relating to, when you relate to me, is my role, then you have no idea of who I really am. So how can you be in relationship with *me*. You may love my role, but do you even know me?

We've already spoken of sacrifice and the meaninglessness of that endeavor. Remember 1st Corinthians 13? Sacrifice is not love. Love is not sacrifice. But somehow we've gotten those terms very confused. When we sacrifice it is really a game. It says I'll give you mine if you'll give me yours. Therefore, we use the word sacrifice, when what we really mean is trade. I'll trade you mine for yours. Then when the other person doesn't give what we thought they were going to give for the trade, we are very hurt and say this means that they don't love us. Further, all of this transaction takes place non-verbally. We may show our partners that we are giving up something we want for them, but we don't make an open trade. We just assume that if we've sacrificed for them then they will sacrifice for us. This is a mental game. Again, sacrifice has nothing to do with love. We can give it all away, and it still may mean nothing if our giving isn't from love.

When we give from love, we love doing it. We are excited about the gift and our passion for giving it. This is not sacrifice. This is not a weary sigh that gives up on something real inside. This is not an expectation for repayment. This is a simple gift with no strings attached. If we could ever take the word sacrifice out of the context of relationships, we would have already moved relationships to a higher plane just by that one act. But we were taught to sacrifice by well-intended but misguided generations before us, who, if we are honest, knew very little about the love that can last a lifetime in a primary relationship. Instead they knew about security, and all the machinations and manipulations necessary to arranging that security. Up until the mid-to-late-1800's most of us were pledged to marry by our parents or married someone because of their money, their farm, their teeth, or some other security issue. We carried that archetype with us into the 20th century and many of us are still living it out in metaphor even into the 21st century. And in some countries it is still the cultural expectation. We must stop listening to these misguided teachers of previous generations and start listening to the Authentic Self if we intend to heal relationships.

Therefore, when people raised in generations past teach us that we need to compromise in relationship and sacrifice for relationship, what they are really saying is, you have to trade off. You have to give up your pound of flesh in order to have the security you need. You have to give up pieces of your soul to have a relationship. Don't let your partner really know who you are. Just keep playing the game; just keep wearing the mask. These same people are now up in arms because marriage is being "threatened" by gays and lesbians. They are also up in arms because of the "alarming" divorce rate.

There has never been an authentic evolution that didn't also create some upheaval. We are now, for the first time in the history of the world, beginning to come to terms with a true concept of what relationship is all about. At least we are asking the right questions and in some cases, we are getting the answers. Here are some of the questions that we, as a collective are asking in earnest:

- What is intimacy?
- What is true commitment?
- How does one open up to the potentialities of long-term love?
- How does one shore-up a floundering relationship?
- What is true and what is false with regard to the mythology surrounding relationship?
- How does one distinguish between love and need; love and fear of loneliness; love and sexual arousal; love and security; love and power; love and control; love and jealousy?

These questions require us to look inside. That is something that down through the generations, we have not been so comfortable doing. How does one, in a relationship in which intimacy holds no promise of existence, answer the first question? Ultimately, one may have to leave that relationship and work on another in order to answer that question. But our evolution requires that we answer that question. And so we go through the necessary upheaval to get our answer. This is true on the collective level as well, ergo, our current high divorce rate. And so, while the righteous nay-sayers take their stand for the status quo, the world evolves anyway. And so it goes.

For those of us seeking authenticity, the answers do not lie in the status quo, nor do they lie in what others think. They can only be found within us. And though the journey may be difficult, the prize to be won is worth it.

Love is not all we need, but love is an authentic connection between my authentic self and another's. When I genuinely love someone I enjoy their company immensely. I choose to be with them often and when I am in their company I am uplifted. I support their authenticity in whatever form it takes and do not wish to change them. I give to them often and freely because my love for them urges me to do so, not because if I don't they will go away, or if I do they'll know I've sacrificed or compromised. We cannot compromise the Self in an authentic relationship, nor can we sacrifice it. When two authentic people are authentically in love, they respect each person's right to be whomever and whatever they are. If then they are to establish a committed long-term relationship, it will have to also include the ingredient of compatibility.

Compatibility means that 90% of what you do is not only tolerated by me, but appreciated by me and vice versa. The other 10% may include the faults you have that irritate me, but they only mildly irritate me, and I may even be able to overlook them entirely. Compatibility means that you are not mystified by my actions and beliefs. Compatibility means that we truly understand and can, without reservation, support each other. Compatibility does not mean that we agree on everything, but that there is an easy flow of understanding between us. I see clients everyday in couples therapy, who are trying and trying and trying to "make it work" between them. They are incompatible people trying to force each other to change so that they can become more compatible. It is simply not going to work. But because they love each other, they think that this gives them license to rail at each other to change so that they can create compatibility where there is none. What a strange arrangement this relationship is!

Compatibility is much more than whether or not we are good for each other in bed, though many have reduced it to just that. In fact, sexual intimacy is something you will teach each other if you are otherwise compatible. Nor does compatibility mean that you share the same religion, though many have also reduced it to that. Compatibility means that you share the same core values. Core values have not so much to do with religion as they have to do with definition and ethics. For example, it is quite common for me to see a couple in therapy who do not share the same definition of relationship. To one, for example, relationship means that the partner is supposed to take care of them in every way, that they are to be joined at the hip and, further, that the partner is just resisting this. To the other, relationship means a strong connection with someone with whom one wants to live and share a life. To this person the partner is possessive and demanding and will not see it any other way. This couple is not compatible because they define relationship entirely differently. Unless they can get on the same page, this relationship will not ever be effective. With regard to ethics, if one partner loves to kick the dog and the other finds this behavior reprehensible, there are going to be problems in this dynamic.

We must have more than love. We must have compatibility. Basically what we are saying about compatibility here is this. *Everyone has faults, but in a long-term, healthy, committed, authentic relationship, both parties have selected persons whose faults are pretty easy to deal with, and which, in fact, they may find somewhat endearing.* Go back and read that sentence again. You see, the reason most of us do not select people with whom we are compatible is because we do not believe that sentence at all. We do not believe that it is really possible to find someone whose faults do not drive us wild with rage sometimes. The real truth is that we do not believe that we deserve such a wonderful arrangement. But I am hereby declaring: Those relationships that really work over the long haul are those in which the above re-read sentence is true.

Compatibility does not mean tolerating the intolerable very well. Nor does it mean doing a really good job of accepting the unacceptable in relationship. It means that I get to select a partner with whom I can pretty easily get along without much friction and really enjoy his/her company most of the time. That means that I'm going to have to pay attention, during the selection process, not only to the yellow flags and red flags, but also to my own preferences and tastes. My own preferences for a partner and tastes in relating matter. They are important aspects of who I am. Therefore, I need to be paying attention, early in the relationship to my own internal reactions to my potential partner's actions. What drives me mad today, will only drive me madder tomorrow. What I find odious, noxious or embarrassing now, will only be multiplied exponentially when I am living with you. Paying attention to how I'm feeling about your behavior, will only help me make a better decision about whether or not I want to commit to you. The decision to commit should definitely include a long hard look at this issue of compatibility.

The third ingredient to a healthy dynamic is two people in the relationship who know how to relate. Each party in the relationship needs to have built a healthy repertoire of relationship skills. This means that each party:

- knows how to be honest, (meaning s/he knows how to speak from authenticity, instead of the role), how to say what s/he is really thinking or feeling;
- can bring integrity (or wholeness and congruity) to the table along with the willingness to negotiate, when it is time for a difficult discussion;
- knows how to recognize a mental or emotional game and avoid such games like the plague;
- has the capacity to show affection openly and freely give to the other;
- can openly express understanding, appreciation and gratitude for and to the other;
- can openly agree and openly disagree without rattling the basic contours and trust in the relationship;
- can take mental and emotional responsibility for his/her own well-being;
- is willing and able to look at him/herself, own his/her mistakes and self-correct;
- is willing and able to self-disclose intimately;
- can build his/her own self-esteem separate from the partner;
- can establish healthy boundaries;
- can be an equal partner in all areas.

We will not magically formulate a long-term healthy commitment with someone just because we love them. We must look for love, yes, but also for compatibility and the ability to relate before we agree to commit. Nothing short of these ingredients will form a healthy, lasting, happy union. We have generally, as a collective, thought that good relationships were formed either by some gigantic stroke of luck or through some miraculous sleight of the hand of God. In other words, they just happened. But this approach does not appear to be working. We must become our own gods here. We must begin to approach commitment with the same care and thoughtfulness that we would approach any other major investment. After all, would you put your $5000.00 into a stock you new very little about? Would you purchase a car that all your friends told you was a lemon? Our hearts are a huge part of our well-being. And it is our job to take care of them. We don't do a good job of taking care of our hearts, when we throw them at whomever seems to have captured our fancy at the moment. We don't do a good job of taking care of them when we listen only to what the other person is saying, instead of watching their behavior, and listening to our own intuition and emotional responses. No matter how much time you have spent with someone, if you haven't listened to yourself in the dynamic, you probably still don't know them. We can't throw our hearts at someone and expect them to handle them with the kind of care we ourselves never gave our own hearts. We have to first take care of our own hearts. Only then will we even recognize good care.

Ponderings: While we are on the subject of primary relationship, let's talk about sexual orientation. Many persons across economic, social strata and politics are concerned about this issue. "Am I gay?" is a question that could be asked by many people at any time of the day, in any nation of the world from all kinds of ethnic backgrounds and childhoods. Therefore, we are going to look at some of the fears and myths surrounding this subject in order that those struggling with the issue may at least *begin* to resolve this, too, as a part of becoming authentic.

In 2004, the American Psychological Association (APA) published an article entitled, *Answers to Your Questions About Sexual Orientation and Homosexuality: Definition of Sexual Orientation.* In this article the APA created a research-based definition to help the public understand the concept of "sexual orientation:"

> Sexual Orientation is an enduring emotional, romantic, sexual or affectional attraction to another person … Sexual orientation exists along a continuum that ranges from exclusive homosexuality to exclusive heterosexuality and includes various forms of bisexuality. Bisexual persons can experience sexual, emotional and affectional attraction to both their own sex and the opposite sex. Persons with a homosexual orientation are sometimes referred to as gay (both men and women) or as lesbian (women only). Sexual orientation is different from sexual behavior because it refers to feelings and self-concept. Persons may or may not express their sexual orientation in their behaviors. (APA, 2004).

In 1973, the American Psychiatric Association took homosexuality out of the Diagnostic and Statistical Manual of Mental Disorders based on their decision that homosexuality is not a mental disorder. Further, in the same article, they say:

> Psychologists, psychiatrists and other mental health professionals agree that homosexuality is not a mental illness, mental disorder or an emotional problem. Over 35 years of objective, well-designed scientific research has shown that homosexuality, in and of itself, is not associated with mental disorders or emotional or social problems. Homosexuality was once thought to be a mental illness because mental health professionals and society had biased information. In the past the studies of gay, lesbian and bisexual people involved only those in therapy, thus biasing the resulting conclusions. When researchers examined data about these people who were not in therapy, the idea that homosexuality was a mental illness was quickly found to be untrue. (APA, 2004).

Because of our bias as a society on this issue, we often look for a cause of homosexuality as a way of telling ourselves that homosexuals are sick. At this moment in time, there is ongoing debate about a "gay gene." Because it is very difficult to pin-point a gene that can be responsible for any complex human behavior, and because homosexuality is such a political issue, it is going to be difficult to give the "gay gene" *complete* credit for gays and lesbians. However, ongoing research continues to indicate that there is an inherited component for sexual orientation. Therefore, though the politicians argue, in the main people are beginning to understand that there is some genetic component to sexual orientation.

Of course, there are a number of non-provable theories too, including those which site reincarnation as the cause. For me, it is enough to recognize that it is a normal human behavior that has some inheritable base. Further, it is a given that as long as we keep asking what makes homosexuals homosexual, we are treating it as if it were not a normal human behavior. After all, there is to date, no one to my knowledge asking why heterosexuals are heterosexual. Based upon this premise then we can begin to assert that *you can be gay without ever having to question your background.* You may explore your background for any dysfunctional behaviors, but your sexual orientation is not, in and of itself, a dysfunctional behavior. The truth is that gays and lesbians come from all kinds of backgrounds, ranging from abusive to quite functional. And the fact is, so do heterosexuals. Looking for the cause of homosexuality is like looking for the cause of eye or skin color or the cause of artistic talent. It is simply a normal way of being which is oriented in all realms of the psyche— mental, emotional, spiritual and physical. Anecdotally, many gays and lesbians say the same thing: "I don't remember *not* being gay." In other words, there is not a time in their lives when they did not have feelings of being gay, whether or not they actually perceived of themselves as gay. They may have worn the heterosexual mask, may have even married and had children while wearing that mask, but something in them always knew they were gay. As time went by, they became more and more aware of it.

Therefore, in order to get clear on sexual orientation, we have to first lay to rest some of our society's long-held biases, which many of us, including gays, lesbians and bisexuals have internalized. So, let's start with clarifying the definitions as they are being used in this book:

- A lesbian is a woman who has an enduring pattern of emotional, romantic, sexual or affectional attraction for women.

- A gay male is a man who has an enduring pattern of emotional, romantic, sexual or affectional attraction for men.
- A bisexual is someone who can experience emotional, romantic, sexual and affectional attraction to both their own sex and the opposite sex.
- The transgendered orientation includes several different types of individuals. It includes the transsexual whose internal experience is one of the opposite gender assigned at birth. It also includes the transgendered and the "drag queen," "drag king," as well as the intersexed person. This entire group of individuals have gone on record as preferring the term "transgendered." The issue for the entire group called transgendered is not necessarily one of sexual orientation, but of gender authenticity.

We will discuss gays, lesbians and bisexuals first, then there will be another section further clarifying bisexuality specifically. Finally, because the transgendered category has not to do so much with relationship as it does with authentic individuality, it will also be separated out for discussion. Some of what you will read below includes all four: gays, lesbians, bisexuals and transgendered persons. When they are lumped together in a group in this manner, they will be referred to as GLBTs. It should also be noted, that in order for us to discuss this issue in a way that is helpful to those who might be confused about it, we have to first lay to rest much of societal bias, misinformation and outright mythology about GLBT persons. And so, we proceed.

Sex is not the issue:

Notice first that we did *not* say that a lesbian is a woman who has sex with women, or a gay man is a man who has sex with men, or a bisexual is a person who has sex with either gender. Notice that we did *not* say that a lesbian woman is a woman who acts like a man, or a gay man is a man who acts like a woman. It is possible to have sex with anyone or anything, and that sexual act does not change your sexual orientation one iota. Having sex is a behavior. It may or may not be authentic. It may or may not have anything whatsoever to do with the heart. Therefore, it is possible to have sex with men, or women, or both, and it still have nothing to do with your sexual orientation. However, many who have had sexual experiences with same-sex partners might tend to believe that they are gay, or bisexual. This is not necessarily true. Sexual orientation goes far deeper than behavior. It goes to the heart of a person. Therefore, we might gain more clarity regarding our sexual orientation if we ask: *With whom do I typically fall in love?*

Before we go any further, we have to pause and reflect on this question for a moment. While it is true that not every attraction ends in "falling in love," falling in love is an easy and accurate way of describing what the APA referred to as: *an enduring pattern of emotional, romantic, sexual or affectional attraction.* Yes it is true that gays, lesbians and bisexuals engage in sexual activity when there is no more than a sexual attraction. It is likewise true that heterosexuals often engage in sexual activity when there is no more than a sexual attraction. It is also true that heterosexuals occasionally have sex with same-sexed partners, and gays, and lesbians sometimes have sex with opposite-sexed partners. Therefore, it doesn't help us to get any clearer on sexual orientation to limit it to sexual attraction, even though sexual attraction in and of itself is definitely a part of the picture. We are therefore, not here denying the fact that it is very possible that the "attraction" can be purely sexual. But that is by *NO* means *ALL* that happens. And this is a *VERY* important distinction that must be made when trying to define one's sexual orientation.

The biased societal definition of the GLBT culture is that it is all about sex. Further, this bias stipulates that it is not only all about sex, but it is all about perverted sex. People who have this opinion simply have never sat down and talked to a gay, lesbian or bisexual person who is in a committed relationship or has recently lost one. If they did, they would hear the gay, lesbian or bisexual person saying the exact same things that the heterosexual says about his/her committed relationship or recent loss of same. And that is wherein the kernel of truth lies that changes everything. Sexual orientation becomes, in this crystallizing moment of understanding, just another love.

Rather than looking to sexual behavior then, in order to gain clarity with regard to sexual orientation, we must begin by looking at this issue of falling in love. Therefore, for the purposes of this book, this will be our point of discovery. Since we can have sex with any one, or anything, this new understanding also makes it a lot easier to clarify one's sexual orientation, without confusing oneself still more by rushing out to have sex with someone to find out one's sexual orientation. Therefore, again, the question: *With whom do I typically fall in love?*

Relationships are founded on much more than pure sexual attraction, though that is a genuine component of the relationship. Let's face it: Heterosexuals get to say that they are lonely and that they desire a long-term, committed relationship. For this reason, they marry. And often, for this reason, they divorce. They want something real. Something enduring, something deeply sexual, spiritual, romantic and intimate. In order to have that, they have to fall in love. Why are GLBTs not allowed to say and feel the same thing? When we reduce gay/lesbian/bisexual orientation to simple sexual attraction, we are internalizing the homophobic concept that gays, lesbians and bisexuals are simply perverting sex into something it was not intended to be. Further, we are denying them the right to have that enduring, deeply sexual, spiritual, romantic and intimate thing that we are all seeking. How does one group of people get the right to so deny another?

But we should also recognize that it is possible to be in relationship with someone, but not be in love. People do this all of the time whether they are gay or straight. Heterosexuals quite often come into therapy after realizing that they were never really in love with their partners. Gays, lesbians and bisexuals quite often come into therapy after realizing that they were never really in love with their partners. When heterosexuals do this it is usually because they have married someone safe, rather than someone they loved. When gays, lesbians and bisexuals do this it is usually because they have committed to someone safe rather than someone they loved. Again, this is the security issue we discussed in the previous section.

The truth is that we are at a juncture in our history in which we can begin to change relationship into a paradigm that actually is all that it is cracked up to be. We have records of people, and we know people throughout history who genuinely loved each other for a lifetime. They lived healthy, happy, committed relationships. But if we are honest with ourselves, we have to admit that these were the exceptions not the rule, even in heterosexual relationships. Many long-term, committed relationships were anything but loving; many feigned commitment through multiple affairs and still others were but cold reflections of a business relationship. Yet most of us are still craving that seemingly illusive long-term commitment that is all about deep, abiding, spiritual, intimate love. And the only thing that gets in the way of it is our own ignorance about how to make it happen. Many gays, lesbians and bisexuals want the same, exact thing. And that is all. How do we, in our ignorance, think that we should have the right to point the finger at the GLBT world and blame it for the "downfall" or "failure" of marriage? If marriage between heterosexuals is failing, it is failing because heterosexuals are ignorant as to how to make it work. If commitment between gays, lesbians and bisexuals is failing, it is because they are ignorant as to how to make it work. It's all the same.

If we are going to seek out long-term love, and go to the trouble to really try to find some answers to the questions put forth in the previous section regarding the nature of intimacy, we will definitely be seeking after someone with whom we can have genuine feelings of being in love. Though for many of us, there is little recognition that we are even engaged in such a process, we nevertheless are. Though there have always been gays, lesbians, and bisexuals, currently we are beginning to understand that relationship has to be authentic if it is to work. For many, if not most gays, lesbians and bisexuals this means that we will seek people of the same sex with whom we can fall in love and maintain an intimate, long-term, committed relationship. For many, if not most heterosexuals, this means we will seek out opposite-sexed persons with whom we can fall in love and maintain an intimate, long-term committed relationship. It definitely is a matter of the heart. Not just the groin.

Sexual Orientation is not about gender role:

I think we will have to also speak to this issue of masculinity and femininity as well now. The 1999 movie, *In and Out,* unwittingly demonstrated evidence of our bias in this arena. The central character in this comedy must consider whether or not he is gay, based *only* on how he walks, talks, moves his hands, his interests in such things as Barbara Streisand and the fact that he was kissed by a man. Never once does the movie even mention the notion that he might fall in love with men. Though the movie was fun, it lacked the appropriate perspective. There are many very "feminine" women, who are lesbian, and many very "masculine" men who are gay. But somehow we have this bias that says, if you are a gay male, you will be effeminate and if you are a lesbian you will be very masculine. Many of the things that we call "feminine" or "masculine" are behaviors motivated by cultural expectations. It is true that there are different hormones, which are specifically masculine or feminine, and these do create physical differences in us and perhaps some differences in our approach to relationships. But the behaviors that we generally consider to be feminine or masculine are defined by things like the way we walk, the way we move our hands, the clothes we wear and the tone of our voice and speech patterns. These are complex human behaviors, but largely attributable to environmental or cultural expectations. However, during this evolutionary phase of our development, and as we become more aware of ourselves and our authentic needs, we often find that these behaviors are becoming more and more androgynous—or an interesting mix of both gender patterns. This means that as time goes by, we may find that we move more toward something that is neither male nor female in its look, or walk, or talk, but rather a mix of both.

In the mean time, perhaps we can begin by detaching our ideas about sexual orientation from our ideas about gender identity. They are very different.

Gender identity is gender role. In other words, I hang my nametag on my gender. How do I do that? I act like people of my gender are supposed to act. I know that I am a girl because not only do I have the biological equipment of a girl, but other people can see my "girl-ness" by the way that I walk and talk and stand and sit and dress. Therefore, I am a girl. It is exactly the same thing as putting on the Scapegoat role. I act, sit, walk, talk like a Scapegoat, I think like a Scapegoat, and so I feel like a Scapegoat and I actually think that this is who I am. If we accepted a more androgynous view of gender identity, it would operate more like gender authenticity. The attachments to gender would then look something like this: I know that I am a girl, because I have the biological equipment of a girl and that gender internally feels authentic to me. But we are still evolving in our awareness of how to define gender. Already in this evolution, among the transgendered population, the notion of gender is changing even beyond the idea of biological equipment to simply what gender internally feels authentic. But whatever else gender means, being gay is not so much about gender identity as it about that question: *With whom do I typically fall in love?*

Nor is being gay, lesbian or bisexual the same as being transgendered. Society's bias is quite ignorant in this regard. The idea of the "drag queen" took hold and was one of the first ways that Hollywood began to introduce society to the issues of sexual orientation. And while I am, frankly, grateful to Hollywood for its ability to open doors to the mind that no one else seems to be able to open, there is yet far more to be discovered. Gay, lesbian and bisexual persons may or may not also be transgendered, just as heterosexuals may or may not also be transgendered. We will study this more later in the section specifically reserved for transgendered issues, but for now suffice it to say that if you are falling in love repeatedly with people of the same sex, but are *not* wishing to live out an identity as the opposite gender, and do *not* wish to dress or act like a gender different from your biological sex, do not let this confuse you. You will come closer to a clear answer to your questions about sexual orientation if you ask the question: *With whom do I typically fall in love?*

So, how does a person know that s/he is gay? What about all the young adults experimenting with sex with both genders these days? Are they gay? Are they bisexual? The issues would, indeed, be so much simpler if they could be reduced to the single act of sex. If, by having sex with someone of the opposite gender, one could know that one were heterosexual, then we could quite easily solve the problem. But, as we have already said, there are many, many people who have even become married and had children with people of the opposite sex, and still learned later that they were gay, or later "came out" to themselves. So, obviously the thing about having sex with someone isn't helping us define ourselves any better. Still, there are countless individuals who think, "If I have sex with someone of my sex and it's like wow, then I'll know I'm gay, right?" Well, I guess first we have to define "like wow."

Falling in love is an attraction that is sexual, but it is also very spiritual. We will define this "like wow" feeling of falling in love in a few minutes, but for now it is important to say that it is hardly the same as meeting someone in a bar and taking them home for sex. This is where we've become quite confused. There are intense feelings of arousal associated with sex all by itself. But they don't hit the same chords of recognition, chords only found in the heart, which falling in love does. But we often get these feelings of arousal mixed up with the feelings of recognition and love that is on a much deeper plane.

Sexual orientation has nothing to do with sexual trauma:

We must mention here, that this may be especially so if we have been sexually traumatized. This is because for many who were molested young, affection and touch became sexualized. For some it was violent, which means that they may have violent associations with sexuality in general. For others it is simply that touch itself is sexualized. For still others affection in any form has become sexualized. These early associations are organic learning links. In other words, our body took on memories of sexualized touch, looks, affection. Therefore, when someone touches some survivors, they tend to sexualize that touch. Deep body memories of either aversion or arousal may come forth, and may bring up deep memories of feelings of horror and torment. This is why many persons who have been sexually traumatized turn off so completely to sex of any kind. Because they have learned that in general touch is sexual, it is also why others are quite sexually promiscuous. Further, when affection is sexualized, then it is very difficult for a person to sort out the subtle distinctions between sexual arousal and falling in love. These things add to the survivor's confusion about sexual orientation. This is another reason why, as therapists, we *must* pull this whole concept of sexual orientation out of the realm of touch and put it into the realm of love. Therapists must also be able to use a language about love and falling in love that separates it out from early associations with sexualized affection. The issue of sexual orientation is confusing enough in a world in which it has been ridiculed and maligned. Sexual trauma adds more to this confusion. Therefore, if you have been sexually traumatized, therapy is recommended. If you have been sexually traumatized and you are also confused about your sexual orientation, for the above reasons, you are encouraged to seek out a therapist who can assist you in separating out the above issues.

There is one more concern with regard to this issue of sexual trauma and sexual orientation that must be exposed and put to rest here. I often see clients who tell me that they fear that they are gay/lesbian or bisexual because their perpetrator was of the same sex and because they were sexually aroused during the rape or molestation. Because the body is biological it is often aroused with touch even when the touch is psychologically disturbing. Therefore, it is not uncommon for people to become aroused during a sexual trauma, or even to have orgasm. This does not have anything to do with your sexual orientation. It only has to do with the biological function of arousal. If your perpetrator was of the same sex and you had orgasm or felt aroused during the sexual abuse, this does not mean that you liked it, or that you are attracted to the same sex. If this is a difficult fact for you to conceptualize, please seek a therapist who is very familiar with sexual trauma to help you work through this.

I also have gay/lesbian/bisexual clients who tell me that they are afraid that their sexual trauma(s) "made" them gay/lesbian/bisexual. This makes them feel "sick" or perverted. My response to that is always to remind them that there are a lot of heterosexuals who have been sexually traumatized. If sexual trauma can turn someone against sex with the opposite gender then why doesn't it do that to everyone? Further, *sexual orientation is not about to whom you have an aversion, but to whom you are attracted.*

While it is true that some persons react to sexual trauma by becoming addicted to sex, this does not specifically have anything to do with sexual orientation. When this happens it is a form of what mental health practitioners call "reenactment." You will often see the phenomenon of reenactment when young children are at play. Something bad happens and they play it out over and over again in their play. What they are trying to do here is reenact their tragedy or trauma again and again until it no longer frightens them. As children grow up this reenactment sometimes takes the form of "acting out" on others. The problem with reenacting a sexual trauma is that sex has its own draw. So you combine the compulsive drive to reenact with the biological/psychological draw of sex itself and you have a pretty strong pull. Ultimately, like any other addiction, it can become life threatening.

Often people who are sexually addicted will have sex with either sex. When I see them in therapy, they will often tell me that they think that they are bisexual because they have sex with both genders. Further they blame their bisexuality on their sexual traumas. But this is not the definition of a true bisexual. We will discuss the definition of true bisexuality in greater detail in the section on bisexuality, but for now let us conclude this: If you are sexually addicted and have sex with both genders, this has nothing do to with your sexual orientation. Sexual addiction is about addiction to sex.

Ultimately what is being conveyed here is that sexual trauma really has nothing whatsoever to do with sexual orientation. Therefore, again, if you have been sexually traumatized, you are encouraged to seek therapy. If you have been sexually traumatized and are also confused about your sexual orientation seek a gay-friendly therapist to help you sort out these issues.

If you are confused about your sexual orientation, the exercise below does not promise to clear up your confusion entirely, but rather to assist you in *beginning* to ask the right questions. If you are not so confused, you may wish to skip over this exercise. If, after you've done this exercise, you still have deep resentment and/or fear of sexuality in general, please talk to your therapist about this as soon as possible. **Fill in the blanks below with your honest answers.**

When I think of my most recent date or sex partner I feel:

_____

Where is that feeling located in my body? _____

When I think of a same-sexed *attraction* I feel: _____

Where is that feeling located in my body? _____

If I could choose anyone in the world to be with right now it would be: _____

Why? _____

I'd like to spend hours talking to: _____

Why? _____

When I think of the person I'd most like to hold, it would be: _____

Why? _____

I wish I could hold hands with: _____

Why? _____

I like to look deeply in the eyes of: _____

Why? _____

The person I most want to take a midnight walk on the beach with is: _____

Why? _____

When I wake up in the morning the first person I think of is: _____

Why? _____

As I am going through my day, I have fantasies about being with: _____

Why? _____

I get so excited about one more opportunity to be with: _____

Why? _____

I am often quite pre-occupied with thoughts of: _____

Why? _____

I imagine what it would feel like to kiss: _____

Why? _____

When I compare the feelings I have for the person I've most mentioned above to feelings I've had for a previous heterosexual partner, I feel: _____

Why? _____

Ponderings: The person you most often named in the above questionnaire is the person with whom you are most likely in love. Often gays and lesbians tell stories of having been in denial about being gay for long periods of
time prior to "coming out of the closet." They told themselves that they just
liked hanging out with so-and-so, but really they were very romantically
drawn to this person. They told themselves that they just felt a deep friendship
with so-and-so, but they were really in love with that person. They found
themselves at gay parties saying, "I just have a lot of gay friends." They told
themselves "just because I have these feelings, well it doesn't really mean anything." Or they told themselves that having these feelings was evil or perverted,
and that they should therefore repress them. But regardless of what they told
themselves the truth was that, until their sexual orientation became authentic,
they were pretty miserable. Being authentic does involve your sexual orientation. Pretense in this area is just as damaging as pretense in any other, perhaps
even more so.

The questionnaire above is just one of the many tools that you can begin to
use to explore your sexual orientation. Suffice it here to say, however, that you
do _not_ have to have sex with someone of the same sex in order to know if you
are gay or straight. You may have sex with them, it may even be quite enjoyable,
but it still will not tell you if you are gay. Now, if you could fall in love with
someone of the same sex that would be different. It is sad but true that I see far
too many people in my practice who have tried this "fail-safe" method (go out
and have same-sex sex) of exploring their sexuality only to end up more confused then ever. When will we ever get it, that it is possible for our bodies to do
one thing, while our hearts are doing another? The heart holds the key to your
sexual orientation, not the groin.

So what is this business about falling in love?

The heart falls in love as a sub-conscious response to another, in which are
aroused feelings of passion, a desire for deep connectedness, and intimacy,
accompanied by sexual desire. The heart may also love without falling in love.
The love that is not falling in love may involve a sense of connection, perhaps
even a passionate connection (meaning one in which there is a certain level of
intensity), accompanied by a desire for some measure of intimacy that does
not necessarily involve a sexual intimacy, though persons who have this kind of
love may also be sexually involved. Love, as opposed to being in love, does not
involve the subconscious element. We can and usually are much more consciously involved in selecting the persons whom we love than we are in select-

ing the persons with whom we are in love. Further this love that is not the same as falling in love, does not have the same obsessive (note, I did not say possessive) quality that falling in love has.

Falling in love is a mood of elation, a relatively but generally safely obsessive mind-set, and a deep desire to be with, to know and be known by the object of attraction. And below that there is a genuine caring for the well-being of the object of attraction, so that we both want them, and care deeply about them. The other feature of falling in love is that it elevates the "lover" to new heights of character, simply through the act of loving the "lovee." In other words, as we've said, when we fall in love with another, we also fall in love with the deeper parts of ourselves.

Falling in love has been ridiculed for its "insanity" because it defies reason and gets us into a "whole lotta trouble." And actually those descriptions are true. But the only reason it gets us in trouble is because we are still learning about love. In fact, the first several times we fall in love, we are still learning about ourselves. Falling in love can help us to learn more about ourselves if we let it, though this is not often how it is used. But it can be helpful in teaching us about ourselves specifically because it is an unconscious act. We do not consciously choose with whom we will fall in love. The unconscious chooses that for us. This unconscious choice has something to do with who will be "good" for us. The intent of this unconscious choice is to help us grow. See the previous section on relationship in general with regard to how falling in love can help us to resolve old unresolved issues.

Let us be clear here, however, that sexual orientation is not an unresolved unconscious issue, unless it is completely repressed. We don't repeatedly fall in love with the same sex because of some unresolved issue; we exhibit a pattern of falling in love with persons of the same sex because we are authentically oriented toward same sex attractions. If I am an acorn I can only grow to be an oak tree. I will not grow to be a willow or a pine. I will grow to be an oak. If I am gay or lesbian I simply cannot fall in love with the opposite gender. I may formulate a relationship with and even marry someone of the opposite gender; I may even love that person very much. But I cannot fall in love with him/her, because I fall in love with people of the same sex. Why? Because I am an oak tree, not a pine or a willow. So, who I fall in love with is only a sign that I may use to discover my sexual orientation, in much the same way that an oak tree might use the fact that it has just dropped an acorn to discover that it is an oak.

Therefore, falling in love can be a unique opportunity to get to know ourselves better, to finish unfinished business, to address authentic needs and desires, indeed, to redeem ourselves from patterns that are no longer effective, by putting in place authentic ways of thinking, feeling, behaving and relating. It may even help us to discover our authentic sexual orientation. It may or may not mean we choose to commit to someone.

Further, same sex relationships still have the same unresolved issues with regard to each partner's family of origin as do heterosexual relationships. A woman may have issues with her father that she projects onto her female partner, just as easily as she may project those same issues onto a man. Or, a man may have issues with his mother, that he projects onto his male partner. The issues that are unfinished, therefore, are not about sexual orientation or about the gender of the parent or primary caregiver but about abuse, abandonment, isolation, indifference, etc. If we have these issues, they WILL come up in relationship. We may count on that as fact. Therefore, falling in love with someone gives us the opportunity to deal with these things. And the truth is that the more we deal with and resolve these things early in our relationship history, whether these are gay or straight relationships, the more we are apt to fall in love with someone later who represents wholeness and has a capacity to relate.

It is most interesting that we have this paradoxical relationship to "falling in love." On the one hand we ridicule it for its ability to lead us astray. On the other we seem to believe that if it happens, we MUST, therefore, commit to the person with whom we are in love, as if it had some mystical, sacred onus to it, that is a command to commit, preferably yesterday. As we have said, we may fall in love with a person with whom we cannot stay in relationship and be authentic. Therefore, we can see that falling in love is just that: falling in love. It means only that a powerful thing is happening in my heart, and I want to pay close attention to what is happening and address it as authentically as possible. As we've said, it does NOT mean I must commit to this person, though, if one falls in love with someone with whom one may have a healthy relationship then marrying, or committing is definitely an option.

Gays and lesbians fall in love with persons of the same sex, with whom they can either address unfinished business or learn to relate intimately, or both. Heterosexuals fall in love with persons of the opposite sex, with whom they can either address unfinished business or learn to relate intimately, or both. So the issues regarding falling in love are the same regardless of sexual orientation. However, as we've said, we get sexual arousal mixed up with falling in love quite often, and again, regardless of sexual orientation. In our modern age of sexual openness, the mythology we live out is often: *If I'm having sex with you, we must be in relationship.* This confusion makes it doubly hard for the gay/lesbian/bisexual, because it blurs the entire issue. Therefore, here is the truth of the matter: A person of any sexual orientation may have sex with someone with whom they *are* in love. A person of any sexual orientation may have sex with someone with whom they *are not* in love.

The difference between gays/lesbians/bisexuals and heterosexuals is that they are drawn through this unconscious response of falling in love, *beyond the barriers* of the assumed sexual orientation, to become involved in primary relationships with persons of the same sex. *The barrier over which every gay, lesbian and bisexual must hurdle, is the assumed belief on the part of most persons living that there is only one sexual orientation: that of heterosexuality.* One can then come to a second assumption: *If the heart can supersede, or persuade, by its passion alone, a person to go beyond such an enormous belief barrier, which as we shall see, is made up of bias, religiosity, condemnation, death threats and outright murder, then a consideration must be made for the authenticity of that response.*

Homophobia:

Basically, we live in a world in which KNOWING has become a principle of safety. We have come to believe that we are safe in this world to the degree to which we KNOW what to expect. Down through the centuries we have learned one central concept about how to organize and orchestrate our lives. We have learned to FEAR. The F-Word! And so, because we know fear, and it is, quite often, the central organizing feature of our lives, we have created all manner of shoulds and should not's around our fears. We fear anything different, unknown, uncertain, the possible, whatever is outside the box. Why? Because to live in fear this way gives us the primary illusion that we CAN and MUST gain the control which will allow us to survive. It is, as we've said, the main reason we put on roles in the first place.

We should, therefore, understand that our tendency to want to KNOW what is right, what is wrong, what is true, what is false, comes from our basic need to feel secure. And this is the source of homophobia. Homophobia is a fear of something that seems different, and thus raises the ugly head of insecurity for us. Homophobia is the fear of homosexuality. However, it very often does not look like fear. If persons who were homophobic would simply say that they were afraid, we could deal with this thing much more honestly. Instead, homophobia often looks like:

-Rage
-Violence
-Self-Righteous Indignation
-Judgment

-Ridicule
-Pretense
-Coldness

But homophobia can also look like:

-Feigned friendship accompanied by acute curiosity.
-Unwillingness to touch or be touched.
-Gossip, back-stabbing, or mocking.
-Even gays, lesbians and bisexuals who are afraid of their own feelings can be
extremely homophobic.

A society that is in large part, homophobic, creates expectations around the
issue of sexual orientation. In other words, we think that we know. And our
thinking this has made us feel more secure. Ergo, we have the huge expectation
that there is only one way to love, there is only one way to relate intimately and
that is the heterosexual way. This makes us all as a society feel more secure. The
problem with that is this: For anyone, particularly a young person, who is trying to determine his/her sexual orientation, these expectations blur the issue.
Persons trying to discover their sexual orientation end up asking about performance, then, rather than authentic orientation. It is as if they have to ask for
a vote, rather than seek authenticity. And if their authenticity is voted down,
they are left struggling internally with feelings that want desperately to find
expression, but cannot due to the internalization of society's vote.

Persons seeking to authentically define their own sexual orientation in a
society, which not only defines it wrongfully, as a way of being sexual, but also
shames and incriminates and "makes sick" these persons; are fighting a life and
death battle. They are being told that they must play a role in order to survive.
That is the entire issue of this book. But for the gay/lesbian/bisexual it becomes
even more complicated, because, unlike persons who are playing an unconscious role, gays and lesbians often KNOW they are being asked to play a role.
And this is a role they must play regardless of any other roles that they have
adopted, such as Runaway, Scapegoat, Superhero, etc. They are in fact being
told that they are evil and sick for having their own very legitimate and
authentic feelings. Given the intensity of adolescent anxt anyway, this added
burden often becomes unbearable for adolescents struggling with sexual orientation. Even those who are adult, find this added burden to be impossible
sometimes. But this book is here to tell those struggling with this issue, that
this is an authentic issue, which deserves an authentic answer. Once that

answer is found, your life will take on its authentic meaning in this arena. And, again, there *is* joy.

But in seeking our own authenticity in this arena, we must know what society says about it, in much the same way that we must know what our role tells us. Because we have often internalized much that society says about this issue, we must be able to create a mental argument with society, in the same way that we created an argument with the role on previous pages. Therefore, we should know that society in large part, gets this whole issue of sexual orientation mixed up with sexuality. In fact, it may be society that named it "sexual" orientation in the first place. It seems that our society thinks that gays and lesbians simply have sex with same sexed partners. This society does not allow much room for there to be an idea that gays and lesbians fall in love with persons of the same sex. That simply makes it too scary for a homophobic society. They believe that if it is something as intangible as falling in love, then it could happen to anyone, and they just don't want to consider that idea. Therefore, because they believe that the issue is one of sex, they also add insult to injury by assuming that this issue of sex includes the myths we are about to discuss.

First it is most important to note that society, as a whole, has more and more people who have accepted the entire issue of diversity in the sexual or relationship realm. From these persons you will receive acceptance and grace. As time goes by and more and more fair legislation is passed and unfair legislation is overturned, it is believed that eventually our society will reach a place of such acceptance, that gays, lesbians and bisexuals will be able to marry and receive all the benefits of marriage. Already several other countries have done so, leaving the U.S. far behind in this arena. How long, after all, can we continue to say that everyone _except_ a few select persons can have these rights and benefits?

Sexual orientation cannot be learned:

However, until then society at large continues to perpetuate the myth that homosexuality can be learned as a behavior, and thereby, chosen. Ergo, homosexuality is all about the behavior of sex. Therefore, gays and lesbians in the United States military must maintain some discretion with the "don't ask, don't tell," policy. The belief is that heterosexuals in a fox hole with a gay persons are at risk, not only for loosing their lives which are dependent on their fox hole mates, and gays can't be depended on because they are basically weak; but also they are at risk for being sexually harassed by their gay fox hole mates. The truth of course is that gays and lesbians think about sex no more or less than heterosexuals and are just as dependable as heterosexuals. The other truth is that if we did not believe that homosexuality was learned we would not be worried about what our fox mates were doing with their thoughts. In other words, because we think it is learned, we fear that *we can learn it*. Therefore, the heterosexual in the fox hole with a homosexual fears that homosexuality is contagious by learning. If the heterosexual is heterosexual, why would he worry about having sex with the homosexual anyway? Only if he worries that it is somehow contagious, would he even be concerned about it. Dispelling this myth then is an important step in becoming authentic in this area.

Because society believes that homosexuality can be learned, many believe that gays are gay because they were sexually traumatized at an early age. We've spoken to this myth earlier, but it should be noted that not only do those who are sexually traumatized fear a connection between their traumas and their orientation, but society at large, in looking for a "cause" assumes that GLBT persons are acting out some sick, distorted desire for molestation. The truth, as we've said, is that if this myth were true, everyone who was sexually traumatized would be a GLBT person. Then we could make a direct correlation, which would make us understand that illusive "cause" we've been looking for. There are many of the GLBT population who were not sexually traumatized, and, in fact, came from quite functional homes. And there are many heterosexuals who have been sexually traumatized and came from extremely dysfunctional homes, but are clearly not GLBT in their orientation.

In other words, women do *not* become attracted to women because they were molested and no longer trust men. And men do *not* become gay because a man molested them. Have you ever stopped to think about this? We twist our biases around the world for the different genders: Women attracted to women are so attracted because they *don't* trust men, but gay men are attracted to men because they *were* molested by a man? From this perspective then, gay men are *attracted to* their molester and gay women are *repelled from* their molester. What absolute hogwash this is, and based totally on bias! And the saddest part of this, is that persons who are GLBT have incorporated this hogwash into their own psyches. Often, when I talk to survivors about this, and mention the one simple fact that if sexual trauma were the cause of homosexuality, then all trauma survivors would be gay, they get this wonderful look of relief on their faces. For in fact, it is becoming authentic in every way, including their own special sexual orientation, that will make them healed and whole. *If you are confused about your sexual orientation, therefore, it is not because you grew up in a dysfunctional home or endured a sexual trauma. It is because it is difficult to accept a part of yourself that society in large part condemns.*

Because society believes that homosexuality is a learned behavior that is all about sex, gay/lesbian/bisexual teachers are suspected of proselytizing or recruiting young people to the "lifestyle." Of course, the fact is that gay/lesbian/bisexual teachers are not seeking out children to recruit anymore than heterosexuals are. Gay/lesbian/bisexual teachers are teaching, in large part, for the same reasons that heterosexual teachers are teaching, because this is the career that they have chosen that best matches their own interests and talents, or because they couldn't think of anything else better. Yet, because we have this homophobic fear, gay/lesbian/bisexual persons in that field must be very discreet and often fear loss of employment regardless of how well they do their jobs, because someone might "figure it out." If homosexuality is useful for recruiting innocents, then would heterosexuality be equally useful for recruiting? Why are we not worried about heterosexual teachers seeking to have sex with opposite-sexed children? Obviously, thus far, this has been more of a problem then gay teachers seeking to have sex with same-sexed children. If the issue is about behavior, then we must consider the behavior of all "sexualities."

Because our society believes that gays, lesbians and bisexuals are practicing learned behaviors that are all about sex, gay/lesbian/bisexual parents are suspected of being incapable of good parenting. In Alabama, in the early spring of 2002, after the state overturned an appeal from a lesbian mother for custody of her children, Chief Justice Roy Moore (Wekipedia, GNU Free Documentation License) put out his own proclamation stating that gays and lesbians should not be allowed to parent, and intimating that they should be jailed and even executed. Many people in Alabama were outraged by his statements and made this public, but there were others who totally agreed with him.

Here is what the American Psychological Association has to say about sexual orientation and parenting, in the same article sited above:

> Studies comparing groups of children raised by homosexual and by heterosexual parents find no developmental differences between the two groups of children in four critical areas: their intelligence, psychological adjustment, social adjustment, and popularity with friends. It is also important to realize that a parent's sexual orientation does not indicate their children's. (APA, 2004).

The fact is that parenting has nothing whatsoever to do with sexual orientation. Parenting is parenting and sexual orientation is sexual orientation. A "good" or a "bad" parent can come from either the heterosexual world or the homosexual world. Parenting and sexuality are two entirely different areas of endeavor. However, several legal precedents have already been set, which stipulate that a gay parent cannot have custody of his/her children simply because s/he is gay, even if the other heterosexual parent would, by any other standards, be considered to be an unfit parent. Therefore, in some areas of the country gay/lesbian/bisexual parents also must show discretion, being very careful to whom they reveal their sexual orientation.

In fact known gay/lesbian/bisexuals (as well as transgendered persons) are sometimes not permitted to touch children, as if they had a highly contagious virus. They are sometimes thought of as pedophiles, even though the facts support a predominately heterosexual population of pedophiles. Pedophilia is pedophilia. It is a mental illness, which does not connote a particular sexual orientation. Generally, pedophiles will take children of either sex, even though the pedophile is heterosexual. Pedophilia is all about predatory sex. Pedophiles are wholly identified as the Bully/Perpetrator. Sexual orientation is simply a way of loving. And transgender authenticity is simply a way of being. These have nothing to do with pedophilia.

Again, the APA, from the same article:

> Another myth about homosexuality is the mistaken belief that gay men have more of a tendency than heterosexual men to sexually molest children. There is no evidence to suggest that homosexuals molest children. (APA, 2004).

Though we *can* separate pedophilia, poor teaching and poor parenting from sexual orientation and transgenderism, we *cannot* so separate childhood itself. Many gays/lesbians report childhood and adolescent emotional experiences of having "fallen in love" with a same sex peer or having crushes on a same-sexed adult. Many gays/lesbians also report very similar experiences as children, with regard to their interest in non-gender-specific hobbies, games, and toys. While there has not been as much research on these experiences among bisexuals, I suspect that they are similar. These experiences seem to indicate that sexual orientation can be a part of many children's childhood experience. Therefore, we need to be able to consider that we impact these children in the negative and in the extreme when we tell them that who they are in terms of their sexual orientation is evil, vile, sick, distorted and should not exist.

Dr. David Brent, Psychiatrist at Western Psychiatric Institute and Clinic in Pittsburgh was noted in an article in the NIH Record, a journal for the National Institute of Health. This is what it had to say:

> Brent described a variety of risk factors for suicidal behavior, among them psychological characteristics such as hopelessness; aggression and impulsivity; a social skills deficit; and homosexuality/bisexuality. He was careful to clarify that "homosexuality and bisexuality are not synonymous with pathology, but the response of society is

deviant. There's so much stigma. Victimization, rejection and bullying place these kids at a much higher risk for suicidal behavior. (Waring, 2006).

Not only are they at greater risk for suicidal behavior but they are also at risk for physical, mental, emotional and/or sexual abuse due to homophobia. Further, they are often at risk for being rejected and even abandoned by their parents for their very authenticity as a gay/lesbian/bisexual (and transgendered) person. *Given these facts, we must begin to understand that sexual orientation is not something that is chosen later in life, but something about which one has no choice and toward which, in spite of that fact, society reacts in a largely punitive manner.*

Because society at large believes that homosexuality is a learned behavior that is all about sex, they often think that all gays, lesbians and bisexuals are constantly engaging in or obsessing about sex. According to this myth, gays, lesbians and bisexuals are always on the prowl, always ready to take their next obsession to bed. Persons who are constantly involved in either obsessing about or being compelled to act out sexual urges are sex addicts. Some heterosexuals are sex addicts. Some homosexuals are sex addicts. But sexual addiction is not the same as homosexuality. Nor is it the same as heterosexuality. It is a disease completely separate from sexual orientation.

Because this is the belief, however, even gays often think that this is "how it's supposed to be," and begin to live that life-style. The "how it's supposed to be" may come from a second myth that gays/lesbians/bisexuals cannot really have a "real" relationship. This, of course, comes from the notion that the lifestyle itself isn't real, but is learned. It can't, after all, be real, or anyone could be gay. Therefore, our society does not allow us to consider the authenticity of being gay, lesbian or bisexual. In fact the majority of the formal and informal education received regarding sexual orientation is very biased against the gay/lesbian/bisexual (and transgendered) population. How then could GLBTs be learning to be GLBT?

The fact is that some gays, lesbians and bisexuals are promiscuous, but there is no evidence that they are, by percentage, any more promiscuous than many heterosexual men and women. However, this myth may create a self-fulfilling prophecy, which may account for much of the sexual promiscuity among gay males, due to the internalization of societal bias. Further, many "heterosexual" men are secretly promiscuous in gay bars. So, sorting out the distinctions becomes extremely difficult from this perspective. But the idea that gays are promiscuous leaves those trying to find their own sexual orientation struggling, confused and frightened of a world they may not want to invest in—a world of drugs, alcohol and sex. Therefore, the path to relationship, which is already seeming remote for the gay/lesbian/bisexual person who has not yet met many others with the same sexual orientation, now begins to seem improbable, even impossible.

The truth is one cannot learn to be gay, lesbian or bisexual. As a matter of fact, in the early stages of coming out, many (especially those who are inculcated with religious dogma that says that they are evil for being who they are) wish they could "un-learn" it. In spite of this fact, some of the religious right have promulgated the false theory that gays, lesbians and bisexuals can convert to heterosexuality through something called reparative therapy. This approach to homosexuality has only to do with homophobia. In the year 2000, the American Psychiatric Association joined with several other professional organizations including the American Academy of Pediatrics, the American Medical Association, the American Psychological Association, the American Counseling Association and the National Association of Social Workers in creating a position statement with regard to reparative therapy, of which the following is a portion:

> As a general principle, a therapist should not determine the goal of treatment either coercively or through subtle influence. Psychotherapeutic modalities to convert or "repair" homosexuality are based on developmental theories whose scientific validity is questionable. Furthermore, anecdotal reports of "cures" are counterbalanced by anecdotal claims of psychological harm. In the last four decades, "reparative" therapists have not produced any rigorous scientific research to substantiate their claims of cure. Until there is such research available, APA recommends that ethical practitioners refrain from attempts to change individuals' sexual orientation, keeping in mind the medical dictum to first, do no harm. (APA, 2006).

The question could be asked: Why, in this current time of prejudice and violence, would one *choose* to be gay? It is a hard life-style, when you consider the bias of our society. So, why would anyone choose it? No, it is not learned and it is not chosen. It simply is. Just like the color of one's skin. It is. Yet, as we've stated, the very fact that in-spite of the negative environment surrounding the issue, gay/lesbian/bisexuals continue to exist and live out their authentic orientation lends even more credence to the idea that this thing is for real.

If you are gay, lesbian or bisexual or if you think you might be, please feel free to go back and work the chapters on barriers to authenticity, keeping in mind that the voice of society has subconsciously, and all too often, become your own mantra about your sexual orientation. Write down your mantra as it pertains to sexual orientation. Then have an argument with that mantra, consider the other barriers to your authenticity, such as your beliefs, your fears, your "if only's" and re-work the exercises on these issues. Do this again and again until you are clear on what YOU believe about your sexual orientation. Your Authentic Self does have these answers for you, just like it has the answers for anything else.

So, how do I know whether or not I am gay? It is a process of unfoldment, in which one explores the roles one has played and the Authentic Self, just like all of the above material. One has to begin to come to awareness. One has to move through feelings of loss of an old identity. One has to question old beliefs, mores, religious values, relationship ideals, etc., that no longer seem authentic. One has to recognize and call to authenticity that which is basically opposed by society. But then authenticity is generally so opposed anyway. Can we change the belief system of the culture? Perhaps, slowly, over time. But we also need to be aware that we cannot stay stuck bargaining with society, instead of moving into our own authenticity. We must, instead begin to move through the stages of acceptance which include denial, anger, bargaining, sorrow (not depression), and acceptance. When we reach acceptance we are finally living comfortably in our own authentic sexual orientation.

Check out the questionnaire below.

What is your greatest fear about sexual orientation?

_____
_____

Prime factor that fear.

Have an argument with yourself. You may need to repeat this exercise several times.

What losses are involved if you decide to authenticate your sexual orientation?

_____
_____
_____

What rituals can you implement which would help you define and honor these losses?

_____
_____
_____

Do you have religious challenges that are difficult to process regarding your sexuality? If so, can you clarify these challenges below?

_____
_____
_____

Where would you like to be in 2 years regarding your sexual orientation? In 5 years, in 10?

_____
_____

What barriers keep you from accomplishing your dreams in this very important area of your life?

_____
_____
_____

Have a dialogue now with the Authentic Self about these barriers. Rework all of the exercises on barriers to living authentically with regard to your sexual orientation.

If you find that you have religious challenges to authentic sexual orientation that are overwhelming and, thereby, prohibitive; or you are having trouble coming out, I've listed a few books below that might help. Also, if you are a student and you have a Gay/Straight Student Alliance at your local college, join this group. It may help. If you have a local Metropolitan Community Church (MCC), a church for GLBTs, you may wish to attend. There are other churches, particularly in metropolitan areas, which are accepting of GLBTs. Some of these are: Unity Church, Unitarian Church, the Episcopal church, and some other churches such as Baptist, Presbyterian and Methodist, who are not affiliated with the larger denominational associations. Some Catholic churches are covertly running a group for gays and lesbians. If you have a local Alternative Bookstore, check it out for many helpful references on the entire issue. Also, you might look through the yellow pages of your city to find therapists who work with gays and lesbians, or as the latest buzzword has it "alternative lifestyles."

What the Bible Really Says About Homosexuality, Daniel Helminiak
Prayer Warriors, Stuart Miller
Coming Out: An Act of Love, Rob Eichberg
Coming Out of Shame: Transforming Gay & Lesbian Lives, Gershen Kaufman, PhD, and
    Lev Raphael, PhD
*Stigma & Sexual Orientation: Understanding Prejudice Against Lesbians, Gay men and
    Bisexuals,* Gregory M. Herek
"… And Then I Became Gay:" Young Men's Stories, Ritch C. Savin-Williams
Coming Out: A Handbook for Men, Orland Outland
There's Something I've Been Meaning to Tell You, Loralee MacPike, Editor
Out in the Workplace: The Pleasures & Perils of Coming Out on the Job, Richard A Rasi &
    Lourdes Rodriquiz-Noques, Editors

Ponderings: Let's add a bit more about bisexuality here. The American Psychological Association, as stated earlier, defines sexual orientation along a continuum, which ranges from homosexuality to heterosexuality, with bisexuality hitting various points between these two poles. However, there is much debate about the definition of the bisexual in both the heterosexual and the homosexual worlds. The heterosexual world tends to believe that a bisexual is someone who has sex with both genders. Many who call themselves bisexuals also subscribe to this definition. In the gay and lesbian worlds, however, many would say that there is no such thing as a true bisexual. By that definition, one is either gay or straight and those who say that they are bisexual are simply in denial about their true sexual orientation. From the perspective of this book, neither definition is correct; rather the APA definition sited above is correct.

We will not here, resolve this debate. However, because it is so debated and each of these worlds may have an influence on someone trying to seek their own true sexual orientation, we need to spend a bit more time for clarifying bisexuality. If a bisexual is someone who can fall in love with either a man or a woman, then all one has to know, in order to live authentically is: With whom am I in love *right now?* I encourage the exploration of the heart. I encourage the exploration of the feelings one has when one says, "I am in love." Again, experimenting with sex, only answers the question: With whom am I having sex? And one can have sex with anyone or anything, and still have no clarity about one's sexual orientation.

The confusion around this issue is perpetuated by the societal myth that sexual orientation is all about sex. And the fact is that many bisexuals are perpetuating this belief. As we've said, we do tend to internalize society's values, even when we seem to be rebelling against them. If I am homophobic, I may categorize any alternate sexual orientation as strictly sexual. From that perspective, the bisexual is defined as someone who is having sex with both genders. If I am gay or lesbian and afraid that someone doesn't fit into the categories I've already discovered, I may think that there is no such thing as a true bisexual. Further, if someone else's bisexual behaviors could disrupt my life or wreck my relationship, then I want to be able to put it in a neat category that is not so scary. In this way, I too, am making the bisexual's sexual orientation all about sex.

I encourage the reader to check out the internet on the subject of bisexuality. You will find, as I did, many sites written by bisexuals or by bisexual groups espousing their beliefs on the subject. Some of the articles espouse such practices as staying married to one's husband or wife, while having sex with a same-sexed partner. Others promote open sex and demand the freedom to be sexual with whomever they chose. Still others encourage readers to discover whether or not they are bisexual based on their sexual appetites. These articles discuss sexual appetites and sexual behavior. There is, in these articles, very little said about falling in love at all. While I would support the equal rights of these persons, as well as their liberty or freedom to conduct their affairs in whatever way they chose, I do think the internalized belief that sexual behavior *is* sexual orientation creates a great deal of confusion for those who are trying to find authenticity in the area of bisexuality.

Bisexuality is not fear of intimacy.

It gets even more confusing for those trying to discover their bisexual orientation when you throw fear of intimacy into the mix. I have treated many in my practice who espouse this internalized belief that sexual behavior is sexual orientation. They want their freedom to behave in any sexual way they choose. And they may either call themselves bisexuals or they will say, "Why do we have to label people? Why do we have to say 'gay' or 'straight' or 'bisexual'?" On the surface, this sounds so politically correct, and, indeed, makes a lot of sense. But an interesting new feature begins to emerge sometimes in these encounters. As I continue talking to them, I often find that this is a very neat rationalization for a deep-seated fear of intimacy. When I look at their histories, I find that at each juncture at which intimacy was offered to them in any kind of way, that's exactly the same time that they chose to bolt and run to the bars, to another person, to an argument which would create a break-up, or at the very least, some distance. However, when it comes to seeking happiness and health, they quite often say that they want a relationship. These persons may be calling themselves bisexual, and ultimately they may be true bisexuals, but right now all we can see is fear of intimacy.

Let me clearly state that I am NOT saying that bisexuals have a problem with intimacy. What I am saying is that at this time in our history in which sex has exploded all over everything, those with a fear of intimacy may use the label of bisexuality to cover up their fear of intimacy. This makes it really confusing for those who are seeking authentic bisexuality. If you are confused about your sexual orientation and think that you might be bisexual but meet up with a person who has a fear of intimacy and is using the label of bisexuality as a cover, you could become quite confused about what it means to be a true bisexual. If you are a person with a fear of intimacy and also confused about a possible bisexual orientation, it may be much more difficult for you to find your authenticity in this area. Therefore, we must discuss this issue.

Those with a fear of intimacy must begin to feel safe in their own internal authentic home in order to begin to formulate real external relationships. Many times, when we begin to explore the area of emotional involvement with persons who fear intimacy, we find that they have great difficulty defining, or naming their emotions at all. If they can stick with the process and really work on moving past their roles and into authentic feeling and thought, they can get some authentic answers about relatedness as well. In the process, however, they will need to work with the chief blocking emotion: fear of intimacy. It should be noted that healing the fear of intimacy will *not* necessarily change someone's definition of their own sexual orientation from bisexual to either gay or straight, though I have seen this happen on occasion. It only means that they can become clear about their true sexual orientation, be it bisexual, gay or straight. They are now ready for a real relationship regardless of the gender of the person with whom they relate.

I have treated gays and lesbians in my practice who have partnered with someone who has this deep-seated fear of intimacy, but calls this fear bisexuality. In the end the partner has informed the client that s/he needs the freedom to have sex with whomever s/he chooses *because* s/he is bisexual. The gay/lesbian client has fallen in love with this person and is unprepared for the on and off, up and down, come here/go away dynamic that is often a part of this kind of interaction. Often, the one who has claimed to be bisexual has used those precious three little words, (I love you) and they are believed. However, the actions of this person are anything but loving. The client then has to come to terms with the fact that though the significant other is using the name "bisexual," the simple truth is that the partner is being allowed to have sex with others and create all manner of chaos for the client. The issue is that the client is involved with someone who, whether or not s/he is actually bisexual, nevertheless lacks the capacity, at least for now, to relate.

For these persons, so identified with the bisexual behavior as a way of avoiding intimacy, there is a psychic split. Therefore, while there may be an unconscious and compulsive loneliness, which seeks to find a significant other, there is also an equally powerful unconscious and compulsive fear of togetherness, which seeks to be alone. Therefore, there is this constant push/pull. There is this seeking out and finding and this pushing away that happen almost simultaneously. And this person identifies with this push/pull, saying that it is who s/he is. Being bisexual then becomes a rationale for not being intimate, in these cases. This then creates an enormous veil, a huge mask behind which the person may be able to live free of commitment and supposedly free of loneliness at the same time. However, there is a certain misery that seems to need to drag other people down into it. These persons and their partners are quite often living miserably, feeling guilty, and angry quite a bit of the time. The person so identified as bisexual feels guilty for not being able to commit and simultaneously angry that someone wants them to. The partner feels guilty for asking for commitment and simultaneously angry that their partner cannot willingly give it. Beyond the relationship aspect of misery, underlying all the acting out behaviors, the person who fears intimacy is genuinely lost and looking for an internal home.

Because there are some people who are using the label of bisexuality to cover up their fear of intimacy, we must begin to understand fear of intimacy and how it works in order to separate true bisexuality or sexual orientation in general from it. Fear of intimacy can be a problem for *any* person of *any* sexual orientation. And there are many ways to avoid intimacy, which we shall discuss below. But for persons using the label of bisexuality as a cover, calling themselves bisexual seems to solve the whole problem of intimacy. *If one is truly bisexual, then the only question one needs to answer with regard to their current life is: Am I in love and with whom?* If I am in love then I can get on with the business of self-discovery or formulating a relationship if that is possible. If I am not then I may choose to date whoever piques my interest regardless of gender until I find someone with whom I am in love. While I am doing this I can stay in the observer mode in order to pay acute attention to my own feelings, desires and attractions. As I do this I may begin to see a pattern emerging. In this way, I begin to answer my own questions about my sexual orientation.

If, however, the problem is one of fear of intimacy, this is something that can be worked through, just like any other fear. And the first step in working through any fear is to decide if one actually has the fear. This is the problem definition phase of problem-solving. Below, we will help you begin to answer the question: Am I genuinely bisexual, or am I simply living this lifestyle in order to avoid intimacy.

When a person fears intimacy, they react to intimacy as if it were a negative thing, which should be avoided at all costs. Some see intimacy as smothering. Others just don't ever allow a relationship to get intimate because they fear their own vulnerability. Intimacy, as defined earlier, requires a willingness to be vulnerable and to trust others. Those with deep fears of intimacy act in certain ways, which preclude the possibility of such vulnerability. Because they are wounded, often having been betrayed and abused by people that they trusted, or because they have been smothered by a parent, or because they have lived with a fear of abandonment perpetuated by one or both parents, they fear becoming involved emotionally with someone, because they fear that they will be wounded again. However, fear of intimacy most often takes the form of behavior, rather than of a conscious feeling of fear. Remember, as you look at the manifestations of this fear below, that these persons are trying to stay *out of touch* with their emotions. It might look something like this (particularly when calling oneself bisexual is a cover-up for fear of intimacy):

- You tell me that we need to talk about something. I say okay, but avoid creating time to do this.
- I ask you to commit to me, but when it gets close to time for our commitment ceremony, I have an affair with someone else.
- I ask you to live with me, but when we really start getting to know each other, I tell you that I've never sewn my "wild oats" and would like to have sex with someone else. I am often quite surprised when you are alarmed at this.
- Every time things get really comfortable between us, I start arguments and/or do things that make you suspect my commitment to you, such as cruise the bars at night, or spend enormous amounts of time talking about and/or being with someone else; or perhaps I'll just say something really hurtful so that there will be more distance between us.
- I tell you that I am gay, in order to get involved with you, but once we are involved I begin to hang out at straight bars and then eventually begin to flirt with and finally have sex with someone else. If I am secretly defining myself as bisexual, my affair will often be with someone of the opposite sex from me and my partner.
- I commit to you, but as I am doing so, I have affairs with others of the opposite sex from you.
- I live with you but begin to tell you that I don't like the label of being "gay" and I'm not sure that I'm willing to give up having sex with people of the opposite sex.
- I get mad at my gay partner for hanging out with his/her friends, but I am not going to stop hanging out at the straight bars or seeking out sex with straights.
- I do not directly answer any of your questions about me or my life, especially in particularly vulnerable areas.
- I avoid conversations in which I have to reveal myself wholly to you.

- When you confront me with my behavior, I turn the issue around to you, blaming you for being suspicious or otherwise keeping the focus on you.
- I may tell you that you are too clingy, or too needy, even when your behaviors do not look this way at all to others.
- Internally, there is just never a firm commitment to another person. I am always, a least in the back of my mind, wondering if I should or I will break up with my partner.
- Sometimes I will have multiple affairs.
- Sometimes I do not get in relationship at all but prefer to have multiple sex partners, though if you asked me, I'd tell you or demonstrate that I'm really lonely.
- I may engage in "pleasing behaviors" to keep you from knowing who I really am.
- Deep down I am terrified that if you get to know me, you'll be disgusted.
- I may appear to be very "shallow," all caught up in the appearance of things, rather than the deeper meaning.
- I will strictly avoid therapy and often go only when I feel you have done something to me, so that I can "tell on" you.
- Often, I will say something like, "I get bored easily," when someone questions me about the number of relationships I've had.
- Sometimes, I am sexually addicted.

If the above applies to you, or to someone with whom you are in relationship, you may be dealing with fear of intimacy. Fear of intimacy, because it takes the form of behavior, rather than feelings, is often difficult to come to terms with. It must first be confronted as behavior that is incongruent with the person's personal desires or at least their expressed desires. Then the person might be willing to consider a fear of intimacy that presents as a behavior pattern that not only keeps them from getting what they want out of life, but also is significantly emotionally abusive to others. It should also be noted that a person can become so identified with their fear of intimacy that it takes on a role. This role would be the Runaway role. You may go back and review the Runaway role to see if it fits for you. If it does, go back and rework, Chapters 2 and 3. The questionnaire below may also prove helpful with regard to discovering a fear of intimacy issue.

Fear of Intimacy Questionnaire:

When was the last time you told someone who is very close to you, something vulnerable about yourself? What happened inside you when you did this?

_____
_____
_____
_____

What happened the last time your partner asked you to talk about a problem?

_____
_____
_____
_____

When you have sexual fantasies, what is most erotic, having sex with your partner, or having sex with a stranger? Why?

_____
_____
_____
_____

Have you ever had an affair? If so, when did that affair occur in the history of your partnership? How were things going in the relationship when you did this?

_____
_____
_____
_____

Have you ever left a relationship because you were bored with your partner? Why? What were you looking for? Did you find it?

_____
_____
_____
_____

Do you find it very, very hard, even frightening to get into a committed relationship? Why? What frightens you most?

_____

_____

_____

_____

Do you dream of a long-term committed relationship, but find that when you get in one, you can't maintain it, or that you, yourself sabotage it? Why?

_____

_____

_____

_____

If fear of intimacy is a problem for you there are many good books on the shelves of your bookstore that can help you get more acquainted with the whole issue. However, working on the issue in therapy is probably the most effective solution. You may find that you also have an intense fear of therapy, which is rationalized as something like, "only crazy people need therapy." Or, "I don't want to be in the same room with someone who only says, 'How does that feel?'" Perhaps the idea of therapy makes you mad. Perhaps this fear of intimacy is not really a problem for you yet. However, you can be assured that it is a major problem for whomever you are in primary relationship. It is often quite difficult to move past this fear to see that you may need help. My suggestion is, go get help, and if, after a year of help, you feel that you still don't need it, quit. It's just an experiment.

If you are confused about your sexual orientation and you feel you may be bisexual, it is very important that you get clear on the distinctions between the wonderful feelings of arousal and the wonderful feelings of falling in love. When one can make these fine inner distinctions, one is definitely in touch with one's own emotions. There are feelings that come with arousal. There are other feelings that come with falling in love. And there are other feelings that come from the need for security, power, control, dependency, or ownership. One has to be intimately acquainted with one's own internal emotional world to know the difference. And one must be in touch with one's own emotions to begin to rely on the wise messages these emotions give us. One cannot be so in touch when one has a deep fear of intimacy, because the real fear of intimacy is fear of one's own emotions. In other words, "I don't want to feel pain if you reject me, therefore, I'll always reject you first." The only way then to answer the question regarding your own sexual orientation is to find out. Go deep inside, work this book all the way through, ask the hard questions, work on all your fears and all other barriers to authenticity. Your Authentic Self has the answer.

Otherwise, the issues of self-discovery regarding true bisexuality are much the same as the issues of self-discovery for the gay or lesbian, with this added twist: The question for the bisexual is not with whom do I typically fall in love, but: *With whom am I in love right now?* Given that you are not in love, then the above suggestions remain. Date whom you are attracted to, and while you are doing so, listen to your own internal messages, your feelings, your sensations and your heart's desire. If you are doing so consistently, you will learn who you are in this area. Further, like the gay or lesbian, you will also have some work to do with regard to removing society's internalized biases regarding bisexuality. Self-acceptance is the name of the game here. Go back and reread the section above on the various societal biases in order to get clearer on which of these you have internalized. Write letters to and from the Authentic Self regarding these internalized biases. In so doing you will get clear on your own truth with regard to your own particular sexual orientation. Self-acceptance is the name of the game here. Bisexuality is just as authentic a way of being as is heterosexuality. Be true to yourself.

Ponderings: Now let's do a little work on the issue of transgender identity affirmation. As we've said the category "transgendered" includes several types of people. It includes, basically, anyone who is identifying or behaving in a manner that is different from the biological sex of that person. To date, it includes the transsexual, the transgendered, the "drag queen," the "drag king," and the intersexed person. We will define each of these separately, keeping in mind that the category itself is in flux and can increase to include others as yet unidentified.

The transsexual is, as we've said, a person of either gender whose internal experience is one of the opposite gender from which s/he was assigned at birth. In other words, the transsexual feels inauthentic in his/her assigned biological sex and wishes to become his or her opposite gender. The issue for transsexuals is not one of sexual orientation, but of gender authenticity. Therefore, the issue for the transsexual is not necessarily one of relationship, though relationship may factor into the equation. In fact, the transsexual may be involved in relationship with either the same or opposite gender. The more authentic the transsexual is, the more authentic the gender of the partner in relationship will be. Most transsexuals have a deep desire to permanently identify as a gender opposite from that assigned at birth. Many desire sex reassignment therapy.

The transgendered person is, in general, a person whose gender identity does not conform to conventional notions of male or female gender or to ones assigned gender. This may include gay males who refer to themselves as female, or dress as females and walk and talk in stereotypically female manners. It may include lesbians who refer to themselves as male, or dress as males and walk and talk in stereotypically male manners. It may also include heterosexuals who dress and act differently from their biological sex. It may include the drag queen or king, typically those of one biological sex who perform on stage as the opposite gender. Of course, they may also keep this role off stage. The transgendered person may or may not desire a permanent identification as the gender opposite from the biological sex. The transgendered person may also identify as both genders, or as bigendered.

The intersexed person is a person born with primary (genitalia) or secondary physical sex characteristics (such as facial hair, chest hair, enlarged breasts, etc.) that are of both sexes. The old term "hermaphrodite" fits here, but has been found to be offensive to intersexed persons, since it implies a "freakish" form. There is still an argument in the medical community about what to call this. However, for the intersexual, the issue is normalization of what has been considered by the medical community to be abnormal. Unless there is a medical necessity, many intersexuals are beginning to refuse any surgical or medical intervention for "correction." Intersexuals have, for centuries, lived in shame and have been shunned by society. They often live with the "freak" stigma. The surgical or medical interventions were meant to erase the social stigma and allow them to live a "normal" life. Now, however, many are coming out of the closet and stand firm in their biological normalcy, establishing healthy relationships and living happy lives.

There are many theories about transgenderism, mostly biased. Whatever theory one espouses, the simple fact is that people wish to live authentically in the gender or gender identity that is most real for them. For example, the transsexual often lives miserably in an existence in which s/he literally feels in the wrong body. There absolutely has to be either an authentic psychological or a physical answer to this dilemma. In order to devise a plan for such a solution, one will have to ask the question: What psychological issues might arise which will effect the outcome of the solution chosen? Of course, before any medical intervention is made to help the transsexual establish the authentic gender, one will have to have therapy, which can answer this question as well as assist the transsexual in adjusting to the reassignment therapy.

Gender Identity Disorder (GID) and Transvestic Fetishism are two disorders listed in the DSM-IV which seem to both help and harm the transsexual in particular and the transgendered in general. On the one hand the diagnosis of GID allows the medical team to evidence medical necessity for the sex reassignment therapy, thus allowing insurance to cover it. On the other hand the diagnosis labels transsexuals as mentally ill. Diagnosing such persons puts them at risk of being further stigmatized and further legitimizes intolerance of gender diversity in much the same way that the diagnosis of homosexuality seemed to legitimize and did in fact perpetuate intolerance for gays, lesbians and bisexuals. Further the diagnosis of Transvestic Fetishism very often does not fit the transgendered person, as it implies that sexual arousal takes place as a result of the change in gender identity. While there are some who are sexually aroused through a change to the opposite gender's typical attire, this is not typically the case for the transgendered person. While more research is definitely needed in this and all other areas of gender identity and sexual orientation, whatever else we don't know about transgenderism, this much is certain: transgendered persons can be authentic.

The assumption on the part of society in general that the transgendered are sick, strange, perverted people is based on the premise that any diversity in gender identity is, in and of itself, not authentic. While it is true that transgendered persons, like anyone else, can be dysfunctional, it is also true that, like anyone else, they can also be authentic. Generally speaking any form of diversity arouses suspicion and bias from others. As we've said, we like to think that we know things. This knowing makes us feel secure. Gender diversity is such a blurry area, for those with rigid expectations and fears regarding gender, that it has been relegated to some form of perversion.

In fact, gender runs far deeper than these simple social mores and rigid expectations. For most of us, whether gay, straight or bisexual, there is a sense of self that is clearly related to an authentic gender. We simply *feel* like the gender we are. This feeling is sensative, emotional and instinctive. When we are living in our authentic gender, we can look in the mirror and not only see the external manifestations of our gender, but also have that congruent sense of self that says that the person we see in the mirror matches the person we sensatively, emotionally and instinctively feel that we are. Unless transgendered persons can find a way to manifest authenticity with regard to gender diversity, they cannot feel this congruence at least not in any permanent way.

For generations this absent sense of authentic gender was thought to mean that one was gay. Because we thought that being gay had to do with masculinity or femininity, we thought that gay people were dissatisfied with their gender. But the fact is that unless a gay person is also transgendered, s/he is perfectly happy with his/her gender. What the transgendered person longs for is an external sense of self that matches the internal sense of self. Again, the transgendered person may have relationships with either gender, but that is not so much the issue, though it can factor into the equation.

For those of us who are very linear in our reasoning, it seems impossible that one could long for a gender one does not biologically possess. This is because linear thinking leads us to look for the empirical. From this same frame of reference love cannot exist because it cannot be empirically proven. But for those of us who look below the level of the external, to the internal, we run into all manner of urgent needs, messages and perceptions that do not come from anything that anyone could call empirical. This sense of self to which we have referred above, is just such an urgent need. The sense of self that must be congruent throughout all of its manifestations is a primal human need. We simply cannot be happy without it. And since happiness is one of the manifestations of living authentically, we have to conclude that in order for one to be happy, one has to experience gender authenticity.

Further, for those with linear reasoning, and rigid expectations regarding gender, there seems to be a belief that if you are born with a particular gender, then that gender is somehow sacred. What we are discovering in our mental and emotional evolution is that biology is not necessarily "right" for a person. Rather it is our internal authenticity that will tell us the truth about who we are in every way, including gender. Therefore, if you experience yourself (either permanently or temporarily) authentically as a female, then you are female, and the same for the male. Authenticity is the answer to every question we can ask.

For example, if you are transsexual, should you consider sex reassignment therapy? While for some transsexuals reassignment is not something that they consider essential to their authenticity, for others, it does seem to be a defining characteristic. The only answer I have is this: If this solution gives genuine peace, it must be authentic. If not, then there is another issue that must be considered. But, of course, the transsexual is going to need to know this answer before the surgery. The answers will come from one's authenticity. Therefore, it behooves anyone who is dealing with this difficult issue, which raises the biases of both the heterosexual and homosexual worlds, to seek fair-minded therapy. Generally, psychological therapy is considered to be a part of the sexual reassignment approach. The therapy should address the issue of authenticity in every area of the person's life in order to facilitate the sensative, emotional and intuitive awareness essential to discovering the authentic self with regard to gender. Take this book with you to therapy. Work and rework the exercises using your authentic gender as the primary question. Ask your therapist to assist you in working these exercises and give yourself the gift of peace.

If you are in any other way transgendered, authenticity is available to you as well. Sometimes finding others like yourself is an incremental part of self-acceptance and living authentically. There are many avenues of support available for transgendered persons, though they may not be found in your typical mental health or medical facility. Try www.transgender.org to get information about support that might be available in your area. Check out the *Transgender Forum* at www.tgforum.com. Try Susan's Place, a data base of transgender related websites and resources, at www.susans.org. Look at NTAC, National Transgender Advocacy Coalition, at www.ntac.org. And look at The Transgender Guide, a national directory of transgender resources at www.tgguide.com.

These resources and others will help you make a start at gaining more information and support. However, if authenticity is your objective, there is more work to be done. If there is any confusion in this area, therapy is recommended, preferably with a therapist who is tg-friendly. When looking for a therapist, simply ask that question: "Are you comfortable dealing with transgenderism?" If a therapist is practicing ethical care, s/he will be honest about his/her experience in this area and/or can refer you to someone who is experienced with transgenderism. Work this book, paying particular attention to any internalized societal values that you might use as a mantra against your own authenticity. Work the sections on barriers to authenticity again and again with regard to your own gender identity. The bottom line here is this: transgendered persons can have the peace of authenticity.

Ponderings: Now let's talk about coming out.

It is most important that the reader understand that this book is NOT going to tell you that if you are among the GLBT population, you have to be "out" as we know it in order to be authentic. "Coming Out" has wrongly been defined as telling the world about your sexual orientation. This is the pop-version of coming out. Actually, coming out is a long process of self-acceptance, in which one slowly rids oneself of internalized homophobia. The first person to accept the self is the self. After that, making clear decisions about what to say and to whom IS being authentic. *It is always a personal and authentic choice as to whether or not we tell anything to anyone about anything.*

Trust is the key word in this regard. And trust is earned. Always. Love can be a given, but trust is earned. And the society that holds GLBT persons in contempt and worthy of no rights, not even, sometimes, the right to life, is not one that has earned trust. Therefore, it is most important to assert here that how much "out" of the closet one is, is definitely a personal choice.

Often a couple will come to see me as a therapist, explaining that the primary issue, meaning the thing that they fight about the most, is the fact that one of them refuses to "come out" to his/her parents. This means that at Christmas, Chanukah, Thanksgiving, Birthdays or other celebrations, the partner cannot be brought into the celebration. It means that often the partner is not acknowledged by the family of the other partner. While it is certain that this could be a difficult arrangement, I am just as clear that coming out is not something that can or should be compelled by another. As stated, coming out is a deeply personal process that happens more internally than externally. Self-acceptance is the goal of coming out. Sometimes telling others is a part of this process. But sometimes telling others creates only more self-loathing. The process simply cannot be rushed.

Therefore, the goal of this section has not been to encourage one to go and tell others about one's sexual orientation, but rather to assist the reader in finding and living out his/her own authentic sexual orientation. The barrier to living authentically in the realm of sexual orientation usually comes down to fear. We fear what others will think, we fear the religious implications or perceived consequences of living a gay life style, we fear that we will lose people that we love because of their homophobia, we fear intimacy, and now, in this society in which the issue has taken a front seat, we fear for our physical safety. Feel free to go back over the chapter on Barriers to Living Authentically and work and rework these pages as they apply to your sexual orientation.

Ponderings: Now, suppose that you already know that you are GLBT and are comfortable in that knowledge, how are you doing with authenticity as it relates to the subculture of the GLBT worlds? Because we live in a society that is biased towards GLBTs, that world has formed a society all its own, a subculture in which gays, lesbians, bisexuals and transgendered persons may know each other, accept each other and have certain (sub)cultural norms and expectations. Even within that more or less alternative culture, there are other subcultures more specific to each orientation. These subcultures within the subculture are somewhat inclusive and somewhat exclusive. For example, lesbians may form their own subculture within the larger subculture. They may include some gays, bisexuals and transgendered persons in the mix, but they seek out other lesbians primarily. In the positive the larger subculture and its break-out subcultures can create an environment in which a person's individuality and connectedness can flourish. If you are a part of this subculture, you already know this. In the negative it can be just another environment in which we are taught to forgo genuine individuality in favor of connectedness.

For a time in history, there was a pattern of dress and mannerism that was expected in this subculture. Lesbians, were not to carry purses, were to dress and act more masculine; gay males were to dress in extravagant, colorful, or see-through attire and walk and talk in very effeminate ways. Same-sex relationships were to take on heterosexual masculine and feminine roles. Now there is a shift in some of the consciousness of the larger subculture, so that there are many lesbians who do not dress in any given pattern or behave in masculine ways, and many gay males who do not dress in any given pattern or behave in feminine ways. There are many same-sex relationships that do not define themselves by the role models put forth by the heterosexual world. This is because so many in the subculture began to develop their own *personal* pattern. I believe that this became possible because society at large opened up to some degree, which allowed more freedom to breathe on both sides of the line between culture and subculture.

The view of the GLBT subculture from the outside larger culture, however, has been one in which there has been an arcane, yet very poignant history, mostly based on the more idiosyncratic versions of the life-style. It has been known as a subculture in which the more outrageous the person, the more easily s/he was defined. This made and continues to make it difficult not only for persons struggling with their own sexual orientation, but for GLBT persons who are confident of their orientation. Persons questioning their own sexual orientation may be left pondering why it is, if they are really GLBT, that they are not more like others they've heard or read about from the subculture. And persons who are more comfortably GLBT may find it difficult to find a group of persons with whom they can associate when they decide to live in a way that isn't just like their peers.

Because the subculture has had to live very closeted, it is only now in its adolescence in terms of its ability to support the authenticity of its members. However, I would hasten to say that society in general does not do a great job of this either. But the whole idea of fitting in can be compared to the adolescent phase of development in which we are asking ourselves about our identity. The problem with so many adolescents is they only ask, "Who am I most like?" This question is a poor substitute for the more authentic question, "Who am I?" This is exactly what is done in the larger culture to some degree and in the GLBT subculture to some degree. The question becomes "Am I more like this group, or this group?" When this is done in the GLBT subculture, you have persons putting on behaviors and affect that no more match their authenticity than pretending to be heterosexual.

Therefore, when we can stop comparing ourselves to others to define our identity, and simply go inside and ask the Authentic Self the questions of the day, then our entire society and subculture will become more authentic by degree. Society is, afterall, only made up of individuals. "What do I feel?" "What do I think?" These are authentic questions, which when asked of the Authentic Self, will be given authentic answers. We can keep pulling bunnies from the hat, by putting on one more mask just to fit into a particular group. Or, we can move out of illusion and into something that rings much more true inside of us. It is hoped that this book will assist the reader in looking at the beliefs s/he has picked up from his/her culture, or subculture and deciding upon his/her own inner truth. This process moves us into individuation, a place from which we can play our own instruments in the orchestra of whatever culture or subculture of which we are a part.

Ponderings: The truth is relatedness is relatedness regardless of its sexual orientation. Are there differences between the heterosexual relationship and the homosexual relationship? Yes, there are, but they are more in the form of rights, and privileges then in the truth of the relatedness itself.

- Straights can show affection in public and be praised for how much they demonstrate love (as long as it's not blatantly sexual).
    - o GLBTs who show affection (even of the mildest nature) in public are often bashed or simply told they are "shoving it in our faces."
- Straights can get married and have all the benefits, both state and federal, of the legal agreement to marry.
    - o In the majority of states, GLBTs cannot marry, and their marriages are never recognized by the federal government, which means that they are hindered by tax and inheritance laws that punish rather than support them.
- Straights have the right to care for their beloved spouses in the hospital intensive care units and to make decisions about their care.
    - o GLBTs are still all too often told that they cannot visit their beloved partners because they are not family; and are often deprived of the right to make decisions about the care of their loved ones.
- Straights can have children and only have those children removed from them when they are neglectful or abusive.
    - o GLBTs who have children must be very careful NOT to involve the courts in custody battles, for they still often loose these battles, even if the other heterosexual party, who wishes custody, IS abusive or neglectful.
- Straights are considered to be normal and healthy simply because they are straight.
    - o GLBTs, no matter how healthy otherwise, are considered to be abnormal (deviant) simply because they are GLBT.
- Therefore, straights often go into marriage or relationship basing their own behaviors on previous role models. In fact, in doing therapy with straight couples it is often quite difficult for them to see that there might be another path to follow other than those cast by their parents roles as "wife" or "husband."

     o   GLBTs, on the other hand, go into relationship with both the blessing and the curse of trying to establish something all their own.

     o   This leaves the door wide open to create something authentic.

     o   However, GLBTs, like straights are often ill-equipped to do this.

If we, as a society are to learn how to relate and continue to relate from love rather obedience to a law, or security issues, we MUST learn how to relate authentically, we must learn the art of intimacy. Therefore, the fact that there are many alternative relationships out there trying to create from nothing a truly intimate, long-term commitment, based on nothing more than their own authenticity, means that some in the GLBT population are offering society the paradigm it needs to learn this lesson of love.

As usual, however, society in general is not taking this lesson very well. Therefore, the world resists its own best paradigm through casting aspersions on the population offering it. However, we are at a unique crossroad, in our evolutionary history. We may pick the challenge of learning to live authentically in relationship, or we may decide to keep fumbling around in the dark, looking for some external rule or custom to show us the way. When each of us individually begins to turn inward for direction, we will form a new habit of relating that is much more authentic for all of us.

In the mean time, right now in our society as a whole, we are in a learning curve regarding love. As we said earlier, we are only now beginning to even investigate this thing called intimacy, which is the essential ingredient of healthy relationships. What does this mean? Our divorce rate is part of what it means. It means that we cannot continue to stay committed to something to which the heart is not committed. But it also means we are redefining love itself. We've recently been through a phase in our culture in which the word "co-dependence" has taken on more meaning than it was ever intended to take on. It has come to mean everything from an over-dependence on the manipulative nature of in-authentic relatedness, to unconditional love. The joke in the therapy community is the guy who comes to see his therapist and says, "Guess what? I've cured my co-dependence!!" The therapist asks how the client did this. The client answers, "Well, last night, my wife had a heart attack and I refused to take her to the hospital!!" All manner of loving-kindnesses have been cast into the ever-growing lake of co-dependence.

And just as we cannot clearly define love as separate from co-dependence, it is difficult for us to define Self separate from our relationships. Therefore, we jump from one extreme to another with regard to the nature of love in relationship. Do I love the self, or do I love the other? If I love the self then I must assert myself and be independent and strong in relationship. If I love the other, then I must sacrifice the self by becoming solely identified as a part of this relationship. We are having trouble defining what is true and false in relationship because we are on a learning curve. But there is hope, for we are finally beginning to ask the right questions. Eventually, through the process of asking and answering these questions, we will learn that love is both self-love and other-love simultaneously. Eventually, we will come to understand that once we love the Authentic Self, we must also love the other, and if we love the other, we must also love the Authentic Self. Because our hearts will then be opened, we cannot help but love the other, as we love the self. We will come to understand that we do not need the other to be whole, but that we are already whole, and that because we are, we can then invest in others who are whole and establish relationships with these persons that invite further self and relatedness exploration, allowing us to grow closer as a couple, and yet, at the same time, more true to ourselves. We will know that *one does not have to lose the self in order to have the other, nor does one have to lose the other in order to have the self.*

In all of the exercises on relatedness we've done in this book, we were learning how to maintain the identity with the Authentic Self while, at the same time maintaining connection with the significant and primary relationships in our lives. It takes practice and commitment to maintain an authentic identity. "I AM" becomes the strongest and most true dictate of our lives when we practice the art of authenticity. And if I am, then I am all that there is of me. I am the manager and lover of all the various aspects of me: my emotions, my thoughts, my intuitions, my desires, my needs, my actions, my words and my relationships. I speak the truth, and I act that truth, because I have come to know the truth of me. From this frame of reference, then, my relationships evolve to just another aspect of my authenticity.

Authenticity
&
Spirituality

Ponderings: It would be all too easy, at this point, to say that career and relationship are the only two adult issues that come into play when it comes to living authentically. But the truth is, and we all already know it, we live by our beliefs. And our beliefs often come down to our relationship to either a spiritual aspect of ourselves, or a relationship to something outside of ourselves of a religious nature. These things are very important, because they either make or break our ability to change beliefs that are ineffective for us. Therefore, these issues must also be brought into question, if we are to consider living authentically.

So, let's be brave and talk about this very often taboo subject. We all know that it takes some form of bravery, as just about every war that's ever been fought on the face of this earth, has some base in belief, and most often religious belief. So, let's set out some parameters first. The first and most important of these is the concept of freedom of religion. Whatever you choose as your religion, whatever you choose as your spirituality, is just that: a choice. Your choices regarding your religious persuasion or lack thereof, are completely respected. This book is not meant to offer you a spiritual premise. Rather it is meant to assist you in finding the spiritual premise that is most authentic for you.

The next thing we must do in order to have this discussion is to define the terms:

> Religion: An organized set of values set out as dogma or creed about something valued as divine, meant to be espoused by a group of people who agree to espouse this dogma and to fit into the culture which is created by this set of values. It is a particular collective response to this dogma, which provides that collective with a sense of hope.

> Spirituality: A personal and often passionate quest for a connection to something valued as divine. An individual response to this connection with the divine, which provides the individual with a sense of wholeness, healing and hope.

The biggest two differences between Religion as defined here and Spirituality as defined here is twofold: 1) Religion is a dogma *about* something valued as divine, whereas spirituality is a quest for a *connection to* something valued as divine; and 2) Religion is meant for a collective; spirituality must first be individual. It is not important here whether or not spirituality lives within a collective culture espousing a dogma. It only matters that there is a very clear distinction between religion and spirituality.

There are all kinds of religions out there. Many of them espouse the belief that theirs is the *only right way*. If you could put yourself on a cloud and look down on that, I'm thinking it would all be pretty humorous. If one could be divine and look down on the enormous numbers of religious groups who have determined that theirs is the only right way, I'm thinking it might be downright hilarious—if it didn't also mean that these religions often take up arms against each other.

Therefore, for the purposes of this book, let us not depend upon religion. Let us then focus only on spirituality. As a matter of fact, the purpose of this chapter in this book is to assist the reader in finding an authentic spirituality rather than just espousing a religion. Let's take it one step further, by saying that religion is just meaningless drivel, unless and until each member of that religious group can connect to his or her own individual spirituality. And anything can become a religion, even our New Ageism, which has also laid down various creeds and dogmas which amount to a "we" mentality. So often our religions, like any other culture, develop a sort of we/they dichotomy that allows those in the "we" category to feel safe by association. If I am in the "we" category then I never want for associates, some of whom may even become my good friends. Whereas, if I am in the "they" category, well then I'll have to go find my own "we" or I'll be all alone.

Spirituality on the other hand is a journey we take alone. We do not have to be physically alone to do it, but it is a journey inward, a journey to the soul of the Authentic Self. Finding one's authentic spirituality means putting aside all of the creeds and dogmas that we have learned and asking ourselves what we really, honestly, in our heart of hearts believe. And beyond beliefs, it is a bridge between my authenticity and something that I call divine. It means asking questions like, "Do I really believe in the God that I've been taught to believe in?"

Often these questions come, in and of themselves, as a result of getting in touch with the Authentic Self. I often see clients who begin to ask these questions but are afraid to discuss them with me because I am a therapist, not a priest. And this is the very reason why I developed a practice in which I do Transpersonal Counseling, because I know that on the way to finding and living the Authentic Self, these questions must be asked and answered. Transpersonal Counseling is counseling which allows the individual to explore beyond the personal identifications of ego. Therefore it allows for individuals to explore their own deeply felt spirituality, without being told by someone else what they should believe or not believe regarding their own truth. The truth is that from a priest or pastor one will get counsel as to how to maintain the religion while trying to turn on the light of authenticity. I've found that sometimes, for some people turning on the light of authenticity, means seeing clearly that the religion previously espoused no longer fits. And I know that there are some who would go so far as to say, "If it doesn't fit your religion, it can't be authentic." My answer to this is: If your religion cannot stand up to some scrutinizing, how will you ever know if it is true for you? And how can one find a true spirituality without the quest that defines it?

I have met and worked with clients whose entire journey toward authenticity is all about letting go of some hard, fast and rigid dogma of a church or religion that no longer fits for the truth of who they are. These individuals end up having to make a choice between the religion that they are steeped in, and the truth of their own existence. One of many examples: persons who are seeking an authentic divorce, who have been brought up and steeped in religion that says, if they divorce they go to hell, and if the spouses they left behind become involved with someone else after the divorce, the spouse will go to hell as well. They then must struggle with the religion's enforced guilt and fear, not only for themselves, but for the well-being of their spouses. The question then is, "Do I really believe that this thing that I've been taught is true?" Another example, and one frequently encountered, is the case of the gay or lesbian individual, who has been taught that to be gay is an abomination to the God of their religion, but who is struggling with suicidal thoughts because they feel trapped by that belief.

It should be known that this quest is very existential in nature. It is all about the meaning of *your* life. Therefore, the exercises that follow are meant to put the reader in touch with these very foundational questions. For example, have you been taught and therefore believe that the meaning of life is to suffer righteousness until you get to another plane of existence in the afterlife, called heaven? Does that belief then run counter to your own newly found authentic belief that life is to be lived fully and passionately, with full regard for the Self and full regard for others? Remember that in all the exercises below, we will be asking you to examine and reexamine what you have been taught, as opposed to what your Authentic Self believes to be true. The first and most important question that must be asked is: Do you believe that what you have been taught is inalterable truth? Do you really believe that, or are you just afraid to ask the question? If you are willing to ask the question, you have just moved beyond the barrier of the F-word, fear, and into a journey, a quest for your own truth, your own naked spirituality.

Shake your head free for a moment. Let go, for just a moment, of everything that you've been taught and try to imagine that God could be exactly what your highest imaginings of it could be. (For all of these exercises we will refer to God as "it" since that removes religious archetype from the entire issue of spirituality.) Then step back and remember what you've been taught that God is. What would your Authentic Self like for God to be like? What have you been taught that God is like? Work the chart below to come up with some honest answers to these questions.

In the area of:	I'd like to believe that: God would	I've been taught that God:
Love		
Providing		
Punishment		
Good and Evil		
Connection to others		

Did you find that there are differences between how you envisioned a God of your Authentic imagining, and the God you've been taught about? Did you find that there were differences in the way the God you've been taught to believe in treats some areas, and the way it treats others? Did you find similar differences between areas for the God you envisioned?

Write a letter to the role, from the Authentic Self, about the God that you envisioned above.

_____

_____

_____

_____

_____

_____

_____

_____

_____

_____

_____

_____

_____

_____

_____

_____

_____

_____

_____

_____

_____

_____

_____

_____

_____

_____

_____

_____

_____

_____

_____

_____

Write a poem about the God that you envisioned above.

_____
_____
_____
_____
_____
_____
_____
_____
_____
_____
_____
_____
_____
_____
_____
_____
_____
_____
_____
_____
_____
_____
_____
_____
_____
_____
_____
_____
_____
_____
_____
_____
_____
_____
_____
_____

What is the feeling that you feel when you think of this God you envisioned? Name that feeling or those feelings and write a story below of what it would be like to have those feelings all the time.

_____
_____
_____
_____
_____
_____
_____
_____
_____
_____
_____
_____
_____
_____
_____
_____
_____
_____
_____
_____
_____
_____
_____
_____
_____
_____
_____
_____
_____
_____
_____
_____
_____

Would you be able to trust the God that you envisioned? If so, what would it be like to live in that kind of trust all the time? Write that story below.

_____
_____
_____
_____
_____
_____
_____
_____
_____
_____
_____
_____
_____
_____
_____
_____
_____
_____
_____
_____
_____
_____
_____
_____
_____
_____
_____
_____
_____
_____
_____
_____

Now, let's talk about the God that you've been taught about. Write a letter from the Authentic Self to the role about this God.

_____

_____

_____

_____

_____

_____

_____

_____

_____

_____

_____

_____

_____

_____

_____

_____

_____

_____

_____

_____

_____

_____

_____

_____

_____

_____

_____

_____

_____

_____

_____

_____

_____

Write a poem about the God you've been taught about.

_____
_____
_____
_____
_____
_____
_____
_____
_____
_____
_____
_____
_____
_____
_____
_____
_____
_____
_____
_____
_____
_____
_____
_____
_____
_____
_____
_____
_____
_____
_____
_____
_____
_____
_____
_____

What is the feeling that you feel when you think of this God? Name that feeling or those feelings and write a story below of what if would be like to have those feelings all the time.

_____

_____

_____

_____

_____

_____

_____

_____

_____

_____

_____

_____

_____

_____

_____

_____

_____

_____

_____

_____

_____

_____

_____

_____

_____

_____

_____

_____

_____

_____

_____

_____

_____

_____

_____

Would you be able to trust the God that you've been taught about? What would it be like to trust that God? Write that story below.

_____
_____
_____
_____
_____
_____
_____
_____
_____
_____
_____
_____
_____
_____
_____
_____
_____
_____
_____
_____
_____
_____
_____
_____
_____
_____
_____
_____
_____
_____
_____
_____

Ponderings: Let's consider a possibility. What if, the God that you envisioned *is* your authentic understanding of God? Okay, let's backtrack a minute. You see, all we have, all we know about God is what we've come to understand about God. And we have come to our understanding mostly based on what others taught us, with perhaps a few verifying experiences, accompanied by our own parental projections. We will discuss the parental projections momentarily, but for now what we are saying here is that we can begin to verify all, or at least a good portion, of our beliefs through authentic experience. The experiencing Authentic Self can be our verifier. When we ask things like, how did we feel in associating our imagination with the God we envisioned, what we are saying is, can you verify on the feeling level the possibility that this God is, in truth, your God. Two associations with this idea of "your God," follow.

In Alcoholics Anonymous the first three steps of the Twelve Step program go like this:

1. We admitted that we were powerless over our addiction to alcohol and that our lives had become unmanageable.
2. We came to believe that there was a power greater than ourselves, which could restore us to sanity.
3. We made a decision to turn our lives and our will over to God as we understood him.

What has this got to do with anything? Well, the second and third steps are very interesting in light of the question: What if the God you envisioned *is* your God? Persons that are addicted have to move through denial to understand that their problem is bigger than they, by themselves, can manage. That is the first step. The second step is stretching beyond what they understand of personal strength and moving to a belief that there is a power greater than themselves that can restore them to balanced living, a manageable life. How do they *come to believe* this? What is this stretch? How does one who feels so powerless over their own actions, move to a position of such strength? And then once they have "come to believe," how do they make a decision to turn their lives and their will over to that power in which they have "come to believe."

There are many, many horrendous stories that one hears when one works in and with an alcohol and drug treatment facility, which I did in different capacities for approximately 10 years. Many of these stories are about God. They come from persons born to pastors and/or highly religious persons, forced to go to church and recite Bible verses, and then severely abused and neglected by the same persons that sent them to church to learn about a God of love and a God of wrath. They made associations, as we shall see that we all do, between the person who told them about this God and the God itself. These persons would do just about anything to avoid making contact with this God again. For this God is an abusive God, who tricks, maligns, confuses and abuses them. This has been their experience of God, because it is blended with the experience of parental abuse. Or, take the examples of persons who were sexually abused by a pastor who told the parents that in order for them to continue to come to that church they had to pay "dues," but that if they couldn't come up with the dues, they could send their daughter around once a week to "work for" the pastor. Or, what about persons sexually abused and exploited by priests. The stories go on and on and on.

How, in the world, do these persons come up with an image of a God in whom they can trust to turn over their lives and will? The answer is that they either move into further self-betrayal, by submitting themselves anew to an image of God that they not only think, but "know" will betray them; they relapse; or they come up with their own personal view of God. And the truth is that without religion, that is exactly what we would all be doing. We would all be tapping into the deeper part of ourselves to find our own personal "higher power." The truth is how we image God is the only "God of our understanding" that we can have, regardless of what religion says.

What we have historically done is what Ruth, of the Bible story, did for Naomi, her mother-in-law. She said, that very famous statement (Ruth 1:16): "Wither thou goest I will go ... thy Gods will be my Gods...." While that statement is very often seen as a very loving statement, it does reflect accurately the mistake we make with regard to finding a God. As we are growing up, instead of seeking and finding our own authentic God, we just accept the God of our parents and family and friends. We do this because God is so important to the fabric of living, that we feel that to betray our parent's version of God is to betray our parents. And we are certain that if we betray our parents they will abandon us. And all of this is figured out on a sub- or unconscious level. The fact is, we hardly ever think about it. What so often happens is we are taught that if we don't believe as our family believes, there are severe consequences. In some cases this would amount to knowing that father or mother would disown us if we believed something different from them. In other cases it is the threat of eternal damnation that makes us comply. So, without even considering any other options, we simply take their Gods to be our Gods. But the truth is that our parents could be encouraging us to find God from an internal frame of reference.

One of the most memorable experiences of my life is the day when I asked my three-year-old son about God. We were in our beautiful wooded backyard, next to a creek bed, into which was flowing, through a large culvert not far from us, a large amount of rainwater from the previous day. It sounded like a lovely waterfall. We were sitting on the grass, playing and talking and I looked at him and said, "Tell me about God." He looked right into my eyes, got very quiet, held up his little finger as if he were silencing me and said, "Do you hear that?" He was referring to the sound of the water pouring into the creek bed. I said, "Yes." He said, "That's God laughing." I put my hand to my heart, began to tear up, then both of us began to laugh together.

What if children already know about God? What if they could find their own authentic God if we but encouraged them a little? Perhaps then they would find it quickly and be able to develop their own trust in this God without further ado. The problem is that we are all so afraid that what they find might be different from what we've found and we might then have to do some real soul searching about this whole thing about God. We've rested our security on having already found the one and only truth. It makes us feel extremely insecure to consider that the seeming truth we've rested our life on may not be valid. Besides, we've already done what Ruth did. We took our parents' Gods to be our Gods. And we say to ourselves, "Everybody can't be wrong, can they?"

Well, most certainly, they can. Think of all the many times that the world changed dramatically because some concept that we'd held to be true just wasn't. Think of Copernicus telling us that the sun did not revolve around the world but vice versa. Or Einstein finding, that unlike what Newton taught, there really are no straight lines here on planet earth, because we live on a sphere. Or what about Columbus, sailing past the horizon on a flat earth? There are many, many, many other examples in which, most certainly, everyone can be wrong. And even our long held beliefs can turn out to be invalid, or at the very least, not authentic for us.

So, why are we still just taking Naomi's God to be our God, instead of finding out who our God really is? And how can we have a personal relationship with someone else's God? How can we relate authentically to something so important, so sacred to our internal life, which is neither internal nor authentic?

In attempting to answer these questions you may run into something else about your image of God that is crucial to finding your own Authentic understanding of God. When we start looking for God, we very often run into something that looks very much like our parents. You see, our parents were our first gods. At least on this physical plane, our parents were our caretakers. Without them we would not survive. Therefore, they became the first images we had of God as well. Now we are talking about something far deeper than merely what we've been taught about God. Now we are talking about a mental image of God. Since none of us has ever seen God, we create a mental image, even a psychological image of God. Even if we were not raised in a particular religion, most of us have formulated some kind of image of God, even if it is only an image we reject as part of atheism or agnosticism.

This image of God becomes our God, whether we like it or not. The question is, where did we get this image? As we've already asserted, this image comes in part from the intellectual image created for us by our religions. But it runs deeper than that. Our image of God also comes from our image of our parents. Here's how it works. If I've been taught that God is loving and kind, but still somehow see God as cold and indifferent, I might have to consider from whence this image of God comes. If I look at my mother, a single parent who was largely cold and indifferent, I might begin to be able to connect the dots a bit.

Let's try that. Close your eyes. Imagine God as you have always imagined it before you started working on your Authenticity. What do you see? Write that down on a clean piece of paper. Now, try to imagine how that God has handled, dealt with, or assisted you in your life circumstances up until now. What did it do? Did you perceive that this God was loving, kind and openly involved in the affairs of your life? Was this God distant, unavailable, and judging? Was this God arbitrarily punitive? Was this God moody and fickle? Regardless of what you read in your religious text, what was your image of God really doing? Now turn to the next page and do the exercise there.

Below, compare your perceptions of the actions of the God you described in the previous paragraph to your perceptions of your parent(s) in response to you as you were growing up and/or now.

Circumstance	Parent's Response	God's Response

What did you find? Did you find similarities between the responses? If so, this particular circumstance represents an area of your life in which you misconceive of God. You have projected your parent(s) onto an image of God in a way that keeps you from seeing an image of your Authentic Self's God. Did you find express differences between the responses? If so this particular circumstance represents an area of your life in which you have evolved or devolved (dependent on what the differences were) to a new understanding of God. Did you see a consistent pattern of similarity? Then the face of your Authentic God is hidden behind the mask of your parents' perceived identity.

If you found it difficult in that exercise to see your God any different from how you see or saw your parents, don't worry, that is very common. Very few of us were lucky enough to have parents who simply mirrored our authenticity. Most of them wanted to mold us into being what they needed for us to be. In so doing they did not help us find an authentic approach to spirituality. And in so doing they acted in ways that left us with some unresolved issues, which we have projected onto our image of God. In much the same way that we end up marrying people who remind of us our parents, we make up a God that reminds of our parents. Why? For the following reasons:

1. It makes us feel safe to maintain some kind of mental image that is familiar to us, even if that image is bred in chaos and conflict. At least it isn't strange.

2. We have unresolved issues with our parents. Those unresolved issues are going to continue to present themselves in some way until we resolve them. They will present in our primary relationships, in our careers and in our spirituality until and unless we resolve them.

3. We imprinted to our parents as the leaders, the caretakers, the love-givers, the authorities in our lives. This imprinting leaves us with mental imaging that is warped along the lines of our parents' behaviors, attitudes and verbalizations towards us. In order for us to resolve this dilemma, we have to go down to the vulnerable spiritual longings of our souls and imprint something different there.

Resolution to these issues is what we have been seeking throughout this book. However, our spirituality is all about those deep, vulnerable inner longings. If we touch those longings, they will tell us something about how we have envisioned God and will tell us where we need to improve our image of God. For example, if I have a deep, inner longing to be an artist, but I see God, like my critical parent, as not really believing in my talent; then I'm not going to really pursue my craft. But if I stop calling that image God and recognize it as just another projection of my parent, then I am able to do two things: 1) I can turn and confront that critical parent on my shoulder, with an argument from the Authentic Self; and 2) I can now set my self free to create an authentic image of God, since that one was never really God in the first place.

This is where spirituality begins. It begins with an authentic search. It is true that if we had all been raised by parents who mirrored our authentic image of God, and society supported that, we would not now have to conduct such a search. But even if our parents were able to do that, society will not have it. This is exactly why the authentic spiritual search is an inward journey that yields an inner understanding of God.

So the search is on to find something real in a God of our own understanding. Use whatever best methods you have of accessing your deep inner longings, whether it be meditation, writing, singing, dancing, yoga, prayer, etc. What you will arrive at, if the search is valid, is the deep, inner, soft tissue of your truest nature. What many have found is that soft vulnerable tissue is like the roots of the tree that do not need the protection of the bark; for the roots are the strongest part of the tree. Here is where we will find God. And from here, we can begin to look at our own particular religious texts with a new eye: What do I believe that this paragraph or poem or sentence is saying to me? Not, what have I been taught that it is saying, not what does my pastor say it means, but what do *I* believe it means. I encourage it. Before you sit down with the text, spend some time with the Authentic Self, either by writing yourself a letter, or by meditating, or just by doing something that makes you feel richly alive. Then sit down with the text and a pen and paper nearby. When you read something that catches your eye, ask the Authentic Self to write down what it thinks this passage means? Or, if you don't want to use the texts of a particular religion, use poetry, use stories. Or, if that doesn't work, sit down with the Authentic Self and write a story about a spiritual journey. Once the spiritual journey is ended on the paper, ask the Authentic Self, what did the character in the story gain on this journey. What you are doing is openly challenging yourself to find your own true spirituality. This matters a great deal, because much of our philosophy about life in general comes from our own beliefs that spring from our spiritual awareness. Without a strong base in this area, we are left to meander between the Gods of all the Naomi's we know. We may be left, in so doing, cursing ourselves, rather than blessing ourselves with our beliefs. It is and it remains all about choice.

Celebrating

Authenticity

Ponderings: We so rarely celebrate our achievements, unless, they are something others will also notice, like winning an Oscar, graduating, getting married or having a funeral. Oh, we might take ourselves out to dinner when we get a promotion, but we rarely celebrate the moments of quiet achievement attained in the dark of the night. In other words, if no one can see the work we are doing, we choose not to see it as well.

If you have worked your way to this far in this book you have just accomplished something quite major. You may have begun to change your perspective on your entire life. Maybe you don't feel all of the external changes that may take place as a result of your internal changes just yet, but if you keep living authentically, you will. Because you will have an inner peace about you that you can feel and others can see, you will put yourself out there in the world in such a way that you will attract to yourself all manner of good things: jobs, positions, relationships, small and large joys. This is no small feat. As a matter of fact, it takes more courage and energy to turn your life into truth than it does to achieve fame and fortune, unless, of course, achieving fame and fortune is your truth. And as we know, the truth sets us free.

Because you have done this work, you are now free to accomplish your life in a way that is genuine. No more need to fake it to please the other guy, or achieve because it is your role to do so, to laugh when you feel like crying, or to sneak around, under and through reality to just eek by. Now, you can have the real deal. As much or as little as you choose. This is definitely worth celebrating. Below you will find a few celebratory exercises. You may wish to implement a few of your own as well. But do celebrate. Do not miss this opportunity to ritualize the beginning of an entirely new life for you.

Below, write a story of the transitions you have made as a result of coming to identify with and rely upon the Authentic Self.

_____

_____

_____

_____

_____

_____

_____

_____

_____

_____

_____

_____

_____

_____

_____

_____

_____

_____

_____

_____

_____

_____

_____

_____

_____

_____

_____

_____

_____

_____

_____

_____

_____

_____

Story (con't)

Below, write a thank you letter to the role, for its early intervention in your life.

_____
_____
_____
_____
_____
_____
_____
_____
_____
_____
_____
_____
_____
_____
_____
_____
_____
_____
_____
_____
_____
_____
_____
_____
_____
_____
_____
_____
_____
_____
_____
_____
_____
_____
_____
_____
_____
_____

Below, write a thank you letter to the Authentic Self, for its activity in your life.

_____
_____
_____
_____
_____
_____
_____
_____
_____
_____
_____
_____
_____
_____
_____
_____
_____
_____
_____
_____
_____
_____
_____
_____
_____
_____
_____
_____
_____
_____
_____
_____
_____
_____

Below, or on a poster board of your choosing, make a collage of the Authentic Self. Feel free to change this collage over the years as you evolve.

Create an audio and/or video tape of the Authentic Self. Call it "The (Your name) Tape." Collect all the songs that you remember or hear which remind you of your Authentic Self, or of the journey of the Authentic Self. Make a duplicate. Keep one in your car to play as often as you'd like, and one at home or in the office, to play as often as you'd like. Make a list of the songs below and say what each of them means to you.

_____
_____
_____
_____
_____
_____
_____
_____
_____
_____
_____
_____
_____
_____
_____
_____
_____
_____
_____
_____
_____
_____
_____
_____
_____
_____
_____
_____
_____

Conduct daily meditations. Upon rising in the morning do a breathing exercise in which you breath deep, quick, cleansing breaths without a pause between them for one half minute. With each breath in, imagine that you are breathing the Authentic Self into all the organs and cells of your body. With each breath out, imagine that you are breathing out the old role. See the old role slipping quickly out of all of the organs and cells of your body and moving rapidly out on your exhalation. See the Authentic Self sliding easily into all of the cells of your body. Then allow yourself to slow down your breathing and focus all of your thoughts on a central place just above your navel. Imagine that this place is the core of your being. See this place as a spiral staircase that you may slowly descend to get deeper and deeper into the core of your being. Keep going down and down until you feel that you can't go any further. Then imagine yourself coming around the last bend of the staircase and out onto a bank next to a deep, beautiful, light-filled river. Sit down on the bank and let your feet dangle in the river. Feel the water on your feet and legs. Then slowly let yourself down into the river and relax. Let the river carry you; let it take you where it will. This river is your authenticity. Surrender to it. Let it carry you to new thoughts, new creative inventions, new ways of being. Then, when you are ready, allow the river to become your blood, carrying your authenticity around inside of you, through your bodily organs, your heart, your brain, your lungs. As you calmly allow yourself to feel the sensations of your authenticity, allow your eyes to open slowly. At the end of your meditation, thank the Authentic Self for taking its proper position in your life. You may change this meditation anyway that you would like, but keep it up daily. You may decide that you want to keep a record of your meditations, what you experienced and what you learned.

Ponderings: I'm sure you already know that the journey does not stop here. Just as you can't go into a treatment center, get cured and forget about it, you can never let yourself forget about working with the Authentic Self either. When I used to direct a treatment center, I would sit in on groups and other activities and I led some groups about how treatment works that remain special in my memory. One of the things that we invariably had to deal with in those groups was a mind-set that sort of said:

> I'm going to walk into treatment and onto a conveyor belt. The whole time I'm on this conveyor belt, the center will be sprinkling pink foo-foo dust on my head. The conveyor belt will carry me from the front door on day one, to the back door on my last day. It will then dump me back into my life and I'll be cured. The pink foo-foo dust will have done the trick and I'll never have to think about this stuff again.

Guess what? It never works this way. The conveyor belt is broken and we are fresh out of the pink stuff. The purpose of doing this work is to get you *started* on an authentic path. If you have done the work of this book, then you have a start. You have begun to see that there is another part of yourself out of which you have never, prior to this time, lived. You have begun to see that part as the truest part of you, the part of you that can be utterly trusted. You have learned how to consult with that part of yourself and get much needed information which then can be used in making decisions and solving problems. You have begun to understand how to relate to others and the world from the base of the Authentic Self. You may have even tapped into a deep layer of peace and joy.

But you have only begun. In order for you to have the life of which you dream, you must continue to do the work of accessing and maintaining direct contact with the Authentic Self. Why? Because when you stop doing this work, it will be terribly easy to slide back into the role. Before you know it, you'll be living out the same old patterns, wondering how in the world you got there. But if you find yourself sliding, just work the special parts of the book that apply again. It is never impossible to get back in touch with the Authentic Self. It is you. It is the true you, the real you. It is always accessible to you, if you just make contact.

Eventually, as you maintain contact with the Authentic Self, you will no longer need to "make contact." You will, by that time, be in constant contact, in fact, you will *be* the Authentic Self. You will be doing what I call "living inside out." In other words, what was once buried and had to be dug up, is now a living, breathing, viable entity, all its own, and needs nothing but for you to keep breathing in and out. At this time, you will be living in joy. You will know what it is like to just be alive and feel free and joyful in that moment. This is living, folks. And nothing short of this can really be called living. It may be surviving. But it isn't living. Living is living inside out. Living is breathing, talking, walking, deciding, declaring, desiring, choosing, problem solving, crying, laughing, all from the Authentic Self. Life is for joy. And joy is only possible in authenticity.

So keep doing the work. Go back and do the whole book over again as often as you'd like. The more you do that, the more you are unlearning all the beliefs, attitudes and roles that have kept you stuck, and the more you are learning how to live. If you run into a snag that seems to be about fear, go back and work the section on fear again. If you run into a seemingly insurmountable problem, have a dialogue with the Authentic Self, listen for its wisdom and follow its guidance. If you have spiritual questions go to the Authentic Self to connect, from there, to your higher power.

Everything comes down to this one thing: Living authentically is life itself. So, live long, and prosper.

And may your God bless you in your journey.

References

American Psychiatric Association. (1994). *Diagnostic and Statistical Manual of Mental Disorders, 4th Edition (DSM-IV)*. Washington, DC: American Psychiatric Association.

American Psychiatric Association. (2006). *Position Statement: COPP position statement on therapies focused on attempts to change sexual orientation (Reparative or Conversion Therapies)*. APA: Arlington, VA. Retrieved March 15, 2006 from the American Psychiatric Association Web site. http://www.psych.org/psych_pract/copptherapyaddendum83100.cfm

American Psychological Association. (2004). *Sexual orientation and homosexuality*. Retreived March 6, 2006 from the APA Help Center: http://www.apahelpcenter.org/articles/article.php?id=31

Cole, Paula. *Me*. (1996). Ensign Music Corporation and Hingface Music. In *Paula Cole: This fire*. Milwaukee, WI: Hal-Leonard Corporation. 49-54.

Fogelberg, Dan. (1974-1982). *Make love stay*, on *Dan Folgelberg greatest hits*. Released by Epic. 1982.

Kübler-Ross, Elizabeth. (1997). *On death and dying*. Reprint edition. NY: Scribner.

Leonard, Linda S. (1983). *The wounded woman: Healing the father-daughter relationship*. Boston, MA: Shambhala Publications.

Waring, Bell, "Brent shares research on adolescent suicide." *NIH Record*. LVIII,No. 6. Retrieved March 24, 2006 from the Web site of the *NIH Record*: http://www.nih.gov/nihrecord/03_24_2006/story02.htm

Wikipedia Foundation, Inc. *Roy Moore.* Retrieved from Wikipedia Free
    Encyclopedia's Web site November 19, 2006: http://en.wikipedia.org/
    wiki/Roy_Moore